Semantic Web for the Working Ontologist

Semantic Web for the Working Ontologist

Modeling in RDF, RDFS and OWL

Dean Allemang

James Hendler

ELSEVIER

AMSTERDAM • BOSTON • HEIDELBERG • LONDON
NEW YORK • OXFORD • PARIS • SAN DIEGO
SAN FRANCISCO • SINGAPORE • SYDNEY • TOKYO
Morgan Kaufmann Publishers is an imprint of Elsevier

MORGAN KAUFMANN PUBL

Publisher: Denise E. M. Penrose
Publishing Services Manager: George Morrison
Project Manager: Marilyn E. Rash
Assistant Editors: Mary E. James
Copyeditor: Debbie Prato
Proofreader: Rachel Rossi
Indexer: Ted Laux
Cover Design: Eric DeCicco
Cover Image: Getty Images
Typesetting/Illustration Formatting: SPi
Interior Printer: Sheridan Books
Cover Printer: Phoenix Color Corp.

Morgan Kaufmann Publishers is an imprint of Elsevier.
30 Corporate Drive, Suite 400, Burlington, MA 01803

This book is printed on acid-free paper.

Library of Congress Cataloging-in-Publication Data

Allemang, Dean
   Semantic web for the working ontologist modeling in RDF, RDFS
      and OWL / Dean Allemang, James A. Hendler.
      p. cm.
   Includes bibliographical references and index.
   ISBN-13: 978-0-12-373556-0 (alk. paper)
   1. Web site development. 2. Metadata. 3. Semantic Web.   I. Hendler,
   James.   II. Title.
   TK5105.888.H465 2008
   025.04—dc22   2007051586

For information on all Morgan Kaufmann publications, visit our
Web site at *www.mkp.com* or *www.books.elsevier.com*.

ISBN-13: 978-0-12-373556-0
Printed in the United States
   10 11 12   5 4 3

For our students

Contents

Preface

In 2003, when the World Wide Web Consortium was working toward the ratification of the Recommendations for the Semantic Web languages RDF, RDFS, and OWL, we realized that there was a need for an industrial-level introductory course in these technologies. The standards were technically sound, but, as is typically the case with standards documents, they were written with technical completeness in mind rather than education. We realized that for this technology to take off, people other than mathematicians and logicians would have to learn the basics of semantic modeling.

Toward that end, we started a collaboration to create a series of trainings aimed not at university students or technologists but at Web developers who were practitioners in some other field. In short, we needed to get the Semantic Web out of the hands of the logicians and Web technologists, whose job had been to build a consistent and robust infrastructure, and into the hands of the practitioners who were to build the Semantic Web. The Web didn't grow to the size it is today through the efforts of only HTML designers, nor would the Semantic Web grow as a result of only logicians' efforts.

After a year or so of offering training to a variety of audiences, we delivered a training course at the National Agriculture Library of the U.S. Department of Agriculture. Present for this training were a wide variety of practitioners in many fields, including health care, finance, engineering, national intelligence, and enterprise architecture. The unique synergy of these varied practitioners resulted in a dynamic four days of investigation into the power and subtlety of semantic modeling. Although the practitioners in the room were innovative and intelligent, we found that even for these early adopters, some of the new ways of thinking required for modeling in a World Wide Web context were too subtle to master after just a one-week course. One participant had registered for the course multiple times, insisting that something else "clicked" each time she went through the exercises.

This is when we realized that although the course was doing a good job of disseminating the information and skills for the Semantic Web, another, more archival resource was needed. We had to create something that students could work with on their own and could consult when they had questions. This was the point at which the idea of a book on modeling in the Semantic Web was conceived. We realized that the readership needed to include a wide variety of people from a number of fields, not just programmers or Web application developers but all the people from different fields who were struggling to understand how to use the new Web languages.

It was tempting at first to design this book to be the definitive statement on the Semantic Web vision, or "everything you ever wanted to know about OWL," **xiii** including comparisons to program modeling languages such as UML, knowledge modeling languages, theories of inferencing and logic, details of the Web infrastructure (URIs and URLs), and the exact current status of all the developing standards (including SPARQL, GRDDL, RDFa, and the new OWL 1.1 effort). We realized, however, that not only would such a book be a superhuman undertaking, but it would also fail to serve our primary purpose of putting the tools of the Semantic Web into the hands of a generation of intelligent practitioners who could build real applications. For this reason, we concentrated on a particular essential skill for constructing the Semantic Web: building useful and reusable models in the World Wide Web setting.

Many of these patterns entail several variants, each embodying a different philosophy or approach to modeling. For advanced cases such as these, we realized that we couldn't hope to provide a single, definitive answer to how these things should be modeled. So instead, our goal is to educate domain practitioners so that they can read and understand design patterns of this sort and have the intellectual tools to make considered decisions about which ones to use and how to adapt them. We wanted to focus on those trying to use RDF, RDFS, and OWL to accomplish specific tasks and model their own data and domains, rather than write a generic book on ontology development. Thus, we have focused on the "working ontologist" who was trying to create a domain model on the Semantic Web.

The design patterns we use in this book tend to be much simpler. Often a pattern consists of only a single statement but one that is especially helpful when used in a particular context. The value of the pattern isn't so much in the complexity of its realization but in the awareness of the sort of situation in which it can be used.

This "make it useful" philosophy also motivated the choice of the examples we use to illustrate these patterns in this book. There are a number of competing criteria for good example domains in a book of this sort. The examples must be understandable to a wide variety of audiences, fairly compelling, yet complex enough to reflect real modeling situations. The actual examples we have encountered in our customer modeling situations satisfy the last condition but either are too specialized—for example, modeling complex molecular biological data; or, in some cases, they are too business-sensitive—for example, modeling particular investment policies—to publish for a general audience.

We also had to struggle with a tension between the coherence of the examples. We had to decide between using the same example throughout the book versus having stylistic variation and different examples, both so the prose didn't get too heavy with one topic, but also so the book didn't become one about how to model—for example, the life and works of William Shakespeare for the Semantic Web.

We addressed these competing constraints by introducing a fairly small number of example domains: William Shakespeare is used to illustrate some of the most basic capabilities of the Semantic Web. The tabular information about products and the manufacturing locations was inspired by the sample data provided with a popular database management package. Other examples come from domains we've worked with in the past or where there had been particular interest among our students. We hope the examples based on the roles of people in a workplace will be familiar to just about anyone who has worked in an office with more than one person, and that they highlight the capabilities of Semantic Web modeling when it comes to the different ways entities can be related to one another.

Some of the more involved examples are based on actual modeling challenges from fairly involved customer applications. For example, the ice cream example in Chapter 7 is based, believe it or not, on a workflow analysis example from a NASA application. The questionnaire is based on a number of customer examples for controlled data gathering, including sensitive intelligence gathering for a military application. In these cases, the domain has been changed to make the examples more entertaining and accessible to a general audience.

We have included a number of extended examples of Semantic Web modeling "in the wild," where we have found publicly available and accessible modeling projects for which there is no need to sanitize the models. These examples can include any number of anomalies or idiosyncrasies, which would be confusing as an introduction to modeling but as illustrations give a better picture about how these systems are being used on the World Wide Web. In accordance with the tenet that this book does not include everything we know about the Semantic Web, these examples are limited to the modeling issues that arise around the problem of distributing structured knowledge over the Web. Thus, the treatment focuses on how information is modeled for reuse and robustness in a distributed environment.

By combining these different example sources, we hope we have struck a happy balance among all the competing constraints and managed to include a fairly entertaining but comprehensive set of examples that can guide the reader through the various capabilities of the Semantic Web modeling languages.

This book provides many technical terms that we introduce in a somewhat informal way. Although there have been many volumes written that debate the formal meaning of words like *inference, representation,* and even *meaning,* we have chosen to stick to a relatively informal and operational use of the terms. We feel this is more appropriate to the needs of the ontology designer or application developer for whom this book was written. We apologize to those philosophers and formalists who may be offended by our casual use of such important concepts.

We often find that when people hear we are writing a new Semantic Web modeling book, their first question is, "Will it have examples?" For this book, the answer is an emphatic "Yes!" Even with a wide variety of examples, however, it is easy to keep thinking "inside the box" and to focus too heavily on the details of the examples themselves. We hope you will use the examples as they were intended: for illustration and education. But you should also consider how the examples could be changed, adapted, or retargeted to model something in your personal domain. In the Semantic Web, Anyone can say Anything about Any topic. Explore the freedom.

Second Printing: Since the first printing there have been advances in several of the technologies we discuss such as SPARQL, OWL 2.0, and SKOS that go beyond the state of affairs at the time of first printing. We have created a web site that covers developing technology standards and changing thinking about best practices for the Semantic Web. You can find it at http://www.workingontologist.org/.

ACKNOWLEDGMENTS

Of course, no book gets written without a lot of input and influence from others. We would like to thank a number of professional colleagues, including Bijan Parsia and Jennifer Golbeck, and the students of the University of Maryland MINDSWAP project, who discussed many of the ideas in this book with us. We thank Irene Polikoff, Ralph Hodgson, and Robert Coyne from TopQuadrant Inc., who were supportive of this writing effort, and our many colleagues in the Semantic Web community, including Tim Berners-Lee, whose vision motivated both of us, and Ora Lassila, Bernardo Cuenca-Grau, Xavier Lopez, Zhe Wu and Guus Schreiber, who gave us feedback on what became the choice of features for RDF-PLUS. We are also grateful to the many colleagues who've helped us as we've learned and taught about Semantic Web technologies.

We would also especially like to thank the reviewers who helped us improve the material in the book: John Bresnick, Ted Slater, and Susie Stephens all gave us many helpful comments on the material, and Mike Uschold of Boeing made a heroic effort in reviewing every chapter, sometimes more than once, and worked hard to help us make this book the best it could be. We didn't take all of his suggestions, but those we did have greatly improved the quality of the material, and we thank him profusely for his time and efforts.

We also want to thank Denise Penrose, who talked us into publishing with Elsevier and whose personal oversight helped make sure the book actually got done on time. We also thank Mary James, Diane Cerra, and Marilyn Rash, who helped in the book's editing and production. We couldn't have done it without the help of all these people.

We also thank you, our readers. We've enjoyed writing this book, and we hope you'll find it not only very readable but also very useful in your World Wide Web endeavors. We wish you all the best of luck.

About the Authors

Dean Allemang is the chief scientist at TopQuadrant, Inc.—the first company in the United States devoted to consulting, training, and products for the Semantic Web. He codeveloped (with Professor Hendler) TopQuadrant's successful Semantic Web training series, which he has been delivering on a regular basis since 2003.

He was the recipient of a National Science Foundation Graduate Fellowship and the President's 300th Commencement Award at the Ohio State University. Allemang has studied and worked extensively throughout Europe as a Marshall Scholar at Trinity College, Cambridge, from 1982 through 1984 and was the winner of the Swiss Technology Prize twice (1992 and 1996).

In 2004, he participated in an international review board for Digital Enterprise Research Institute—the world's largest Semantic Web research institute. He currently serves on the editorial board of the *Journal of Web Semantics* and has been the Industrial Applications chair of the International Semantic Web conference since 2003.

Jim Hendler is the Tetherless World Senior Constellation Chair at Rensselaer Polytechnic Institute where he has appointments in the Departments of Computer Science and the Cognitive Science. He also serves as the associate director of the Web Science Research Initiative headquartered at the Massachusetts Institute of Technology. Dr. Hendler has authored approximately 200 technical papers in the areas of artificial intelligence, Semantic Web, agent-based computing, and high-performance processing.

One of the inventors of the Semantic Web, he was the recipient of a 1995 Fulbright Foundation Fellowship, is a former member of the U.S. Air Force Science Advisory Board, and is a Fellow of the American Association for Artificial Intelligence and the British Computer Society. Dr. Hendler is also the former chief scientist at the Information Systems Office of the U.S. Defense Advanced Research Projects Agency (DARPA), was awarded a U.S. Air Force Exceptional Civilian Service Medal in 2002, and is a member of the World Wide Web Consortium's Semantic Web Coordination Group. He is the Editor-in-Chief of *IEEE Intelligent Systems* and is the first computer scientist to serve on the Board of Reviewing Editors for *Science*.

What Is the Semantic Web?

This book is about something we call the Semantic Web. From the name, you can probably guess that it is related somehow to the famous World Wide Web (WWW) and that it has something to do with semantics. Semantics, in turn, has to do with understanding the nature of meaning, but even the word *semantics* has a number of meanings. In what sense are we using the word *semantics*? And how can it be applied to the Web?

This book is also about a working ontologist. That is, the aim of this book is not to motivate or pitch the Semantic Web but to provide the tools necessary for working with it. Or, perhaps more accurately, the World Wide Web Consortium (W3C) has provided these tools in the forms of standard Semantic Web languages, complete with abstract syntax, model-based semantics, reference implementations, test cases, and so forth. But these are like a craftsman's tools: In the hands of a novice, they can produce clumsy, ugly, barely functional output, but in the hands of a skilled craftsman, they can produce works of utility, beauty, and durability. It is our aim in this book to describe the craft of building Semantic Web systems. We go beyond coverage of the fundamental tools to show how they can be used together to create semantic models, sometimes called *ontologies,* that are understandable, useful, durable, and perhaps even beautiful.

WHAT IS A WEB?

The idea of a web of information was once a technical idea accessible only to highly trained, elite information professionals: IT administrators, librarians, information architects, and the like. Since the widespread adoption of the WWW, it is now common to expect just about anyone to be familiar with the idea of a web of information that is shared around the world. Contributions to this web come from every source, and every topic you can think of is covered.

Essential to the notion of the Web is the idea of an open community: Anyone can contribute their ideas to the whole, for anyone to see. It is this openness that has resulted in the astonishing comprehensiveness of topics covered by the Web. An information "web" is an organic entity that grows from the interests and energy of the community that supports it. As such, it is a hodgepodge of different analyses, presentations, and summaries of any topic that suits the fancy of anyone with the energy to publish a webpage. Even as a hodgepodge, the Web is pretty useful. Anyone with the patience and savvy to dig through it can find support for just about any inquiry that interests them. But the Web often feels like it is "a mile wide but an inch deep." How can we build a more integrated, consistent, deep Web experience?

SMART WEB, DUMB WEB

Suppose you consult a Webpage, looking for a major national park, and you find a list of hotels that have branches in the vicinity of the park. In that list you see that Mongotel, one of the well-known hotel chains, has a branch there. Since you have a Mongotel rewards card, you decide to book your room there. So you click on the Mongotel website and search for the hotel's location. To your surprise, you can't find a Mongotel branch at the national park. What is going on here? "That's so dumb," you tell your browsing friends. "If they list Mongotel on the national park website, shouldn't they list the national park on Mongotel's website?"

Suppose you are planning to attend a conference in a far-off city. The conference website lists the venue where the sessions will take place. You go to the website of your preferred hotel chain and find a few hotels in the same vicinity. "Which hotel in my chain is nearest to the conference?" you wonder. "And just how far off is it?" There is no shortage of websites that can compute these distances once you give them the addresses of the venue and your own hotel. So you spend some time copying and pasting the addresses from one page to the next and noting the distances. You think to yourself, "Why should I be the one to copy this information from one page to another? Why do I have to be the one to copy and paste all this information into a single map?

Suppose you are investigating our solar system, and you find a comprehensive website about objects in the solar system: Stars (well, there's just one of those), planets, moons, asteroids, and comets are all described there. Each object has its own webpage, with photos and essential information (mass, albedo, distance from the sun, shape, size, what object it revolves around, period of rotation, period of revolution, etc.). At the head of the page is the object category: planet, moon, asteroid, comet. Another page includes interesting lists of objects: the moons of Jupiter, the named objects in the asteroid belt, the planets that revolve around the sun. This last page has the nine familiar planets, each linked to its own data page.

One day, you read in the newspaper that the International Astronomical Union (IAU) has decided that Pluto, which up until 2006 was considered a planet, should be considered a member of a new category called a "dwarf planet"! You rush to the Pluto page, and see that indeed, the update has been made: Pluto is listed as a dwarf planet! But when you go back to the "Solar Planets" page, you still see nine planets listed under the heading "Planet." Pluto is still there! "That's dumb." Then you say to yourself, "Why didn't they update the webpages consistently?"

What do these examples have in common? Each of them has an apparent representation of data, whose presentation to the end user (the person operating the Web browser) seems "dumb." What do we mean by "dumb"? In this case, "dumb" means inconsistent, out of synch, and disconnected. What would it take to make the Web experience seem smarter? Do we need smarter applications or a smarter Web infrastructure?

Smart Web Applications

The Web is full of intelligent applications, with new innovations coming every day. Ideas that once seemed futuristic are now commonplace; search engines make matches that seem deep and intuitive; commerce sites make smart recommendations personalized in uncanny ways to your own purchasing patterns; mapping sites include detailed information about world geography, and they can plan routes and measure distances. The sky is the limit for the technologies a website can draw on. Every information technology under the sun can be used in a website, and many of them are. New sites with new capabilities come on the scene on a regular basis.

But what is the role of the Web infrastructure in making these applications "smart"? It is tempting to make the infrastructure of the Web smart enough to encompass all of these technologies and more. The smarter the infrastructure, the smarter the Web's performance, right? But it isn't practical, or even possible, for the Web infrastructure to provide specific support for all, or even any, of the technologies that we might want to use on the Web. Smart behavior in the Web comes from smart applications on the Web, not from the infrastructure.

So what role does the infrastructure play in making the Web smart? Is there a role at all? We have smart applications on the Web, so why are we even talking about enhancing the Web infrastructure to make a smarter Web if the smarts aren't in the infrastructure?

The reason we are improving the Web infrastructure is to allow smart applications to perform to their potential. Even the most insightful and intelligent application is only as smart as the data that is available to it. Inconsistent or contradictory input will still result in confusing, disconnected, "dumb" results, even from very smart applications. The challenge for the design of the Semantic Web is not to make a web infrastructure that is as smart as possible; it is to make an infrastructure that is most appropriate to the job of integrating information on the Web.

The Semantic Web doesn't make data smart because smart data isn't what the Semantic Web needs. The Semantic Web just needs to get the right data to the right place so the smart applications can do their work. So the question to ask is not "How can we make the Web infrastructure smarter?" but "What can the Web infrastructure provide to improve the consistency and availability of Web data?"

A Connected Web Is a Smarter Web

Even in the face of intelligent applications, disconnected data result in dumb behavior. But the Web data don't have to be smart; that's the job of the applications. So what can we realistically and productively expect from the data in our Web applications? In a nutshell, we want data that don't surprise us with inconsistencies that make us want to say, "This doesn't make sense!" We don't need a smart Web infrastructure, but we need a Web infrastructure that lets us connect data to smart Web applications so that the whole Web experience is enhanced. The Web *seems* smarter because smart applications can get the data they need.

In the example of the hotels in the national park, we'd like there to be coordination between the two webpages so that an update to the location of hotels would be reflected in the list of hotels at any particular location. We'd like the two sources to stay synchronized, then we won't be surprised at confusing and inconsistent conclusions drawn from information taken from different pages of the same site.

In the mapping example, we'd like the data from the conference website and the data from the hotels website to be automatically understandable to the mapping website. It shouldn't take interpretation by a human user to move information from one site to the other. The mapping website already has the smarts it needs to find shortest routes (taking into account details like toll roads and one-way streets) and to estimate the time required to make the trip, but it can only do that if it knows the correct starting and end points.

We'd like the astronomy website to update consistently. If we state that Pluto is no longer a planet, the list of planets should reflect that fact as well. This is the sort of behavior that gives a reader confidence that what they are reading reflects the state of knowledge reported in the website, regardless of how they read it.

None of these things is beyond the reach of current information technology. In fact, it is not uncommon for programmers and system architects, when they first learn of the Semantic Web, to exclaim proudly, "I implemented something very like that for a project I did a few years back. We used. . . ." Then they go on to explain how they used some conventional, established technology such as relational databases, XML stores, or object stores to make their data more connected and consistent. But what is it that these developers are building?

What is it about managing data this way that made it worth their while to create a whole subsystem on top of their base technology to deal with it? And where are these projects two or more years later? When those same developers are asked whether they would rather have built a flexible, distributed, connected data model support system themselves or to have used a standard one that someone else optimized and supported, they unanimously chose the latter. Infrastructure is something that one would rather buy than build.

SEMANTIC DATA

In the Mongotel example, there is a list of hotels at the national park and another list of locations for hotels. The fact that these lists are intended to represent the presence of a hotel at a certain location is not explicit anywhere; this makes it difficult to maintain consistency between the two representations. In the example of the conference venue, the address appears only as text typeset on a page so that human beings can interpret it as an address. There is no explicit representation of the notion of an address or the parts that make up an address. In the case of the astronomy webpage, there is no explicit representation of the status of an object as a planet. In all of these cases, the data describe the presentation of information rather than describe the entities in the world.

Could it be some other way? Can an application organize its data so that they provide an integrated description of objects in the world and their relationships rather than their presentation? The answer is "yes," and indeed it is common good practice in website design to work this way. There are a number of well-known approaches.

One common way to make Web applications more integrated is to back them up with a relational database and generate the webpages from queries run against that database. Updates to the site are made by updating the contents of the database. All webpages that require information about a particular data record will change when that record changes, without any further action required by the Web maintainer. The database holds information about the entities themselves, while the relationship between one page and another (presentation) is encoded in the different queries.

Consider the case of the national parks and hotel. If these pages were backed by the same database, the national park page could be built on the query "Find all hotels with location = national park," and the hotel page could be built on the query "Find all hotels from chain = Mongotel." If Mongotel has a location at the national park, it will appear on both pages; otherwise, it won't appear at all. Both pages will be consistent. The difficulty in the example given is that it is organizationally very unlikely that there could be a single database driving both of these pages, since one of them is published and maintained by the National Park Service and the other is managed by the Mongotel chain.

The astronomy case is very similar to the hotel case, in that the same information (about the classification of various astronomical bodies) is accessed from two different places, ensuring consistency of information even in the face of diverse presentation. It differs in that it is more likely that an astronomy club or university department might maintain a database with all the currently known information about the solar system.

In these cases, the Web applications can behave more robustly by adding an organizing query into the Web application to mediate between a single view of the data and the presentation. The data aren't any less dumb than before, but at least what's there is centralized, and the application or the webpages can be made to organize the data in a way that is more consistent for the user to view. It is the webpage or application that behaves smarter, not the data. While this approach is useful for supporting data consistency, it doesn't help much with the conference mapping example.

Another approach to making Web applications a bit smarter is to write program code in a general-purpose language (e.g., C, Perl, Java, Lisp, Python, or XSLT) that keeps data from different places up to date. In the hotel example, such a program would update the National Park webpage whenever a change is made to a corresponding hotel page. A similar solution would allow the planet example to be more consistent. Code for this purpose is often organized in a relational database application in the form of *stored procedures*; in XML applications, it can be affected using a transformational language like XSLT.

These solutions are more cumbersome to implement, since they require special-purpose code to be written for each linkage of data, but they have the advantage over a centralized database that they do not require all the publishers of the data to agree on and share a single data source. Furthermore, such approaches could provide a solution to the conference mapping problem by transforming data from one source to another. Just as in the query/presentation solution, this solution does not make the data any smarter; it just puts an informed infrastructure around the data, whose job it is to keep the various data sources consistent.

The common trend in these solutions is to move away from having the presentation of the data (for human eyes) be the primary representation of the data; that is, they move from having a website be a collection of pages to having a website be a collection of data, from which the webpage presentations are generated. The application focuses not on the presentation but on the subjects of the presentation. It is in this sense that these applications are semantic applications; they explicitly represent the relationships that underlie the application and generate presentations as needed.

A Distributed Web of Data

The Semantic Web takes this idea one step further, applying it to the Web as a whole. The current Web infrastructure supports a distributed network of webpages that can refer to one another with global links called Uniform Resource Locators (URLs). As we have seen, sophisticated websites replace this structure locally with a database or XML backend that ensures consistency within that page.

The main idea of the Semantic Web is to support a distributed Web at the level of the data rather than at the level of the presentation. Instead of having one webpage point to another, one data item can point to another, using global references called Uniform Resource Identifiers (URIs). The Web infrastructure provides a data model whereby information about a single entity can be distributed over the Web. This distribution allows the Mongotel example and the conference hotel example to work like the astronomy example, even though the information is distributed over websites controlled by more than one organization. The single, coherent data model for the application is not held inside one application but rather is part of the Web infrastructure. When Mongotel publishes information about its hotels and their locations, it doesn't just publish a human-readable presentation of this information but instead a distributable, machine-readable description of the data. The data model that the Semantic Web infrastructure uses to represent this distributed web of data is called the Resource Description Framework (RDF) and is the topic of Chapter 3.

This single, distributed model of information is the contribution that the Semantic Web infrastructure brings to a smarter web. Just as is the case with data-backed Web applications, the Semantic Web infrastructure allows the data to drive the presentation so that various webpages (presentations) can provide views into a consistent body of information. In this way, the Semantic Web helps data not be so dumb.

Features of a Semantic Web

The World Wide Web was the result of a radical new way of thinking about sharing information. These ideas seem familiar now, as the Web itself has become pervasive. But this radical new way of thinking has even more profound ramifications when it is applied to a web of data like the Semantic Web. These ramifications have driven many of the design decisions for the Semantic Web Standards and have a strong influence on the craft of producing quality Semantic Web applications.

Give Me a Voice . . .

On the World Wide Web, publication is by and large in the hands of the content producer. People can build their own webpage and say whatever they want on it. A wide range of opinions on any topic can be found; it is up to the reader to come to a conclusion about what to believe. The Web is the ultimate example of the warning *caveat emptor* ("Let the buyer beware"). This feature of the Web is so instrumental in its character that we give it a name: the *AAA Slogan*: "**A**nyone can say **A**nything about **A**ny topic."

In a web of documents, the AAA slogan means that anyone can write a page saying whatever they please, and publish it to the Web infrastructure. In the case of the Semantic Web, it means that our data infrastructure has to allow any individual to express a piece of data about some entity in a way that can be combined with information from other sources. This requirement sets some of the foundation for the design of RDF.

It also means that information is not managed as usual for a large, corporate data center, where one database administrator rules with an iron hand over any addition or modification to the database. A distributed web of data, in contrast, is an organic system, with contributions coming from all sources. It was this freedom of expression on the document Web that allowed it to take off as a bottom-up, grassroots phenomenon.

... *So I May Speak!*

In the early days of the document Web, it was common for skeptics, hearing for the first time about the possibilities of a worldwide distributed web full of hyperlinked pages on every topic, to ask, "But who is going to create all that content? Someone has to write those webpages!"

To the surprise of those skeptics, and even of many proponents of the Web, the answer to this question was that *everyone* would provide the content. Once the Web infrastructure was in place (so that Anyone could say Anything about Any topic), people came out of the woodwork to do just that. Soon every topic under the sun had a webpage, either official or unofficial. It turns out that a lot of people had something to say, and they were willing to put some work into saying it.

The document Web grew because of a virtuous cycle that is called the *network effect*. In a network of contributors like the Web, the infrastructure made it *possible* for anyone to publish, but what made it *desirable* for them to do so? At one point in the Web, when Web browsers were a novelty, there was not much incentive to put a page on this new thing called "the Web"; after all, who was going to read it? Why do I want to communicate to them? Just as it isn't very useful to be the first kid on the block to have a fax machine (whom do you exchange faxes with?), it wasn't very interesting to be the first kid with a Web server.

But because a few people did have Web servers, and a few more got Web browsers, it became more attractive to have both webpages and Web browsers. Content providers found a larger audience for their work; content consumers found more content to browse. As this trend continued, it became more and more attractive, and more people joined in, on both sides. This is the basis of the network effect: The more people who are playing now, the more attractive it is for new people to start playing.

A good deal of the information that will populate the Semantic Web is already available on the Web, typically in the form of tables, spreadsheets, or databases. Who will do the work of converting this data to RDF for distributed access? In the earliest days of the Semantic Web, there was little incentive to do so. As more and more data is available in RDF form, it becomes more useful to write applications that utilize this distributed data. The Semantic Web has been designed to benefit from the same network effect that drove the document Web.

What about the Round-Worlders?

The network effect has already proven to be an effective and empowering way to muster the effort needed to create a massive information network like the World Wide Web; in fact, it is the only method that has actually succeeded in creating such a structure. The AAA slogan enables the network effect that made the rapid growth of the Web possible. But what are some of the ramifications of such an open system? What does the AAA slogan imply for the content of an organically grown web?

For the network effect to take hold, we have to be prepared to cope with a wide range of variance in the information on the Web. Sometimes the differences will be minor details in an otherwise agreed-on area; at other times, differences may be essential disagreements that drive political and cultural discourse in our society. This phenomenon is apparent in the document web today; for just about any topic, it is possible to find webpages that express widely differing opinions about that topic. The ability to disagree, and at various levels, is an essential part of human discourse and a key aspect of the Web that makes it successful. Some people might want to put forth a very odd opinion on any topic; someone might even want to postulate that the world is round, while others insist that it is flat. The infrastructure of the Web must allow both of these (contradictory) opinions to have equal availability and access.

There are a number of ways in which two speakers on the Web may disagree. We will illustrate each of them with the example of the status of Pluto as a planet:

They may fundamentally disagree on some topic. While the IAU has changed its definition of *planet* in such a way that Pluto is no longer included, it is not necessarily the case that every astronomy club or even national body agrees with this categorization. Many astrologers, in particular, who have a vested interest in considering Pluto to be a planet, have decided to continue to consider Pluto as a planet. In such cases, different sources will simply disagree.

Someone might want to intentionally deceive. Someone who markets posters, models, or other works that depict nine planets has a good reason to delay reporting the result from the IAU and even to spreading uncertainty about the state of affairs.

Someone might simply be mistaken. Websites are built and maintained by human beings, and thus they are subject to human error. Some website might erroneously list Pluto as a planet or, indeed, might even erroneously fail to list one of the eight "nondwarf" planets as a planet.

Some information may be out of date. There are a number of displays around the world of scale models of the solar system, in which the status of the planets is literally carved in stone; these will continue to list Pluto as a planet until such time as there is funding to carve a new description for the ninth object. Websites are not carved in stone, but it does take effort to update them; not everyone will rush to accomplish this.

While some of the reasons for disagreement might be, well, disagreeable (wouldn't it be nice if we could stop people from lying?), in practice there isn't any way to tell them apart. The infrastructure of the Web has to be able to cope with the fact that information on the Web will disagree from time to time and that this is not a temporary condition. It is in the very nature of the Web that there be variations and disagreement.

To Each Their Own

How can the Web infrastructure support this sort of variation of opinion? That is, how can two people say different things, about the same topic? There are two approaches to this issue. First, we have to talk a bit about how one can make any statement at all in a web context.

The IAU can make a statement in plain English about Pluto, such as "Pluto is a dwarf planet," but such a statement is fraught with all the ambiguities and contextual dependencies inherent in natural language. We think we know what "Pluto" refers to, but how about "dwarf planet"? Is there any possibility that someone might disagree on what a "dwarf planet" is? How can we even discuss such things?

The first requirement for making statements on a global web is to have a global way of identifying the entities we are talking about. We need to be able to refer to "the notion of Pluto as used by the IAU" and "the notion of Pluto as used by the American Federation of Astrologers" if we even want to be able to discuss whether the two organizations are referring to the same thing by these names.

In addition to Pluto, another object was also classified as a "dwarf planet." This object is sometimes known as UB313 and sometimes known by the name Xena. How can we say that the object known to the IAU as UB313 is the same object that its discoverer Michael Brown calls "Xena"?

One way to do this would be to have a global arbiter of names decide how to refer to the object. Then Brown and the IAU can both refer to that "official" name and say that they use a private "nickname" for it. Of course, the IAU itself is a good candidate for such a body, but the process to name the object has already taken over two years. Coming up with good, agreed-on global names is not always easy business.

In the absence of such an agreement, different Web authors will select different URIs for the same real-world resource. Brown's Xena is IAU's UB313. When information from these different sources is brought together in the distributed network of data, the Web infrastructure has no way of knowing that these need to be treated as the same entity. The flip side of this is that we cannot assume that just because two URIs are distinct, they refer to distinct resources. This feature of the Semantic Web is called the *Nonunique Naming Assumption*; that is, we have to assume (until told otherwise) that some Web resource might be referred to using different names by different people.

There's Always One More

In a distributed network of information, as a rule we cannot assume at any time that we have seen all the information in the network, or even that we know everything that has been asserted about one single topic. This is evident in the history of Pluto and UB313. For many years, it was sufficient to say that a *planet* was defined as "any object orbiting the sun of a particular size." Given the information available during that time, it was easy to say that there were nine planets around the sun. But the new information about UB313 changed that; if a planet is defined to be any body that orbits the sun of a particular size, then UB313 had to be considered a planet, too. Careful speakers in the late twentieth century, of course, spoke of the "known" planets, since they were aware that another planet was not only possible but even suspected (the so-called "Planet X," which stood in for the unknown but suspected planet for many years).

The same situation holds for the Semantic Web. Not only might new information be discovered at any time (as is the case in solar system astronomy), but, because of the networked nature of the Web, at any one time a particular server that holds some unique information might be unavailable. For this reason, on the Semantic Web we can rarely conclude things like "there are nine planets," since we don't know what new information might come to light.

In general, this aspect of a Web has a subtle but profound impact on how we draw conclusions from the information we have. It forces us to consider the Web as an *Open World* and to treat it using the *Open World Assumption*. An open world in this sense is one in which we must assume at any time that new information could come to light, and we may draw no conclusions that rely on assuming that the information available at any one point is all the information available.

For many applications, the open world assumption makes no difference; if we draw a map of all the Mongotel hotels in Boston, we get a map of all the ones we know of at the time. The fact that Mongotel might have more hotels in Boston (or might open a new one) does not invalidate the fact that it has the ones it already lists. In fact, for a great deal of Semantic Web applications, we can ignore the open world assumption and simply understand that a semantic application, like any other webpage, is simply reporting on the information it was able to access at one time.

The openness of the Web only becomes an issue when we want to draw conclusions based on distributed data. If we want to place Boston in the list of cities that are not served by Mongotel (e.g., as part of a market study of new places to target Mongotels), then we cannot assume that just because we haven't found a Mongotel listing in Boston, no such hotel exists.

As we shall see in the following chapters, the Semantic Web includes features that correspond to all the ways of working with open worlds that we have seen in the real world. We can draw conclusions about missing Mongotels if we say that some list is a comprehensive list of all Mongotels. We can have an anonymous "Planet X" stand in for an unknown but anticipated entity. These techniques allow us to cope with the open world assumption in the Semantic Web, just as they do in the open world of human knowledge.

SUMMARY

The aspects of the Web we have outlined here—the AAA slogan, the network effect, nonunique naming and the open world assumption—already hold for the document Web. As a result, the Web today is something of an unruly place, with a wide variety of different sources, organizations, and styles of information. Effective and creative use of search engines is something of a craft; efforts to make order from this include community efforts like social bookmarking and community encyclopedias to automated methods like statistical correlations and fuzzy similarity matches.

For the Semantic Web, which operates at the finer level of individual statements about data, the situation is even wilder. With a human in the loop, contradictions and inconsistencies in the document Web can be dealt with by the process of human observation and application of common sense. With a machine combining information, how do we bring any order to the chaos? How can one have any confidence in the information we merge from multiple sources? If the document Web is unruly, then surely the Semantic Web is a jungle—a rich mass of interconnected information, without any roadmap, index, or guidance.

How can such a mess become something useful? That is the challenge that faces the working ontologist. Their medium is the distributed web of data; their tools are the Semantic Web languages RDF, RDFS, and OWL. Their craft is to make sensible, usable, and durable information resources from this medium. We call that craft *modeling*, and it is the centerpiece of this book.

The cover of this book shows a system of channels with water coursing through them. If we think of the water as the data that are on the Web, the channels are the model. If not for the model, the water would not flow in any systematic way; there would simply be a vast, undistinguished expanse of water. Without the water, the channels would have no dynamism; they have no moving parts in and of themselves. Put the two together, and we have a dynamic system. The water flows in an orderly fashion, defined by the structure of the channels. This is the role that a model plays in the Semantic Web.

Without the model, there is an undifferentiated mass of data; there is no way to tell which data can or should interact with other data. The model itself has no significance without data to describe it. Put the two together, however, and you have a dynamic web of information, where data flow from one point to another in a principled, systematic fashion. This is the vision of the Semantic Web—an organized worldwide system where information flows from one place to another in a smooth but orderly way.

Fundamental Concepts

The following fundamental concepts were introduced in this chapter.

The AAA slogan—Anyone can say Anything about Any topic. One of the basic tenets of the Web in general and the Semantic Web in particular.

Open world/closed world—A consequence of the AAA slogan is that there could always be something new that someone will say; this means that we must assume that there is always more information that could be known.

Nonunique naming—Since the speakers on the Web won't necessarily coordinate their naming efforts, the same entity could be known by more than one name.

The network effect—The property of a web that makes it grow organically. The value of joining in increases with the number of people who have joined, resulting in a virtuous cycle of participation.

Semantic Modeling $\Big|\,2$

What would you call a world in which any number of people can speak, when you never know who has something useful to say, and when someone new might come along at any time and make a valuable but unexpected contribution? What if just about everyone had the same goal of advancing the collaborative state of knowledge of the group, but there was little agreement (at first, anyway) about how to achieve it?

If your answer is "That sounds like the Semantic Web!" you are right (and you must have read Chapter 1). If your answer is "It sounds like any large group trying to understand a complex phenomenon," you are even more right. The jungle that is the Semantic Web is not a new thing; this sort of chaos has existed since people first tried to make sense of the world around them.

What intellectual tools have been successful in helping people sort through this sort of tangle? Any number of analytical tools has been developed over the years, but they all have one thing in common: They help people understand their world by forming an abstract description that hides certain details while illuminating others. These abstractions are called *models*, and they can take many forms.

How do models help people assemble their knowledge? Models assist in three essential ways:

1. *Models help people communicate.* A model describes the situation in a particular way that other people can understand.

2. *Models explain and make predictions.* A model relates primitive phenomena to one another and to more complex phenomena, providing explanations and predictions about the world.

3. *Models mediate among multiple viewpoints.* No two people agree completely on what they want to know about a phenomenon; models represent their commonalities while allowing them to explore their differences.

The Semantic Web standards have been created not only as a medium in which people can collaborate by sharing information but also as a medium in which **15** people can collaborate on models. Models that they can use to organize the information that they share. Models that they can use to advance the common collection of knowledge.

How can a model help us find our way through the mess that is the Web? How do these three features help? The first feature, human communication, allows people to collaborate on their understanding. If someone else has faced the same challenge that you face today, perhaps you can learn from their experience and apply it to yours. There are a number of examples of this in the Web today, of newsgroups, mailing lists, and wikis where people can ask questions and get answers. In the case in which the information needs are fairly uniform, it is not uncommon for a community or a company to assemble a set of "Frequently Asked Questions," or FAQs, that gather the appropriate knowledge as answers to these questions. As the number of questions becomes unmanageable, it is not uncommon to group them by topic, by task, by affected subsystem, and so forth. This sort of activity, by which information is organized for the purpose of sharing, is the simplest and most common kind of modeling, with the sole aim of helping a group of people collaborate in their effort to sort through a complex set of knowledge.

The second feature, explanation and prediction, helps individuals make their own judgments based on information they receive. FAQs are useful when there is a single authority that can give clear answers to a question, as is the case for technical assistance for using some appliance or service. But in more interpretive situations, someone might want or need to draw a conclusion for themselves. In such a situation, a simple answer as given in a FAQ is not sufficient. Politics is a common example from everyday life. Politicians in debate do not tell people how to vote, but they try to convince them to vote in one way or another. Part of that convincing is done by explaining their position and allowing the individual to evaluate whether that explanation holds true to their own beliefs about the world. They also typically make predictions: If we follow this course of action, then a particular outcome will follow. Of course, a lot more goes into political persuasion than the argument, but explanation and prediction are key elements of a persuasive argument.

Finally, the third feature, mediation of multiple viewpoints, is essential to fostering understanding in a web environment. As the web of opinions and facts grows, many people will say things that disagree slightly or even outright contradict what others are saying. Anyone who wants to make their way through this will have to be able to sort out different opinions, representing what they have in common as well as the ways in which they differ. This is one of the most essential organizing principles of a large, heterogeneous knowledge set, and it is one of the major contributions that modeling makes to helping people organize what they know.

Astrologers and the IAU agree on the planethood of Mercury, Venus, Earth, Mars, Jupiter, Saturn, Uranus, and Neptune. The IAU also agrees with astrologers that Pluto is a planet, but it disagrees by calling it a dwarf planet. Astrologers (or classical astronomers) do not accept the concept of dwarf planets, so they are not in agreement with the IAU, which categorizes UB313 and Ceres as such. A model for the Semantic Web must be able to organize this sort of variation, and much more, in a meaningful and manageable way.

MODELING FOR HUMAN COMMUNICATION

Models used for human communication have a great advantage over models that are intended for use by computers; they can take advantage of the human capacity to interpret signs to give them meaning. This means that communication models can be written in a wide variety of forms, including plain language or ad hoc images. A model can be explained by one person, amended by another, interpreted by a third person, and so on. Models written in natural language have been used in all manner of intellectual life, including science, religion, government, and mathematics.

But this advantage is a double-edged sword; when we leave it to humans to interpret the meaning of a model, we open the door for all manner of abuse, both intentional and unintentional. Legislation provides a good example of this. A governing body like a parliament or a legislature enacts laws that are intended to mediate rights and responsibilities between various parties. Legislation typically sets up some sort of model of a situation, perhaps involving money (e.g., interest caps, taxes); access rights (who can view what information, how can information be legally protected); personal freedom (how freely can one travel across borders, when does the government have the right to restrict a person's movements); or even the structure of government itself (who can vote and how are those votes counted, how can government officials be removed from office). These models are painstakingly written in natural language and agreed on through an elaborate process (which is also typically modeled in natural language).

It is well known to anyone with even a passing interest in politics that good legislation is not an easy task and that crafting the words carefully for a law or statute is very important. The same flexibility of interpretation that makes natural language models so flexible also makes it difficult to control how the laws will be interpreted in the future. When someone else reads the text, they will have their own background and their own interests that will influence how they interpret any particular model. This phenomenon is so widespread that most government systems include a process (usually involving a court magistrate and possibly a committee of citizens) whereby disputes over the interpretation of a law or its applicability can be resolved.

When a model relies on particulars of the context of its reader for interpretation of its meaning, as is the case in legislation, we say that a model is *informal*. That is, the model lacks a formalism whereby the meaning of terms in the model can be uniquely defined.

In the document web today, there are informal models that help people communicate about the organization of the information. It is common for commerce websites to organize their wares in catalogs with category names like "webcams," "Oxford shirts," and "Granola." In such cases, the communication is primarily one-way; the catalogue designer wants to communicate to the buyers the information that will help them find what they want to buy. The interpretation of these words is up to the buyers. The effectiveness of such a model is measured by the degree to which this is successful. If enough people interpret the categories in a way similar enough to the intent of the cataloguer, then they will find what they want to buy. There will be the occasional discrepancy like "Why wasn't that item listed as a *webcam*?" or "That's not granola, that's just plain cereal!" But as long as the interpretation is close enough, the model is successful.

A more collaborative style of document modeling comes in the form of community tagging. A number of websites have been successful by allowing users to provide meaningful symbolic descriptions of their content in the form of *tags*. A tag in this sense is simply a single word or short phrase that describes some aspect of the content. Examples of tagging systems include Flickr for photos and del.icio.us for Web bookmarks. The idea of community tagging is that each individual who provides content will describe it using tags of their own choosing. If any two people use the same tag, this becomes a common organizing entity; anyone who is browsing for content can access information from both contributors under that tag. The tagging infrastructure shows which tags have been used by many people. Not only does this help browsers determine what tags to use in a search, but it also helps content providers to find commonly used tags that they might want to use to describe new content. Thus, a tagging system will have a certain self-organizing character, whereby popular tags become more popular and unpopular tags remain unpopular—something like evolution by artificial selection of tags.

Tagging systems of this sort provide an informal organization to a large body of heterogeneous information. The organization is informal in the sense that the interpretation of the tags requires human processing in the context of the consumer. Just because a tag is popular doesn't mean that everyone is using it in the same way. In fact, the community selection process actually selects tags that are used in several different ways, whether they are compatible or not. As more and more people provide content, the popular tags saturate with a wide variety of content, making them less and less useful as discriminators for people browsing for content. This sort of problem is inherent in information modeling systems; since there isn't an objective description of the meaning of a symbol outside the context of the provider and consumer of the symbol, the communication power of that symbol degrades as it is used in more and more contexts.

Formality of a model isn't a black-and-white judgment; there can be degrees of formality. This is clear in legal systems, where it is common to have several layers of legislation, each one giving objective context for the next. A contract between two parties is usually governed by some regional law that provides standard definitions for terms in the contract. Regional laws are governed by national laws, which provide constraints and definitions for their terms. National laws have their own structure, in which a constitution or a body of case law provides a framework for new decisions and legislation. Even though all these models are expressed in natural language and fall back on human interpretation in the long run, they can be more formal than private agreements that rely almost entirely on the interpretation of the agreeing parties.

This layering of informal models sometimes results in a modeling style that is reminiscent of Talmudic scholarship. The content of the Talmud includes not only the original scripture but also interpretative comments on the scripture by authoritative sources (classical rabbis). Their comments have gained such respect that they are traditionally published along with the original scripture for comment by later rabbis, whose comments in turn have become part of the intellectual tradition. The original scripture, along with all the authoritative comments, is collectively called the Talmud, and it is the basis of a classical Jewish education to this day.

A similar effect happens with informal models. The original model is appropriate in some context, but as its use expands beyond that context, further models are required to provide common context to explicate the shared meaning. But if this further exposition is also informal, then there is the risk that its meaning will not be clear, so further modeling must be done to clarify that. This results in heavily layered models, in which the meaning of the terms is always subject to further interpretation. It is the inherent ambiguity of natural language at each level that makes the next layer of commentary necessary until the degree of ambiguity is "good enough" that no more levels are needed. When it is possible to choose words that are evocative and have considerable agreement, this process converges much more quickly.

Human communication, as a goal for modeling, allows it to play a role in the ongoing collection of human knowledge. The levels of communication can be quite sophisticated, including the collection of information used to interpret other information. In this sense, human communication is the fundamental requirement for building a Semantic Web. It allows people to contribute to a growing body of knowledge and then draw from it. But communication is not enough; to empower a web of human knowledge, the information in a model needs to be organized in such a way that it can be useful to a wide range of consumers.

EXPLANATION AND PREDICTION

Models are used to organize human thought in the form of explanations. When we understand how a phenomenon results from other basic principles, we gain a number of advantages. Not least is the feeling of confidence that we have actually understood it; people often claim to "have a grasp on" or "have their head around" an idea when they finally understand it. Explanation plays a major role in this sort of understanding. Explanation also assists in memory; it is easier to remember that putting a lid on a flaming pot can quench the flame if one knows the explanation that fire requires air to burn. Most important for the context of the Semantic Web, explanation makes it easier to reuse a model in whole or in part; an explanation relates a conclusion to more basic principles. Understanding how a pot lid quenches a fire can help one understand how a candle snuffer works. Explanation is the key to understanding when a model is applicable and when it is not.

Closely related to this aspect of a model is the idea of prediction. When a model provides an adequate explanation of a phenomenon, it can also be used to make predictions. This aspect of models is what makes their use central to the scientific method, where falsification of predictions made by models forms the basis of the methodology of inquiry.

Explanation and prediction typically require models with a good deal more formality than is usually required for human communication. An explanation relates a phenomenon to "first principles"; these principles, and the rules by which they are related, do not depend on interpretation by the consumer but instead are in some objective form that stands outside the communication. Such an objective form, and the rules that govern how it works, is called a *formalism*.

Formal models are the bread and butter of mathematical modeling, in which very specific rules for calculation and symbol manipulation govern the structure of a mathematical model and the valid ways in which one item can refer to another. Explanations come in the form of proofs, in which steps from premises (stated in some formalism) to conclusions are made according to strict rules of transformation for the formalism. Formal models are used in many human intellectual endeavors, wherever precision and objectivity are required.

Formalisms can also be used for predictions. Given a description of a situation in some formalism, the same rules that govern transformations in proofs can be used to make predictions. We can explain the trajectory of an object thrown out of a window with a formal model of force, gravity, speed, and mass, but given the initial conditions of the object thrown, we can also compute, and thus predict, its trajectory.

Formal prediction and explanation allow us to evaluate when a model is applicable. Furthermore, the formalism allows that evaluation to be independent of the listener. One can dispute the result that $2 + 2 = 4$ by questioning just what the terms "2," "4," "+," and "=" mean, but once people agree on what they mean, they cannot (reasonably) dispute that this formula is correct.

Formal modeling therefore has a very different social dynamic than informal modeling; because there is an objective reference to the model (the formalism), there is no need for the layers of interpretation that result in Talmudic modeling. Instead of layers and layers of interpretation, the buck stops at the formalism.

As we shall see, the Semantic Web standards include a small variety of modeling formalisms. Because they are formalisms, modeling in the Semantic Web need not become a process of layering interpretation on interpretation. Also, because they are formalisms, it is possible to couch explanations in the Semantic Web in the form of proofs and to use that proof mechanism to make predictions. This aspect of Semantic Web models goes by the name *inference*, and it will be discussed in detail in Chapter 5.

Mediating Variability

In any Web setting, variability is to be expected and even embraced. The dynamics of the network effect require the ability to represent a variety of opinions. A good model organizes those opinions so that the things that are common can be represented together, while the things that are distinct can be represented as well.

Let's take the case of Pluto as an example. From 1930 until 2006, it was considered to be a planet by astronomers and astrologers alike. After the redefinition of *planet* by the IAU in 2006, Pluto was no longer considered to be a planet but more specifically a *dwarf planet* by the IAU and by astronomers who accept the IAU as an authority. Astrologers, however, chose not to adopt the IAU convention, and they continued to consider Pluto a planet. Some amateur astronomers, mostly for nostalgic reasons, also continued to consider Pluto a planet. How can we accommodate all of these variations of opinion on the Web?

One way to accommodate them would be to make a decision as to which one is "preferred" and to control the Web so that only that position is supported. This is the solution that is most commonly used in corporate data centers, where a small group or even a single person acts as the database administrator and decides what data are allowed to live in the corporate database. This solution is not appropriate for the Web because it does not allow for the AAA slogan (see Chapter 1) that leads to the network effect.

Another way to accommodate these different viewpoints would be to simply allow each one to be represented separately, with no reference to one another at all. It would be the responsibility of the information consumer to understand how these things relate to one another and to make any connections as appropriate. This is the basis of an informal approach, and it indeed describes the state of the document web as it is today. A Web search for Pluto will turn up a wide array of articles, in which some call it a planet (e.g., astrological ones or astronomical ones that have not been updated), some call it a dwarf planet (IAU official websites), and some that are still debating the issue. The only way a reader can come to understand what is common among these things—the notion of a planet, of the solar system, or even of Pluto itself—is through reader interpretation.

How can a model help sort this out? How can a model describe what is common about the astrological notion of a planet, the twentieth-century astronomical notion of a planet, and the post-2006 notion of a planet? The model must also allow for each of these differing viewpoints to be expressed.

Variation and Classes

This problem is not a new one; it is a well-known problem in software engineering. When a software component is designed, it has to provide certain functionality, determined by information given to it at runtime. There is a trade-off in such a design; the component can be made to operate in a wide variety of circumstances, but it will require a complex input to describe just how it should behave at any one time. Or the system could be designed to work with very simple input but be useful in only a small number of very specific situations. The design of a software component inherently involves a model of the commonality and variability in the environment in which it is expected to be deployed. In response to this challenge, software methodology has developed the art of object modeling (in the context of Object-Oriented Programming, or OOP) as a means of organizing commonality and variability in software components.

One of the primary organizing tools in OOP is the notion of a hierarchy of classes and subclasses. Classes high up in the hierarchy represent functionality that is common to a large number of components; classes farther down in a hierarchy represent more specific functionality. Commonality and variability in the functionality of a set of software components is represented in a class hierarchy.

The Semantic Web standards also use this idea of class hierarchy for representing commonality and variability. Since the Semantic Web, unlike OOP, is not focused on software representation, classes are not defined in terms of behaviors of functions. But the notion of classes and subclasses remains, and it plays much the same role. High-level classes represent commonality among a large variety of entities, whereas lower-level classes represent commonality among a small, specific set of things.

Let's take Pluto as an example. The 2006 IAU definition of *planet* is quite specific in requiring these three criteria for a celestial body to be considered a planet:

1. It is in orbit around the sun.
2. It has sufficient mass to be nearly round.
3. It has cleared the neighborhood around its orbit.

The IAU goes further to state that a dwarf planet is a body that satisfies conditions 1 and 2 (and not 3); a body that satisfies only condition 1 is a *small solar system body (SSSB)*. These definitions make a number of things clear: The classes SSSB, dwarf planet, and planet are all mutually exclusive; no body is a member of any two classes. However, there is something that all of them have in common: They all are in orbit around the sun.

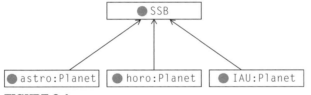

FIGURE 2-1

Subclass diagram for different notions of *planet.*

Twentieth-century astronomy and astrology are not quite as organized as this; they don't have such rigorous definitions of the word *planet.* So how can we relate these notions to the twenty-first-century notion of *planet?*

The first thing we need is a way to talk about the various uses of the word *planet:* the IAU use, the astrological use, and the twentieth-century astronomical use. This seems like a simple requirement, but until it is met, we can't even talk about the relationship among these terms. We will see details of the Semantic Web solution to this issue in Chapter 3, but for now, we will simply prefix each term with a short abbreviation of its source—for example, use `IAU:Planet` for the IAU use of the word, `horo:Planet` for the astrological use, and `astro:Planet` for the twentieth-century astronomical use.

The solution begins by noticing what it is that all three notions of *planet* have in common; in this case, it is that the body orbits the sun. Thus, we can define a class of the things that orbit the sun, which we may as well call *solar system body,* or *SSB* for short. All three notions are subclasses of this notion. This can be depicted graphically as in Figure 2-1.

We can go further in this modeling when we observe that there are only eight `IAU:Planet`s, and each one is also a `horo:Planet` and an `astro:Planet`. Thus, we can say that `IAU:Planet` is a subclass of both `horo:Planet` and `astro:Planet`, as shown in Figure 2-2. We can continue in this way, describing the relationships among all the concepts we have mentioned so far: `IAU:dwarf planet` and `IAU:SSSB`. As we go down the tree, each class refers to a more restrictive set of entities. In this way, we can model the commonality among entities (at the high level) while respecting their variation (at a low level).

Variation and Layers

Classes and subclasses are a fine way to organize variation when there is a simple, known relationship between the modeled entities and it is possible to determine a clear ordering of classes that describes these relationships. In a Web setting, however, this usually is not the case. Each contributor can have something new to say that may fit in with previous statements in a wide variety of ways. How can we accommodate variation of sources if we can't structure the entities they are describing into a class model?

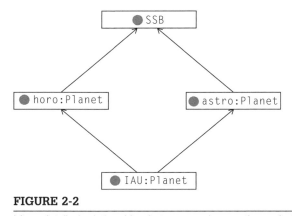

FIGURE 2-2

More detailed relationships between various notions of *planet*.

The Semantic Web provides an elegant solution to this problem. The basic idea is that any model can be built up from contributions from multiple sources. One way of thinking about this is to consider a model to be described in layers. Each layer comes from a different source. The entire model is the combination of all the layers, viewed as a single, unified whole.

Let's have a look at how this could work in the case of Pluto. Figure 2-3 illustrates how different communities could assert varying information about Pluto. In part (a) of the figure, we see some information about Pluto that is common among astrologers—namely, that Pluto signifies rebirth and regeneration and that the preferred symbol for referring to Pluto is the glyph indicated. Part (b) shows some information that is of concern to astronomers, including the composition of the body Pluto and their preferred symbol. How can this variation be accommodated in a web of information? The simplest way is to simply merge the two models into a single one that includes all the information from each model, as shown in part (c).

Merging models in this way is a conceptually simple thing to do, but how does it cope with variability? In the first place, it copes in the simplest way possible: It allows the astrologers and the astronomers to both have their say about Pluto (remember the AAA slogan!). For any party that is interested in both of these things (perhaps someone looking for a spiritual significance for elements?), the information can be viewed as a single, unified whole.

But merging models in this way has a drawback as well. In Figure 2-3(c), there are two distinct glyphs, each claiming to be the "preferred" symbol for Pluto. This brings up issues of consistency of viewpoints. On the face of it, this appears to be an inconsistency because, from its name, we might expect that there can be exactly one preferred symbol (prefSymbol) for any body. But how can a machine know that? For a machine, the name prefSymbol can't be treated any differently from any other label—for instance, madeOf or signifies. In such a context, how can we even tell that this is an inconsistency? After all,

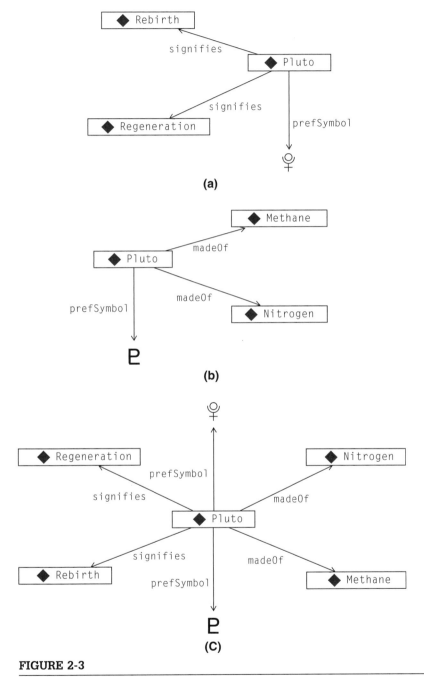

FIGURE 2-3

Layers of modeled information about Pluto.

we don't think it is an inconsistency that Pluto can be composed of more than one chemical compound or that it can signify more than one spiritual theme. Do we have to describe this in a natural language commentary on the model?

Detailed answers to questions like these are exactly the reason why we need to publish models on the Semantic Web. When two (or more!) viewpoints come together in a web of knowledge, there will typically be overlap, disagreement, and confusion before there is synergy, cooperation, and collaboration. If the infrastructure of the Web is to help us to find our way through the wild stage of information sharing, an informal notion of how things fit together, or should fit together, will not suffice. It is easy enough to say that we have an intuition that states there is something special about `prefSymbol` that makes it different from `madeOf` or `signifies`. If we can inform our infrastructure about this distinction in a sufficiently formal way, then it can, for instance, detect discrepancies of this sort and, in some cases, even resolve them.

This is the essence of modeling in the Semantic Web: providing an infrastructure where not only can anyone say anything about any topic but the infrastructure can help a community work through the resulting chaos. A model can provide a framework (like classes and subclasses) for representing and organizing commonality and variability of viewpoints when they are known. But in advance of such an organization, a model can provide a framework for describing what sorts of things we can say about something. We might not agree on the symbol for Pluto, but we can agree that it should have just one preferred symbol.

Expressivity in Modeling

There is a trade-off when we model, and although anyone can say anything about any topic, not everyone will want to say certain things. There are those who are interested in saying details about individual entities, like the preferred symbol for Pluto or the themes in life that it signifies. Others (like that IAU) are interested in talking about categories, what belongs in a category, and how you can tell the difference. Still others (like lexicographers, information architects, and librarians) want to talk about the rules for specifying information, such as whether there can be more than one preferred label for any entity. All of these people have contributions to make to the web of knowledge, but the kinds of contributions they make are very different, and they need different tools. This difference is one of *level of expressivity.*

The idea of different levels of expressivity is as well known in the history of collaborative human knowledge as modeling itself. Take as an example the development of models of a water molecule, as shown in Figure 2-4. In part (a), we see a model of the water molecule in terms of the elements that make up the molecule and how many of each is present—namely, two hydrogen atoms and one oxygen atom. This model expresses important information about

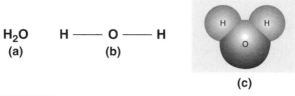

H_2O H —— O —— H

(a)   (b)

(c)

FIGURE 2-4

Different expressivity of models of a water molecule.

the molecule, it and can be used to answer a number of basic questions about water, such as calculating the mass of the molecule (given the masses of its component atoms) and what components would have to be present to be able to construct water from constituent parts.

In Figure 2-4(b), we see a model with more expressivity. Not only does this model identify the components of water and their proportions, but it also shows how they are connected in the chemical structure of the molecule. The oxygen molecule is connected to each of the hydrogen molecules, which are not (directly) connected to one another at all. This model is somewhat more expressive than the model in part (a); it can answer further questions about the molecule. From (b), it is clear that when the water molecule breaks down into smaller molecules, it can break into single hydrogen atoms (H) or into oxygen-hydrogen ions (OH) but not into double-hydrogen atoms (H_2) without some recombination of components after the initial decomposition.

Finally, the model shown in Figure 2-4(c) is more expressive still in that it shows not only the chemical structure of the molecule but also the physical structure. The fact that the oxygen atom is somewhat larger than the hydrogen atoms is shown in this model. Even the angle between the two hydrogen atoms as bound to the oxygen atom is shown. This information is useful for working out the geometry of combinations of water molecules, as is the case, for instance, in the crystalline structure of ice.

Just because one model is more expressive than another does not make it superior; different expressive modeling frameworks are different tools for different purposes. The chemical formula for water is simpler to determine than the more expressive, but more complex, models, and it is useful for resolving a wide variety of questions about chemistry. In fact, most chemistry textbooks go for quite a while working only from the chemical formulas without having to resort to more structural models until the course covers advanced topics.

The Semantic Web provides a number of modeling languages that differ in their level of expressivity; that is, they constitute different tools that allow different people to express different sorts of information. In the rest of this book, we will cover these modeling languages in detail. The Semantic Web standards are organized so that each language level builds on the one before so the languages themselves are layered. The following are the languages of the Semantic Web from least expressive to most expressive.

RDF—The Resource Description Framework. This is the basic framework that the rest of the Semantic Web is based on. RDF provides a mechanism for allowing anyone to make a basic statement about anything and layering these statements into a single model. Figure 2-3 shows the basic capability of merging models in RDF. RDF has been a recommendation from the W3C since 2003.

RDFS—The RDF Schema language. RDFS is a language with the expressivity to describe the basic notions of commonality and variability familiar from object languages and other class systems—namely classes, subclasses, and properties. Figures 2-1and 2-2 illustrated the capabilities of RDFS. RDFS has been a W3C recommendation since 2003.

RDFS-Plus. RDFS-Plus is a subset of OWL that is more expressive than RDFS but without the complexity of OWL. There is no standard in progress for RDFS-Plus, but there is a growing awareness that something between RDFS and OWL could be industrially relevant. We have selected a particular subset of OWL functionality to present the capabilities of OWL incrementally. RDFS-Plus includes enough expressivity to describe how certain properties can be used and how they relate to one another. RDFS-Plus is expressive enough to show the utility of certain constructs beyond RDFS, but it lacks the complexity that makes OWL daunting to many beginning modelers. The issue of uniqueness of the preferred symbol is an example of the expressivity of RDFS-Plus.

OWL. OWL brings the expressivity of logic to the Semantic Web. It allows modelers to express detailed constraints between classes, entities, and properties. OWL was adopted as a recommendation by the W3C in 2003.

SUMMARY

The Semantic Web, just like the document web that preceded it, is based on some radical notions of information sharing. These ideas—the AAA slogan, the open world assumption, and nonunique naming—provide for an environment in which information sharing can thrive and a network effect of knowledge synergy is possible. But this style of information gathering creates a chaotic landscape rife with confusion, disagreement and conflict. How can the infrastructure of the Web support the development from this chaotic state to one characterized by information sharing, cooperation and collaboration?

The answer to this question lies in modeling. Modeling is the process of organizing information for community use. Modeling supports this in three ways: It provides a framework for human communication, it provides a means for explaining conclusions, and it provides a structure for managing varying viewpoints. In the context of the Semantic Web, modeling is an ongoing process.

At any point in time, some knowledge will be well structured and understood, and these structures can be represented in the Semantic Web modeling language. At the same time, other knowledge will still be in the chaotic, discordant stage, where everyone is expressing himself differently. And typically, as different people provide their own opinions about any topic under the sun, the Web will simultaneously contain organized and unorganized knowledge about the very same topic. The modeling activity is the activity of distilling communal knowledge out of a chaotic mess of information.

The next several chapters of the book introduce each of the modeling languages of the Semantic Web and illustrate how they approach the challenges of modeling in a Semantic Web context. For each modeling language—RDF, RDFS and OWL—we will describe the technical details of how the language works, with specific examples "in the wild" of the standard in use.

Fundamental Concepts

The following fundamental concepts were introduced in this chapter.

Modeling—Making sense of unorganized information.

Formality/Informality—The degree to which the meaning of a modeling language is given independent of the particular speaker or audience.

Commonality and *Variability*—A fundamental aspect of the Semantic Web that a model can represent.

Expressivity—The ability of a modeling language to describe certain aspects of the world. More expressive modeling language can express a wider variety of statements about the model. Modeling languages of the Semantic Web—*RDF, RDFS,* and *OWL*—differ in their levels of expressivity.

RDF—The Basis of the Semantic Web

3

When we speak of the "semantics" of a programming language, we usually refer to the mapping from the language syntax to some formalism that expresses the "meaning" of that language. For programming languages, this could be an abstract machine or a specification in some operational calculus. When we speak of "semantics" of natural language, we often refer to something about what it means to understand the utterance—how to go from the structured letters or sounds in a language to some kind of meaning behind them.

Perhaps the most primitive part of this notion of semantics is a representation of the linkage of a term in a statement to the entity in the world that the term refers to. This primitive notion of semantics—as referential semantics—is the one that motivates the Semantic Web. While the study of symbols or "signs" and their relationship to the world they represent has been studied extensively as the field of semiotics, this book (and the Semantic Web) is about modeling as a craft, rather than a semiotic exploration of the nature of modeling. That is, given that symbols can refer to things in the world, how can we build models from those symbols that help us to capture, understand, and communicate what we know about relationships between those things?

The Web that we are accustomed to is made up of documents that are linked to one another. Any connection between a document and the thing(s) in the world it describes is made only by the person who reads the document. There could be a link from a document about Shakespeare to a document about Stratford-on-Avon, but there is no notion of an entity that is Shakespeare or linking it to the thing that is Stratford.

In the Semantic Web we refer to the things in the world as *resources*; a *resource* can be anything that someone might want to talk about. Shakespeare, Stratford, "the value of X," and "all the cows in Texas" are all examples of things someone might talk about and that can be resources in the Semantic Web. This is admittedly a pretty odd use of the word *resource,* but alternatives like *entity* or *thing,* which might be more accurate, have their own issues. In any case, *resource* is the word used in the Semantic Web standards. In fact, the name of the base technology in the Semantic Web (RDF) uses this word in an essential way. *RDF* stands for Resource Description Framework. **31**

In a web of information, anyone can contribute to our knowledge about a resource. It was this aspect of the current Web that allowed it to grow at such an unprecedented rate. To implement the Semantic Web, we need a model of data that allows information to be distributed over the Web.

DISTRIBUTING DATA ACROSS THE WEB

Data are most often represented in tabular form, in which each row represents some item we are describing and each column represents some property of those items. The cells in the table are the particular values for those properties. Table 3-1 shows a sample of some data about works completed around the time of Shakespeare.

Let's consider a few different strategies for how this data could be distributed over the Web. In all of these strategies, some part of the data will be represented on one computer, while other parts will be represented on another. Figure 3-1 shows one strategy for distributing information over many machines. Each networked machine is responsible for maintaining the information about one or more complete rows from the table. Any query about an entity can be answered by the machine that stores its corresponding row. One machine is responsible for information about "Sonnet 78" and *Edward II,* whereas another is responsible for information about *As You Like It.*

This distribution solution provides considerable flexibility, since the machines can share the load of representing information about several individuals. But because it is a distributed representation of data, it requires some coordination between the servers. In particular, each server must share information about the columns. Does the second column on one server correspond to

Table 3-1 Tabular Data about Elizabethan Literature and Music

ID	Title	Author	Medium	Year
1	*As You Like It*	Shakespeare	Play	1599
2	*Hamlet*	Shakespeare	Play	1604
3	*Othello*	Shakespeare	Play	1603
4	"Sonnet 78"	Shakespeare	Poem	1609
5	*Astrophil and Stella*	Sir Phillip Sidney	Poem	1590
6	*Edward II*	Christopher Marlowe	Play	1592
7	*Hero and Leander*	Christopher Marlowe	Poem	1593
8	*Greensleeves*	Henry VIII Rex	Song	1525

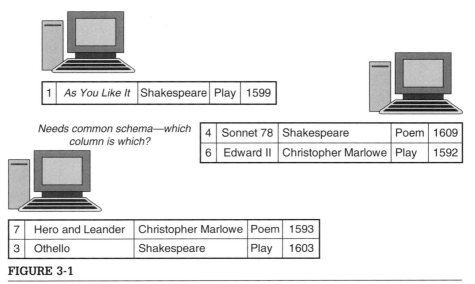

FIGURE 3-1

Distributing data across the Web, row by row.

the same information as the second column on another server? This is not an insurmountable problem, and, in fact, it is a fundamental problem of data distribution. There must be some agreed-on coordination between the servers. In this example, the servers must be able to, in a global way, indicate which property each column corresponds to.

Figure 3-2 shows another strategy, in which each server is responsible for one or more complete columns from the original table. In this example, one server is responsible for the publication dates and medium, and another server is responsible for titles. This solution is flexible in a different way from the solution of Figure 3-1. The solution in Figure 3-2 allows each machine to be responsible for one kind of information. If we are not interested in the dates of publication, we needn't consider information from that server. If we want to specify something new about the entities (say, how many pages long the manuscript is), we can add a new server with that information without disrupting the others.

This solution is similar to the solution in Figure 3-1 in that it requires some coordination between the servers. In this case, the coordination has to do with the identities of the entities to be described. How do I know that row 3 on one server refers to the same entity as row 3 on another server? This solution requires a global identifier for the entities being described.

The strategy outlined in Figure 3-3 is a combination of the previous two strategies, in which information is neither distributed row by row nor column by column but instead is distributed cell by cell. Each machine is responsible for some number of cells in the table. This system combines the flexibility of both

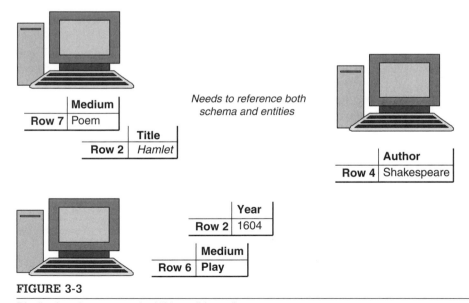

Year	Medium
1599	Play
1604	Play
1603	Play
1609	Poem
1590	Poem
1592	Play
1593	Poem
1525	Song

Needs to reference entities—which thing are we talking about?

Author
Shakespeare
Shakespeare
Shakespeare
Shakespeare
Sir Phillip Sidney
Christopher Marlowe
Christopher Marlowe
Henry VIII Rex

Title
As You Like It
Hamlet
Othello
"Sonnet 78"
Astrophil and Stella
Edward II
Hero and Leander
Greensleeves

FIGURE 3-2

Distributing data across the Web, column by column.

	Medium
Row 7	Poem

	Title
Row 2	*Hamlet*

Needs to reference both schema and entities

	Author
Row 4	Shakespeare

	Year
Row 2	1604

	Medium
Row 6	Play

FIGURE 3-3

Distributing data across the Web, cell by cell.

of the previous strategies. Two servers can share the description of a single entity (in the figure, the year and title of *Hamlet* are stored separately), and they can share the use of a particular property (in Figure 3-3, the Mediums of rows 6 and 7 are represented on different servers).

This flexibility is required if we want our data distribution system to really support the AAA slogan that "Anyone can say Anything about Any topic." If we take the AAA slogan seriously, any server needs to be able to make a statement about any entity (as is the case in Figure 3-2), but also any server needs to be able to specify any property of an entity (as is the case in Figure 3-1). The solution in Figure 3-3 has both of these benefits.

But this solution also combines the costs of the other two strategies. Not only do we now need a global reference for the column headings, but we also need a global reference for the rows. In fact, each cell has to be represented with three values: a global reference for the row, a global reference for the column, and the value in the cell itself. This third strategy is the strategy taken by RDF. We will see how RDF resolves the issue of global reference later in this chapter, but for now, we will focus on how a table cell is represented and managed in RDF.

Since a cell is represented with three values, the basic building block for RDF is called the *triple*. The identifier for the row is called the *subject* of the triple (following the notion from elementary grammar, since the subject is the thing that a statement is about). The identifier for the column is called the *predicate* of the triple (since columns specify properties of the entities in the rows). The value in the cell is called the *object* of the triple. Table 3-2 shows the triples in Figure 3-3 as subject, predicate, and object.

Triples become more interesting when more than one triple refers to the same entity, such as in Table 3-3. When more than one triple refers to the same thing, sometimes it is convenient to view the triples as a *directed graph* in which each triple is an edge from its subject to its object, with the predicate as the label on the edge, as shown in Figure 3-4. The graph visualization in Figure 3-4 expresses the same information presented in Table 3-3, but everything we know about Shakespeare (either as subject or object) is displayed at a single node.

Table 3-2 Sample Triples

Subject	Predicate	Object
Row 7	Medium	Poem
Row 2	Title	Hamlet
Row 2	Year	1604
Row 4	Author	Shakespeare
Row 6	Medium	Play

Table 3-3 Sample Triples

Subject	Predicate	Object
Shakespeare	Wrote	King Lear
Shakespeare	Wrote	Macbeth
Anne Hathaway	Married	Shakespeare
Shakespeare	Lived In	Stratford
Stratford	Is in	England
Macbeth	Set in	Scotland
England	Part of	The UK
Scotland	Part of	The UK

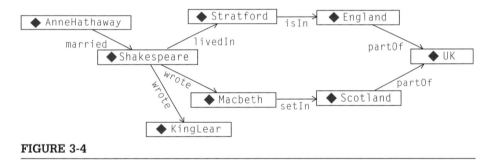

FIGURE 3-4

Graph display of triples from Table 3-3. Eight triples appear as eight labeled edges.

MERGING DATA FROM MULTIPLE SOURCES

We started off describing RDF as a way to distribute data over several sources. But when we want to use that data, we will need to merge those sources back together again. One value of the triples representation is the ease with which this kind of merger can be accomplished. Since information is represented simply as triples, merged information from two graphs is as simple as forming the graph of all of the triples from each individual graph, taken together. Let's see how this is accomplished in RDF.

Suppose that we had another source of information that was relevant to our example from Table 3-3—that is, a list of plays that Shakespeare wrote or a list of parts of the United Kingdom. These would be represented as triples as in Table 3-4. Each of these can also be shown as a graph, just as in the original table, as shown in Figure 3-5.

Table 3-4 Triples about Shakespeare's Plays

Subject	Predicate	Object
Shakespeare	Wrote	*As You Like It*
Shakespeare	Wrote	*Henry V*
Shakespeare	Wrote	*Love's Labours Lost*
Shakespeare	Wrote	*Measure for Measure*
Shakespeare	Wrote	*Twelfth Night*
Shakespeare	Wrote	*The Winter's Tale*
Shakespeare	Wrote	*Hamlet*
Shakespeare	Wrote	*Othello*
		etc.

What happens when we merge together the information from these three sources? We simply get the graph of all the triples that show up in Figures 3-4 and 3-5. Merging graphs like those in Figure 3-4 and Figure 3-5 to create a combined graph like the one shown in Figure 3-6 is a straightforward process—but only when it is known which nodes in each of the source graphs match.

NAMESPACES, URIs, AND IDENTITY

The essence of the merge comes down to answering the question "When is a node in one graph *the same node* as a node in another graph?" In RDF, this issue is resolved through the use of Uniform Resource Identifiers (URIs).

In the figures so far, we have labeled the nodes and edges in the graphs with simple names like *Shakespeare* or *Wales*. On the Semantic Web, this is not sufficient information to determine whether two nodes are really the same. Why not? Isn't there just one thing in the universe that everyone agrees refers to as *Shakespeare*? When referring to agreement on the Web, never say, "everyone." Somewhere, someone will refer not to the historical Shakespeare but to the title character of the feature film *Shakespeare in Love,* which bears very little resemblance to the historical figure. And "Shakespeare" is one of the more stable concepts to appear on the Web; consider the range of referents for a name like "Washington" or "Bordeaux." To merge graphs in a Semantic Web setting, we have to be more specific: In what sense do we mean the word *Shakespeare*?

RDF borrows its solution to this problem from foundational Web technology—in particular, the URI. The syntax and format of a URI is familiar even to

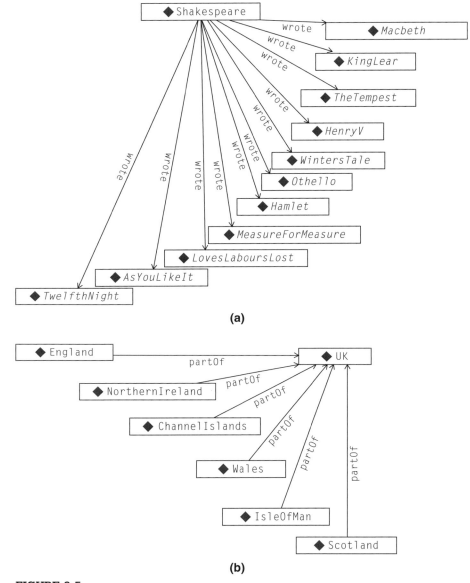

FIGURE 3-5

Graphic representation of triples describing Shakespeare's plays and parts of the United Kingdom.

casual users of the Web today because of the special, but typical, case of the URL—for example, *http://www.WorkingOntologist.org/Examples/Chapter3/ Shakespeare.owl#Shakespeare*. But the significance of the URI as a global identifier for a Web resource is often not appreciated. A URI provides a global

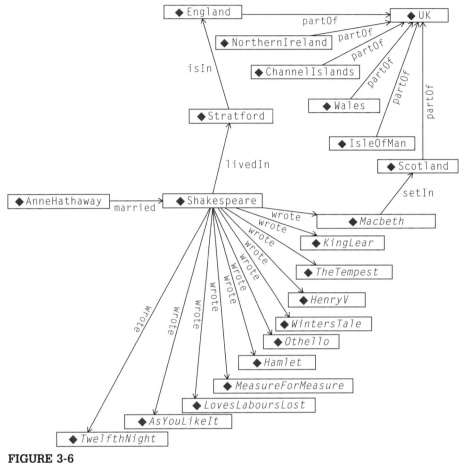

FIGURE 3-6

Combined graph of all triples about Shakespeare and the United Kingdom.

identification for a resource that is common across the Web. If two agents on the Web want to refer to the same resource, recommended practice on the Web is for them to agree to a common URI for that resource. This is not a stipulation that is particular to the Semantic Web but to the Web in general; global naming leads to global network effects.

URIs and URLs look exactly the same, and in fact, a URL is just a special case of the URI. Why does the Web have both of these ideas? Simplifying somewhat, the URI is an identifier with global (i.e., "World Wide" in the "World Wide Web" sense) scope. Any two Web applications in the world can refer to the same thing by referencing the same URI. But the syntax of the URI makes it possible to "dereference" it—that is, to use all the information in the URI (which specifies things like server name, protocol, port number, file name, etc.) to locate a file (or a location in a file) on the Web.[1] This dereferencing succeeds if all these parts work; the protocol locates the specified server running on the specified port and so on. When this is the case, we can say that the URI is not just a URI, but it also is a URL. From the point of view of modeling, the distinction is not important. But from the point of view of having a model on the Semantic Web, the fact that a URI can potentially be dereferenced allows the models to participate in a global Web infrastructure.

RDF applies the notion of the URI to resolve the identity problem in graph merging. The application is quite simple: A node from one graph is merged with a node from another graph—exactly, if they have the same URI. On the one hand, this may seem disingenuous, "solving" the problem of node identity by relying on another standard to solve it. On the other hand, since issues of identity appear in the Web in general and not just in the Semantic Web, it would be foolish not to use the same strategy to resolve the issue in both cases.

Expressing URIs in Print

URIs work very well for expressing identity on the World Wide Web, but they are typically a bit of a pain to write out in detail when expressing models, especially in print. So for the examples in this book, we use a simplified version of a URI abbreviation scheme called *qnames*. In its simplest form, a URI expressed as a qname has two parts: a namespace and an identifier, written with a colon between. So the qname representation for the identifier *England* in the namespace *geo* is simply `geo:England`. The RDF/XML standard includes elaborate rules that allow programmers to map namespaces to other URI representations (such as the familiar *http://*notation). For the examples in this book, we will use the simple qname form for all URIs. It is important, however, to note that qnames are *not* global identifiers on the Web, but only fully qualified URIs (e.g., *http://www.WorkingOntologist.org/Examples/Chapter3/ Shakespeare.owl#Shakespeare*) are global Web names. Thus, any representation of a qname must, in principle, be accompanied by a declaration of the namespace correspondence.

It is customary on the Web in general and part of the XML specification to insist that URIs contain no embedded spaces. For example, an identifier "part of" is typically not used in the web. Instead, we follow the InterCap convention (sometimes called CamelCase), whereby names that are made up of multiple

---

[1]We are primarily discussing files here, but a URI can refer to other resources. The Wikipedia article on URIs includes more than 50 different resource types that can be referenced by URIs—see *http://en.wikipedia.org/wiki/URI_scheme*.

words are transformed into identifiers without spaces by capitalizing each word. Thus, "part of" becomes `partOf`, "Great Britain" becomes `GreatBritain`, "Measure for Measure" becomes `MeasureForMeasure`, and so on.

There is no limitation on the use of multiple namespaces in a single source of data, or even in a single triple. Selection of namespaces is entirely unrestricted as far as the data model and standards are concerned. It is common practice, however, to refer to related identifiers in a single namespace. For instance, all of the literary or geographical information from Table 3-4 or Table 3-5 would be placed into one namespace per table, with a suggestive name—say, *lit* or *geo*—respectively. Strictly speaking, these names correspond to fully qualified URIs—example, *lit* stands for *http://www.WorkingOntologist.com/Examples/Chapter3/Shakespeare.owl#*, and *geo* stands for *http://www.WorkingOntologist.com/Examples/Chapter3/geography.owl#*.

For the purposes of explaining modeling on the Semantic Web, the detailed URIs behind the qnames are not important, so for the most part, we will omit these bindings from now on. In many examples, we will take this notion of abbreviation one step further; in the cases when we use a single namespace throughout one example, we will assume there is a *default* namespace declaration that allows us to refer to URIs simply with a symbolic name preceded by a colon (:), such as `:Shakespeare`, `:JamesDean`, `:Researcher`.

Using qnames, our triple sets now look as shown in Tables 3-6. and 3-7. Compare Table 3-6 with Table 3-4, and compare Table 3-7 with Table 3-5. But it isn't always that simple; some triples will have to use identifiers with different namespaces, as in the example in Table 3-8, which was taken from Table 3-3.

In Table 3-8, we introduced a new namespace, *bio:*, without specifying the actual URI to which it corresponds. For this model to participate on the Web, this information must be filled in. But from the point of view of modeling, this

Table 3-5 Triples about the Parts of the United Kingdom

Subject	Predicate	Object
Scotland	part Of	The UK
England	part Of	The UK
Wales	part Of	The UK
Northern Ireland	part Of	The UK
Channel Islands	part Of	The UK
Isle of Man	part Of	The UK

Table 3-6 Plays of Shakespeare with qnames

Subject	Predicate	Object
lit:Shakespeare	lit:wrote	lit:AsYouLikeIt
lit:Shakespeare	lit:wrote	lit:HenryV
lit:Shakespeare	lit:wrote	lit:LovesLaboursLost
lit:Shakespeare	lit:wrote	lit:MeasureForMeasure
lit:Shakespeare	lit:wrote	lit:TwelfthNight
lit:Shakespeare	lit:wrote	lit:WintersTale
lit:Shakespeare	lit:wrote	lit:Hamlet
lit:Shakespeare	lit:wrote	lit:Othello
		etc.

Table 3-7 Geographical Information as qnames

Subject	Predicate	Object
geo:Scotland	geo:partOf	geo:UK
geo:England	geo:partOf	geo:UK
geo:Wales	geo:partOf	geo:UK
geo:NorthernIreland	geo:partOf	geo:UK
geo:ChannelIslands	geo:partOf	geo:UK
geo:IsleOfMan	geo:partOf	geo:UK

Table 3-8 Triples Referring to URIs with a Variety of Namespaces

Subject	Predicate	Object
lit:Shakespeare	lit:wrote	lit:KingLear
lit:Shakespeare	lit:wrote	lit:MacBeth
bio:AnneHathaway	bio:married	lit:Shakespeare
bio:AnneHathaway	bio:livedWith	lit:Shakespeare
lit:Shakespeare	bio:livedIn	geo:Stratford
geo:Stratford	geo:isIn	geo:England
geo:England	geo:partOf	geo:UK
geo:Scotland	geo:partOf	geo:UK

detail is unimportant. For the rest of this book, we will assume that the prefixes of all qnames are defined, even if that definition has not been specified explicitly in print.

Standard Namespaces

Using the URI as a standard for global identifiers allows for a worldwide reference for any symbol. This means that we can tell when any two people anywhere in the world are referring to the same thing.

This property of the URI provides a simple way for a standards organization (like the W3C) to specify the meaning of certain terms in the standard. As we will see in coming chapters, the W3C standards provide definitions for terms such as `type`, `subClassOf`, `Class`, `inverseOf`, and so forth. But these standards are intended to apply globally across the Semantic Web, so the standards refer to these reserved words in the same way as they refer to any other resource on the Semantic Web, as URIs.

The W3C has defined a number of standard namespaces for use with Web technologies, including `xsd:` for XML schema definition; `xmlns:` for XML namespaces; and so on. The Semantic Web is handled in exactly the same way, with namespace definitions for the major layers of the Semantic Web. Following standard practice with the W3C, we will use qnames to refer to these terms, using the following definitions for the standard namespaces.

rdf: Indicates identifiers used in RDF. The set of identifiers defined in the standard is quite small and is used to define types and properties in RDF. The global URI for the *rdf* namespace is *http://www.w3.org/1999/02/22-rdf-syntax-ns#*.

rdfs: Indicates identifiers used for the RDF Schema language, RDFS. The scope and semantics of the symbols in this namespace are the topics of future chapters. The global URI for the *rdfs* namespace is *http://www.w3.org/2000/01/rdf-schema#*.

owl: Indicates identifiers used for the Web Ontology Language, OWL. The scope and semantics of the symbols in this namespace are the topics of future chapters. The global URI for the *owl* namespace is *http://www.w3.org/2002/07/owl#*.

These URIs provide a good example of the interaction between a URI and a URL. For modeling purposes, any URI in one of these namespaces (e.g., *http://www.w3.org/2000/01/rdf-schema#subClassOf*, or `rdfs:subClassOf` for short) refers to a particular term that the W3C makes some statements about in the RDFS standard. But the term can also be dereferenced—that is, if we look at the server *www.w3.org*, there is a page at the location 2000/01/rdf-schema with an entry about `subClassOf`, giving supplemental information about this resource. From the point of view of modeling, it is not necessary that it be possible to dereference this URI, but from the point of view of Web integration, it is critical that it is.

IDENTIFIERS IN THE RDF NAMESPACE

The RDF data model specifies the notion of triples and the idea of merging sets of triples as just shown. With the introduction of namespaces, RDF uses the infrastructure of the Web to represent agreements on how to refer to a particular entity. The RDF standard itself takes advantage of the namespace infrastructure to define a small number of standard identifiers in a namespace defined in the standard, a namespace called *rdf*.

`rdf:type` is a property that provides an elementary typing system in RDF. For example, we can express the relationship between several playwrights using type information, as shown in Table 3-9. The subject of `rdf:type` in these triples can be any identifier, and the object is understood to be a type. There is no restriction on the usage of `rdf:type` with types; types can have types ad infinitum, as shown in Table 3-10.

Table 3-9   Using `rdf:type` to Describe Playwrights

Subject	Predicate	Object
lit:Shakespeare	rdf:type	lit:Playwright
lit:Ibsen	rdf:type	lit:Playwright
lit:Simon	rdf:type	lit:Playwright
lit:Miller	rdf:type	lit:Playwright
lit:Marlowe	rdf:type	lit:Playwright
lit:Wilder	rdf:type	lit:Playwright

Table 3-10   Defining Types of Names

Subject	Predicate	Object
lit:Playwright	rdf:type	bus:Profession
bus:Profession	rdf:type	hr:Compensation

Table 3-11 `rdf:Property` Assertions for Tables 3-5 to 3-8

Subject	Predicate	Object
lit:wrote	rdf:type	rdf:Property
geo:partOf	rdf:type	rdf:Property
bio:married	rdf:type	rdf:Property
bio:livedIn	rdf:type	rdf:Property
bio:livedWith	rdf:type	rdf:Property
geo:isIn	rdf:type	rdf:Property

When we read a triple out loud (or just to ourselves), it is understandably tempting to read it (in English, anyway) in subject/predicate/object order so that the first triple in Table 3-9 would read, "Shakespeare type Playwright." Unfortunately, this is pretty fractured syntax no matter how you inflect it. It would be better to have something like "Shakespeare has type Playwright" or maybe "The type of Shakespeare is Playwright."

This issue really has to do with the choice of name for the `rdf:type` resource; if it had been called `rdf:isInstanceOf` instead, it would have been much easier to read out loud in English. But since we never have control over how other entities (in this case, the W3C) chose their names, we don't have the luxury of changing these names. When we read out loud, we just have to take some liberties in adding in connecting words. So this triple can be pronounced, "Shakespeare [has] type Playwright," adding in the "has" (or sometimes, the word "is" works better) to make the sentence into somewhat correct English.

`rdf:Property` is an identifier that is used as a type in RDF to indicate when another identifier is to be used as a predicate rather than as a subject or an object. We can declare all the identifiers we have used as predicates so far in this chapter as shown in Table 3-11.

CHALLENGE: RDF AND TABULAR DATA

We began this chapter by motivating RDF as a way to distribute data over the Web—in particular, tabular data. Now that we have all of the detailed mechanisms of RDF (including namespaces and triples) in place, we can revisit tabular data and show how to represent it consistently in RDF.

Challenge 1   Given a table from a relational database, describing products, suppliers, and stocking information about the products (see Table 3-12), produce an RDF graph that reflects the content of Table 3-12 in such a way that the information intent is preserved but the data are now amenable for RDF operations like merging and RDF query.

SOLUTION

Each row in the table describes a single entity, all of the same type. That type is given by the name of the table itself, *Product*. We know certain information about each of these items, based on the columns in the table itself, such as the model number, the division, and so on. We want to represent this data in RDF.

Since each row represents a distinct entity, each row will have a distinct URI. Fortunately, the need for unique identifiers is just as present in the database as it is in the Semantic Web, so there is a (locally) unique identifier

Table 3-12   Sample Tabular Data for Triples

				Product		
ID	Model Number	Division	Product Line	Manufacture Location	SKU	Available
1	ZX-3	Manufacturing support	Paper machine	Sacramento	FB3524	23
2	ZX-3P	Manufacturing support	Paper machine	Sacramento	KD5243	4
3	ZX-3S	Manufacturing support	Paper machine	Sacramento	IL4028	34
4	B-1430	Control Engineering	Feedback line	Elizabeth	KS4520	23
5	B-1430X	Control Engineering	Feedback line	Elizabeth	CL5934	14
6	B-1431	Control Engineering	Active sensor	Seoul	KK3945	0
7	DBB-12	Accessories	Monitor	Hong Kong	ND5520	100
8	SP-1234	Safety	Safety valve	Cleveland	HI4554	4
9	SPX-1234	Safety	Safety valve	Cleveland	OP5333	14

available—namely, the primary table key, in this case the column called *ID*. For the Semantic Web, we need a globally unique identifier. The simplest way to form such an identifier is by having a single URI for the database itself (perhaps even a URL if the database is on the Web). Use that URI as the namespace for all the identifiers in the database. Since this is a database for a manufacturing company, let's call that namespace `mfg:`.

Then we can create an identifier for each line by concatenating the table name "Product" with the unique key and expressing this identifier in the mfg: namespace, resulting in identifiers `mfg:Product1`, `mfg:Product2`, and so on.

Each row in the table says several things about that item—namely, its model number, its division, and so on. To represent this in RDF, each of these will be a property that will describe the Products. But just as is the case for the unique identifiers for the rows, we need to have global unique identifiers for these properties. We can use the same namespace as we did for the individuals, but since two tables could have the same column name (but they aren't the same properties!), we need to combine the table name and the column name. This results in properties like `mfg:Product_ModelNo`, `mfg:Product_Division`, and so on.

With these conventions in place, we can now express all the information in the table as triples. There will be one triple per cell in the table—that is, for n rows and c columns, there will be $n \times c$ triples. The data shown in Table 3-12 has 7 columns and 9 rows, so there are 63 triples, as shown in Table 3-13.

The triples in the table are a bit different from the triples we have seen so far. Although the subject and predicate of these triples are RDF resources (complete with qname namespaces!), the objects are not resources but literal data—that is, strings, integers, and so forth. This should come as no surprise, since, after all, RDF is a data representation system. RDF borrows from XML all the literal data types as possible values for the object of a triple; in this case, the types of all data are strings
or integers.

The usual interpretation of a table is that each row in the table corresponds to one individual and that the type of these individuals corresponds to the name of the table. In Table 3-12, each row corresponds to a Product. We can represent this in RDF by adding one triple per row that specifies the type of the individual described by each row, as shown in Table 3-14.

The full complement of triples from the translation of the information in Table 3-12 is shown in Figure 3-7. The types (i.e., where the predicate is `rdf:type`, and the object is the class `mfg:Product`) are shown as links in the graph; triples in which the object is a literal datum are shown (for sake of compactness in the figure) within a box labeled by their common subject.

Table 3-13 Triples Representing Some of the Data in Table 3-12

Subject	Predicate	Object
mfg:Product1	mfg:Product_ID	1
mfg:Product1	mfg:Product_ModelNo	ZX-3
mfg:Product1	mfg:Product_Division	Manufacturing support
mfg:Product1	mfg:Product_Product_Line	Paper machine
mfg:Product1	mfg:Product_Manufacture_Location	Sacramento
mfg:Product1	mfg:Product_SKU	FB3524
mfg:Product1	mfg:Proudct_Available	23
mfg:Product2	mfg:Product_ID	2
mfg:Product2	mfg:Product_ModelNo	ZX-3P
mfg:Product2	mfg:Product_Division	Manufacturing support
mfg:Product2	mfg:Product_Product_Line	Paper machine
mfg:Product2	mfg:Product_Manufacture_Location	Sacramento
mfg:Product2	mfg:Product_SKU	KD5243
mfg:Product2	mfg:Product_Available	4...

Table 3-14 Triples Representing Type of Information from Table 3-12

Subject	Predicate	Object
mfg:Product1	rdf:type	mfg:Product
mfg:Product2	rdf:type	mfg:Product
mfg:Product3	rdf:type	mfg:Product
mfg:Product4	rdf:type	mfg:Product
mfg:Product5	rdf:type	mfg:Product
mfg:Product6	rdf:type	mfg:Product
mfg:Product7	rdf:type	mfg:Product
mfg:Product8	rdf:type	mfg:Product
mfg:Product9	rdf:type	mfg:Product

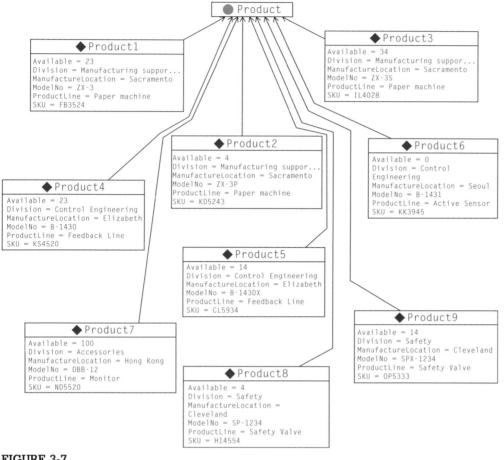

FIGURE 3-7

Graphical version of the tabular data from Table 3-12.

HIGHER-ORDER RELATIONSHIPS

It is not unusual for someone who is building a model in RDF for the first time to feel a bit limited by the simple subject/predicate/object form of the RDF triple. They don't want to just say that *Shakespeare wrote Hamlet*, but they want to qualify this statement and say that *Shakespeare wrote Hamlet in 1604* or that *Wikipedia states that Shakespeare wrote Hamlet in 1604*. In general, these are cases in which it is, or at least seems, desirable to make a statement about another statement. This process is called *reification*.

Reification is not a problem specific to Semantic Web modeling; the same issue arises in other data modeling contexts like relational databases and object systems. In fact, one approach to reification in the Semantic Web is to simply borrow the standard solution that is commonly used in relational database schemas, using the conventional mapping from relational tables to RDF given in the preceding challenge. In a relational database table, it is possible to simply create a table with more columns to add additional information about a triple. So the statement *Shakespeare wrote Hamlet* is expressed (as in Table 3-1) in a single row of a table, where there is a column for the author of a work and another column for its title. Any further information about this event is done with another column (again, just as in Table 3-1). When this is converted to RDF according to the example in the Challenge, the row is represented by a number of triples, one triple per column in the database. The subject of all of these triples is the same: a single resource that corresponds to the row in the table.

An example of this can be seen in Table 3-13, where several triples have the same subject and one triple apiece for each column in the table. This approach to reification has a strong pedigree in relational modeling, and it has worked well for a wide range of modeling applications. It can be applied in RDF even when the data have not been imported from tabular form. That is, the statement *Shakespeare wrote Hamlet in 1601* (disagreeing with the statement in Table 3-2) can be expressed with these three triples:

```
bio:n1 bio:author lit:Shakespeare.
bio:n1 bio:title "Hamlet".
bio:n1 bio:publicationDate 1601.
```

This approach works well for examples like *Shakespeare wrote Hamlet in 1601*, in which we want to express more information about some event or statement. It doesn't work so well in cases like *Wikipedia says Shakespeare wrote Hamlet,* in which we are expressing information about the statement itself, *Shakespeare wrote Hamlet.* This kind of metadata about statements often takes the form of provenance (information about the source of a statement, as in this example), likelihood (expressed in some quantitative form like probability, such as *It is 90 percent probable that Shakespeare wrote* Hamlet), context (specific information about a project setting in which a statement holds, such as *Kenneth Branagh played Hamlet in the movie*), or time frame (Hamlet *plays on Broadway January 11 through March 12*). In such cases, it is useful to explicitly make a statement about a statement. This process, called *explicit reification*, is supported by the W3C RDF standard with three resources called `rdf:subject`, `rdf:predicate`, and `rdf:object`.

Let's take the example of *Wikipedia says Shakespeare wrote Hamlet*. Using the RDF standard, we can refer to a triple as follows:

```
q:n1 rdf:subject lit:Shakespeare ;
    rdf:predicate lit:wrote ;
    rdf:object lit:Hamlet .
```

Then we can express the relation of Wikipedia to this statement as follows:

```
web:Wikipedia m:says q:n1 .
```

Notice that just because we have asserted the reification triples about q:n1, it is not necessarily the case that we have also asserted the triple itself:

```
lit:Shakespeare lit:wrote lit:Hamlet .
```

This is as it should be; after all, if an application does not trust information from Wikipedia, then it should not behave as though that triple has been asserted. An application that does trust Wikipedia will want to behave as though it had.

ALTERNATIVES FOR SERIALIZATION

So far, we have expressed RDF triples in subject/predicate/object tabular form or as graphs of boxes and arrows. Although these are simple and apparent forms to display triples, they aren't always the most compact forms, or even the most human-friendly form, to see the relations between entities.

The issue of representing RDF in text doesn't only arise in books and documents about RDF; it also arises when we want to publish data in RDF on the Web. In response to this need, there are multiple ways of expressing RDF in textual form.

N-Triples

The simplest form is call *N-Triples* and corresponds most directly to the raw RDF triples. It refers to resources using their fully unabbreviated URIs. Each URI is written between angle brackets ($<$ and $>$). Three resources are expressed in subject/predicate/object order, followed by a period (.). For example, if the namespace mfg corresponds to ***http://www.WorkingOntologist.org/Examples/Chapter3Manufacture.rdf#***, then the first triple from Table 3-14 is written in ntriples as follows:

```
<http://www.WorkingOntologist.org/Examples/Chapter3Manufacture.rdf#Product1>

<http://www.w3.org/1999/02/22-rdf-syntax-ns#type>

<http://www.WorkingOntologist.org/Examples/Chapter3Manufacture.rdf#Product>
```

It is fortunate that the ntriples serialization allows new lines between resources; only the period at the end indicates the end of a triple. Otherwise, it would often be difficult to fit a triple onto a single line!

Notation 3 RDF (N3)

In this book, we use a more compact serialization of RDF called *Notation 3 RDF* (or *N3* for short), developed by Tim Berners-Lee. N3 combines the apparent display of triples from ntriples with the terseness of qnames. We will introduce N3 in this section and describe just the subset required for the current examples. We will describe more of the language as needed for later examples. For a full description of N3, see Chapter 2.

Since N3 uses qnames, there must be a binding between the (local) qnames and the (global) URIs. Hence, N3 begins with a preamble in which these bindings are defined; for example, we can define the qnames needed in the Challenge example with the following preamble:

```
@prefix mfg:
<http://www.WorkingOntologist.com/Examples/Chapter3/
  Manufacturing.rdf#>
@prefix rdf: <http://www.w3.org/1999/02/22-rdf-syntax-ns#>
```

Once the local qnames have been defined, N3 provides a very simple way to express a triple by listing three resources, using qname abbreviations, in subject/predicate/object order, followed by a period, such as the following:

```
mfg:Product1 rdf:type mfg:Product .
```

It is quite common (especially after importing tabular data) to have several triples that share a common subject. N3 provides for a compact representation of such data. It begins with the first triple in subject/predicate/object order, as before; but instead of terminating with a period, it uses a semicolon (;) to indicate that another triple with the same subject follows. For that triple, only the predicate and object need to be specified (since it is the same subject from before). The information in Tables 3-13 and 3-14 about Product1 and Product2 appears in N3 as follows:

```
mfg:Product1 rdf:type mfg:Product;
    mfg:Product_Division "Manufacturing support";
    mfg:Product_ID "1";
    mfg:Product_Manufacture_Location "Sacramento";
    mfg:Product_ModelNo "ZX-3";
    mfg:Product_Product_Line "Paper Machine";
    mfg:Product_SKU "FB3524";
    mfg:Product_Available "23."
```

```
mfg:Product2 rdf:type mfg:Product;
mfg:Product_Division "Manufacturing support";
mfg:Product_ID "2";
mfg:Product_Manufacture_Location "Sacramento";
mfg:Product_ModelNo "ZX-3P";
mfg:Product_Product_Line "Paper Machine";
mfg:Product_SKU "KD5243";
mfg:Product_Available "4."
```

When there are several triples that share both subject and predicate, N3 provides a compact way to express this as well so that neither the subject nor the predicate needs to be repeated. N3 uses a comma (,) to separate the objects. So the fact that Shakespeare had three children named Susanna, Judith and Hamnet can be expressed as follows:

```
lit:Shakespeare b:hasChild b:Susanna , b:Judith , b:Hamnet .
```

There are actually three triples represented here—namely:

```
lit:Shakespeare b:hasChild b:Susanna .
lit:Shakespeare b:hasChild b:Judith .
lit:Shakespeare b:hasChild b:Hamnet .
```

N3 provides some abbreviations to improve terseness and readability; in this book, we use just a few of these. One of most widely used abbreviation is to use the word *a* to mean "`rdf:type.`" The motivation for this is that in common speech, we are likely to say, "`Product1` is *a* Product" or "Shakespeare is *a* playwright" for the triples,

```
mfg:Product1 rdf:type mfg:Product .
lit:Shakespeare rdf:type lit:Playwright .
```

respectively. Thus we will usually write instead:

```
mfg:Product1 a mfg:Product .
lit:Shakespeare a lit:Playwright .
```

RDF/XML

While N3 is convenient for human consumption and is more compact for the printed page, many Web infrastructures are accustomed to representing information in HTML or, more generally, XML. For this reason, the W3C has recommended the use of an XML serialization of RDF called RDF/XML. The information about `Product1` and `Product2` just shown looks as follows in RDF/XML. In this example, the subjects (`Product1` and `Product2`) are referenced using the XML attribute `rdf:about`; the triples with each of these as subjects appear as subelements within these definitions. The complete details of the RDF/XML syntax are beyond the scope of this discussion and can be found in *http://www.w3.org/TR/rdf-syntax-grammar/*.

```
<rdf:RDF

xmlns:mfg="http://www.WorkingOntologist.com/Examples/Chap-
ter3/Manufacturing.rdf#"
    xmlns:rdf="http://www.w3.org/1999/02/22-rdf-syntax-ns#">
    <mfg:Product
rdf:about="http://www.WorkingOntologist.com/Examples/Chap-
ter3/Manufacturing.rdf#Product1">
    <mfg:Available>23</mfg:Available>
    <mfg:Division>Manufacturing support</mfg:Division>
    <mfg:ProductLine>Paper machine</mfg:ProductLine>
    <mfg:SKU>FB3524</mfg:SKU>
    <mfg:ModelNo>ZX-3</mfg:ModelNo>
    <mfg:ManufactureLocation>Sacramento</mfg:Manufacture
    Location>
    </mfg:Product>
    <mfg:Product
rdf:about="http://www.WorkingOntologist.com/Examples/Chap-
ter3/Manufacturing.rdf#Product2">
    <mfg:SKU>KD5243</mfg:SKU>
    <mfg:Division>Manufacturing support</mfg:Division>
    <mfg:ManufactureLocation>Sacramento</mfg:Manufacture
    Location>
    <mfg:Available>4</mfg:Available>
    <mfg:ModelNo>ZX-3P</mfg:ModelNo>
    <mfg:ProductLine>Paper machine</mfg:ProductLine>
    </mfg:Product>
</rdf:RDF>
```

The same information is contained in the RDF/XML form as in the N3, including the declarations of the qnames for mfg: and rdf:. RDF/XML includes a number of rules for determining the fully qualified URI of a resource mentioned in an RDF/XML document. These details are quite involved and will not be used for the examples in this book.

BLANK NODES

So far, we have described how RDF can represent sets of triples, in which each subject, predicate, and object is either a resource or (in the case of the object of a triple) a literal data value. Each resource is given an identity according to the Web standard for identity, the URI. RDF also allows for resources that do not have any Web identity at all. But why would we want to represent a resource that has no identity on the Web?

Sometimes we know that something exists, and we even know some things about it, but we don't know its identity. For instance, suppose we want to represent the fact that Shakespeare had a mistress, whose identity remains unknown. But we know a few things about her; she was a woman, she lived in England, and she was the inspiration for "Sonnet 78."

It is simple enough to express these statements in RDF, but we need an identifier for the mistress. In N3, we could express them as follows:

```
lit:Mistress1 rdf:type bio:Woman;
   bio:LivedIn geo:England .
lit:Sonnet78 lit:hasInspiration lit:Mistress1 .
```

But if we don't want to have an identifier for the mistress, how can we proceed? RDF allows for a "blank node," or *bnode* for short, for such a situation. If we were to indicate a bnode with a ?, the triples would look as follows:

```
? rdf:type bio:Woman;
   bio:livedIn geo:England .
lit:Sonnet78 lit:hasInspiration ? .
```

The use of the bnode in RDF can essentially be interpreted as a logical statement, "there exists." That is, in these statements we assert "there exists a woman, who lived in England, who was the inspiration for 'Sonnet78.'"

But this notation (which does *not* constitute a valid N3 expression) has a problem: If there is more than one blank node, how do we know which "?" references which node? For this reason, N3 instead includes a compact and unambiguous notation for describing blank nodes. A blank node is indicated by putting all the triples of which it is a subject between square brackets ([and]) so:

```
[ rdf:type bio:Woman;
  bio:livedIn England ]
```

It is customary, though not required, to leave blank space after the opening bracket to indicate that we are acting *as if* there were a subject for these triples, even though none is specified.

We can refer to this blank node in other triples by including the entire bracketed sequence in place of the blank node. Furthermore, the abbreviation of "a" for `rdf:type` is particularly useful in this context. Thus, our entire statement about the mistress who inspired "Sonnet 78" looks as follows in N3:

```
lit:Sonnet78 lit:hasInspiration [ a :Woman;
                                 bio:livedIn :England] .
```

This expression of RDF can be read almost directly as plain English: that is, "Sonnet78 has [as] inspiration a `Woman` [who] lived in `England`." The identity of the woman is indeterminate. The use of the bracket notation for blank nodes will become particularly important when we come to describe OWL, the Web Ontology Language, since it makes very particular use of bnodes.

Ordered Information in RDF

The children of Shakespeare appear in a certain order on the printed page, but from the point of view of RDF, they are in no order at all; there are just three triples, one describing the relationship between Shakespeare and each of his children. What if we did want to specify an ordering. How would we do it in RDF?

RDF provides a facility for ordering elements in a list format. An ordered list can be expressed quite easily in N3 as follows:

```
lit:Shakespeare b:hasChild (b:Susanna b:Judith b:Hamnet) .
```

This translates into the following triples, where _:a, _:b, and _:c are bnodes:

```
lit:Shakespeare b:hasChild _:a .
_:a rdf:first b:Susanna .
_:a rdf:rest _:b .
_:b rdf:first b:Judith .
_:b rdf:rest _:c .
_:c rdf:rest rdf:nil .
_:c rdf:first b:Hamnet .
```

This rendition preserves the ordering of the objects but at a cost of considerable complexity of representation. Fortunately, the N3 representation is quite compact, so it is not usually necessary to remember the details of the RDF triples behind it.

SUMMARY

RDF is, first and foremost, a system for modeling data. It gives up in compactness what it gains in flexibility. Every relationship between any two data elements is explicitly represented, allowing for a very simple model of merging data. There is no need to arrange the columns of tables so that they "match up" or to worry about data "missing" from a particular column. A relationship (expressed in a familiar form of subject/predicate/object) is either present or it is not. Merging data is thus reduced to a simple matter of considering all such statements from all sources, together in a single place.

The only challenge that remains in such a system is the challenge of *identity*. How do we have a global notation for the identity of any entity? Fortunately, this problem is not unique to the RDF data model. The infrastructure of the Web itself has the same issue and has a standard solution: the URI. RDF borrows this solution.

Since RDF is a Web language, a fundamental consideration is the distribution of information from multiple sources, across the Web. On the Web, the AAA slogan holds: Anyone can say Anything about Any topic. RDF supports this slogan by allowing any data source to refer to resources in any namespace. Even a single triple can refer to resources in multiple namespaces.

As a data model, RDF provides a clear specification of what has to happen to merge information from multiple sources. It does not provide algorithms or technology to implement those processes. These technologies are the topic of the next chapter.

Fundamental Concepts

The following fundamental concepts were introduced in this chapter.

RDF (Resource Description Framework)—This distributes data on the Web.

Triple—The fundamental data structure of RDF. A triple is made up of a subject, predicate, and object.

Graph—A nodes-and-links structural view of RDF data.

Merging—The process of treating two graphs as if they were one.

URI (Uniform Resource Indicator)—A generalization of the URL (Uniform Resource Locator), which is the global name on the Web.

namespace—A set of names that belongs to a single authority. Namespaces allow different agents to use the same word in different ways.

qname—An abbreviated version of a URI, it is made up of a namespace identifier and a name, separated by a colon.

`rdf:type`—The relationship between an instance and its type.

`rdf:Property`—The type of any property in RDF.

Reification—The practice of making a statement about another statement. It is done in RDF using `rdf:subject`, `rdf:predicate`, and `rdf:object`.

N-triples, N3, RDF/XML—The serialization syntaxes for RDF.

Blank nodes—RDF nodes that have no URI and thus cannot be referenced globally. They are used to stand in for anonymous entities.

Semantic Web Application Architecture

4

So far, we have seen how RDF can represent data in a distributed way across the Web. As such, it forms the basis for the Semantic Web, a web of data in which Anyone can say Anything about Any topic. The focus of this book is modeling on the Semantic Web: describing and defining distributed data in such a way that the data can be brought back together in a useful and meaningful way. In a book about only modeling, one could say that there is no room for a discussion of system architecture—the components of a computer system that can actually use these models in useful applications. But this book is for the working ontologist who builds models so that they can be used. But used for what? These models are used to build some application that takes advantage of information distributed over the Web. In short, to put the Semantic Web to work, we need to describe, at least at a high level, the structure of a Semantic Web application—in particular, the components that comprise it, the kinds of inputs it gets (and from where), how it takes advantage of RDF, and why this is different from other application architectures.

Many of the components of a Semantic Web application are provided both as supported products by companies specializing in Semantic Web technology or by free software under a variety of licenses. New software is being developed both by research groups as well as product companies on an ongoing basis. We do not describe any particular tools in this chapter, but rather we discuss the types of components that make up a Semantic Web deployment and how they fit together.

RDF Parser/Serializer We have already seen a number of serializations of RDF, including the W3C standard serialization in XML. An RDF parser reads text in one (or more) of these formats and interprets it as triples in the RDF data model. An RDF serializer does the reverse; it takes a set of triples and creates a file that expresses that content in one of the serialization forms.

RDF Store We have seen how RDF distributes data in the form of triples. An RDF store (sometimes called a triple store) is a database that is tuned for **59**

storing and retrieving data in the form of triples. In addition to the familiar functions of any database, an RDF store has the additional ability to merge information from multiple data sources, as defined by the RDF standard.

RDF Query Engine   Closely related to the RDF store is the RDF Query engine. The query engine provides the capability to retrieve information from an RDF store according to structured queries.

Application   An application has some work that it performs with the data it processes: analysis, user interaction, archiving, and so forth. These capabilities are accomplished using some programming language that accesses the RDF store via queries (processed with the RDF query engine).

Most of these components have corresponding components in a familiar relational data-backed application. The relational database itself corresponds to the RDF store in that it stores the data. The database includes a query language that corresponds to the query engine for accessing this data. In both cases, the application itself is written using a general-purpose programming language that makes queries and processes their results. The parser/serializer has no direct counterpart in a relational data-backed system, at least as far as standards go. There is no standard serialization of a relational database that will allow it to be imported into a competing relational database system without a change of semantics. (This is a key advantage of RDF stores over traditional data stores.)

In the following sections, we examine each of these capabilities in detail. Since new products in each of these categories are being developed on an ongoing basis, we describe them generically and do not refer to specific products.

RDF PARSER/SERIALIZER

How does an RDF-based system get started? Where do the triples come from? There are a number of possible answers for this, but the simplest one is to find them directly on the web.

At the time of this writing, Google was able to find millions of files with the extension `.rdf`. Any of these could be a source of data for an RDF application. But these files are useless unless we have a program that can read them. That program is an RDF parser. RDF parsers take as their input a file in some RDF format. Most parsers support the standard RDF/XML format, which is compatible with the more widespread XML standard. An RDF parser takes such a file as input and converts it into an internal representation of the triples that are expressed in that file. At this point, the triples are stored in the triple store and are available for all the operations of that store.

The triples at this point could also be serialized back out, either in the same text form or in another text form. This is done using the reverse operation of the parser: the serializer. It is possible to take a "round-trip" with triples using a parser and serializer; if you serialize a set of triples, then you parse the resulting string with a corresponding parser (e.g., an N3 parser for an N3 serialization), and the result is the same set of triples that the process began with. Notice that this is not necessarily true if you start with a text file that represents some triples. Even in a single format, there can be many distinct files that represent the same set of triples. Thus, it is not, in general, possible to read in an RDF file, export it again, and be certain that the resulting file will be identical (character by character) to the input file.

Other Data Sources—Converters and Scrapers

Parsers and serializers based on the standard representations of RDF are useful for the systematic processing and archiving of data in RDF. While there is considerable data available in these formats, even more data are not already available in RDF. Fortunately, for many common data formats (e.g., tabular data), it is quite easy to convert these formats into RDF triples.

We already saw how tabular data can be mapped into triples in a natural way. This approach can be applied to relational databases or spreadsheets. Tools to perform a conversion based on this mapping, though not strictly speaking parsers, play the same role as a parser in a semantic solution: They connect the triple store with sources of information in the form of triples. Most RDF systems include a table input converter of some sort. Some tools specifically target relational databases, including appropriate treatment of foreign key references, whereas others work more directly with spreadsheet tables. Tools of this sort are called *converters*, since they typically convert information from some form into RDF and often into a standard form of RDF like RDF/XML. This allows them to be used with any other tools that respect the RDF/XML standard.

Another rich source of data for the Semantic Web can be found in existing webpages—that is, in HTML pages. Such pages often include structured information, like contact information, descriptions of events, product descriptions, publications, and so on. This information can be combined in novel ways on the Semantic Web once it is available in RDF. There are two different approaches to the problem of using HTML sources for RDF data. The first approach assumes that the original author of the HTML document might have no interest in or knowledge of RDF and the Semantic Web, and will create content accordingly. This means that no annotations correspond to predicates and no special structure of the HTML makes it especially "RDF-ready." The second approach assumes that the content author is willing to put in a bit of effort to mark up the content in such a way that in addition to its use for display as HTML, it can also include information that allows the data to be interpreted also as RDF.

Not surprisingly, the first approach received the most attention, especially as the Semantic Web began the bootstrapping process of gathering enough RDF data to begin the network effect. Legacy data had been represented in HTML before anyone knew anything about RDF. How could that information be made available to the Semantic Web as RDF triples?

The most "hands-off" approach to this problem is to use a program called a *scraper*. A scraper is a program that reads a source that was intended for human reading, typically an HTML page, and produces from it an RDF representation of that data. The name scraper was inspired by the image of "scraping" useful information from a complex display like a webpage.

Scraper technology is continuing to develop. We will illustrate the basics with an early scraper system called Solvent, which has been developed as part of the Simile project at MIT. Solvent provides a user interface for highlighting selected parts of a webpage and translating the content into RDF. Figure 4-1 shows

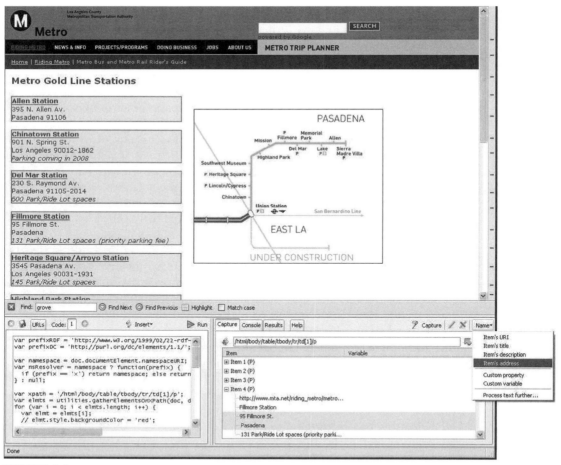

FIGURE 4-1

Example of the Solvent interface working with the Los Angeles Metro webpage.

Solvent at work on a webpage from the Los Angeles Metro Rail site. Solvent is implemented as a Firefox plug-in, and it appears as an extra panel at the bottom of the Firefox window. Solvent provides the basic functions of a scraper. First, it allows the user to select an item on the webpage; in the figure, the user has selected the name and address of one station. The scraper then highlights all the items on the page that it determines to be "the same kind" of item; in this case, we see that Solvent has highlighted all the addresses of stations on the page in yellow.

The scraper then provides a way for the user to describe the selected data; in this example, the user specifies that "Allen Station" is the name of the first item and that the next two lines "395 N. Allen Av., Pasadena 91106" is the address of the item. The scraper extrapolates this information to find the name and address of all the stations. The details of how the Solvent user interface does this are not important; the fundamental idea is that a user specifies information about a single item on a webpage, and the system uses that information to mark up all the information on the page. The result is then expressed in RDF; in this example, Solvent produces the following RDF triples:

```
metro:item0 rdf:type metro:Metro;
    dc:title "Allen Station";
    simile:address "395 N. Allen Av., Pasadena 91106".
  metro:item1 rdf:type metro:Metro;
    dc:title "Chinatown Station";
    simile:address "901 N. Spring St., Los Angeles 90012-1862".
  metro:item2 rdf:type metro:Metro;
    dc:title "Del Mar Station";
    simile:address "230 S. Raymond Av., Pasadena 91105-2014".
    (etc.)
```

Scrapers differ in their user interfaces (for allowing users to specify items and their descriptions) and the sophistication with which they determine "similar" items on a page.

A new development in webpage deployment is a trend that goes by the name of *microformats*. The idea of a microformat is that some webpage authors might be willing to put some structured information into their webpage to express its intended structure. To enable them to do this, a standard vocabulary (usually embedded in HTML as special tag attributes that have no impact on how a browser displays a page) is developed for commonly used items on a webpage. Some of the first microformats were for business cards (including, in the controlled vocabulary, names, positions, companies, and phone numbers) and events (including location, start time, and end time). The growing popularity of microformats indicates that at least some Web developers are willing to put in some extra effort to encode structured information into their HTML.

The W3C has outlined a specification called GRDDL (Gleaning Resource Descriptions from Dialects of Languages) that provides a standard way to express a mapping from a microformat, or other structured markup, to RDF.

GRDDL makes it possible to specify, within an HTML document, a recipe for translating the HTML data into RDF resources. The transformations themselves are typically written in the XML stylesheet transformation language XSLT. Existing XHTML documents can be made available to the Semantic Web simply by marking up the preamble to the documents with a few simple references to transformations.

The W3C is also pursuing an alternate approach for allowing HTML authors to include semantic information in their webpages. One limitation of microformats is the need to specify a controlled vocabulary and write an XSLT script for GRDDL to use with that vocabulary. Wouldn't it be better if, instead, someone (like the W3C) would simply specify a single syntax for marking up HTML pages with RDF data? Then there would be a single processing script for all microformats.

The W3C has proposed just such a format called RDFa. The idea behind RDFa is quite simple: use the attribute tags in HTML to embed information that can be parsed into RDF. Just like microformats, RDFa has no effect on how a browser displays a page. Current versions of RDFa are somewhat difficult to use, but better tools are being developed. It is unclear whether the microformat approach or the RDFa approach to embedding RDF information into webpages will dominate (or indeed, if either of them will; there really is no reason for the webpage development industry to make a choice, and something else might turn out to catch on better than either of them).

All of these methods that allow webpage developers to include structured information in their webpages have two advantages over scrapers and converters. First, from the point of view of the system developer, it is easier to harvest the RDF data from pages that were marked up with structure data extraction in mind. But, more important, from the point of view of the content author, it ensures that the interpretation of the information in the document, when rendered as RDF, matches the intended meaning of the document. This really is the spirit of the word *semantic* in the Semantic Web—that page authors be given the capability of expressing what they mean in a webpage for a machine to read and use.

RDF STORE

A database is a program that stores the data, making them available for future use. An RDF data storage solution is no different; the RDF data are kept in a system called an *RDF store*. It is typical for an RDF data store to be accompanied by a parser and a serializer to populate the store and publish information from the store, respectively. Just as is the case for conventional (e.g., relational) data stores, an RDF store may also include a query engine, as described in the next section. Conventional data stores are differentiated, based on a variety of performance features, including the volume of data that can be stored, the speed with which data can be accessed or updated, and the variety of query languages supported by the query engine. These features are equally relevant when applied to an RDF store.

In contrast to a relational data store, an RDF store includes as a fundamental capability the ability to merge two data sets together. Because of the flexible nature of the RDF data model, the specification of such a merge operation is clearly defined. Each data store represents a set of RDF triples; a merger of two (or more) datasets is the single data set that includes all and only the triples from the source data sets. Any resources with the same URI (regardless of the originating data source) are considered to be equivalent in the merged data set. Thus, in addition to the usual means of evaluating a data store, an RDF store can be evaluated on the efficiency of the merge process.

RDF store implementations range from custom programmed database solutions to fully supported off-the-shelf products from specialty vendors. Conceptually, the simplest relational implementation of a triple store is as a single table with three columns, one each for the subject, predicate, and object of the triple. The information about the Los Angeles Metro given in Figure 4-1 would be stored as in Table 4-1.

This representation should look familiar, as it is exactly the representation we used to introduce RDF triples in Chapter 3. Since this fits in a relational database representation, it can be accessed using conventional relational database tools such as SQL. An experienced SQL programmer would have no problem writing a query to answer a question like "List the dc:title of every instance of metro:Metro in the table." As an implementation representation, it has a number of apparent problems, including the replication of information in the first column and the difficulty of building indices around string values like URIs.

Table 4-1 Names and Addresses of Los Angeles Metro Stations

Subject	Predicate	Object
metro:item0	rdf:type	metro:Metro
metro:item0	dc:title	"Allen Station"
metro:item0	simile:address	"395 N. Allen Av., Pasadena 91106
metro:item1	rdf:type	metro:Metro
metro:item1	dc:title	"Chinatown Station"
metro:item1	simile:address	"901 N. Spring St., Los Angeles 90012–1862"
metro:item2	rdf:type	metro:Metro
metro:item2	dc:title	Del Mar Station
metro:item2	simile:address	"230 S. Raymond Av., Pasadena 91105–2014"

On the other hand, in situations in which SQL programming experience is plentiful, this sort of representation has been used to create a custom solution in short order.

It is not the purpose of this discussion to go into details of the possible optimizations of the RDF store. These details are the topic of the particular (often patented) solutions provided by a vendor of an off-the-shelf RDF store. In particular, the issue of building indices that work on URIs can be solved with a number of well-understood data organization algorithms. Serious providers of RDF stores differentiate their offerings based on the scalability and efficiency of these indexing solutions.

RDF Data Standards and Interoperability of RDF Stores

RDF stores bear considerable similarity to relational stores, especially in terms of how the quality of a store is evaluated. A notable distinction of RDF stores results from the standardization of the RDF data model and RDF/XML serialization syntax. Several competing vendors of relational data stores dominate the market today, and they have for several decades. While each of these products is based on the same basic idea of the relational algebra for data representation, it is a difficult process to transfer a whole database from one system to another. That is, there is no standard serialization language with which one can completely describe a relational database in such a way that it can be automatically imported into a competitor's system. Such a task is possible, but it typically requires a database programmer to track down the particulars of the source database to ensure that they are represented faithfully in the target system.

The standardization effort for RDF makes the situation very different when it comes to RDF stores. Just as for relational stores, there are several competing vendors and projects. In stark contrast to the situation for relational databases, the underlying RDF data model is shared by all of these products, and, even more specifically, all of them can import and export their data sets in the RDF/XML format. This makes it a routine task to transfer an RDF data set—or several RDF data sets—from one RDF store to another. This feature, which is a result of an early and aggressive standardization process, makes it much easier to begin with one RDF store, secure in the knowledge that the system can be migrated to another as the need arises. It also simplifies the issue of federating data that is housed in multiple RDF stores, possibly coming from different vendor sources.

RDF Query Engines and SPARQL

An RDF store may be differentiated based on its performance, but it is typically accessed using a query language. In this sense, an RDF store is similar to a relational database or an XML store. Not surprisingly, in the early days of RDF, a number of different query languages were available, each supported by some RDF-based product or open-source project. From the common features of these query languages, the W3C has undertaken the process of standardizing an RDF query language called SPARQL. We cover the highlights of the SPARQL query language in this section.

While these highlights are typical of RDF query languages in general, each query language has its own distinguishing features, some of which we expect will be incorporated in due course into the W3C standard recommendation. We will describe SPARQL by example, based on the following set of 19 triples, shown here in N3 and in Figure 4-2 as a graph.

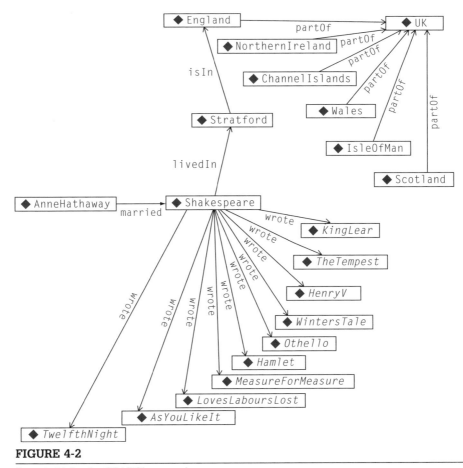

FIGURE 4-2

Sample triples for SPARQL examples.

```
lit:Shakespeare lit:wrote lit:AsYouLikeIt;
    lit:wrote lit:TwelfthNight;
    lit:wrote lit:KingLear;
    lit:wrote lit:LovesLaboursLost;
    lit:wrote lit:Hamlet;
    lit:wrote lit:TheTempest;
    lit:wrote lit:WintersTale;
    lit:wrote lit:HenryV;
    lit:wrote lit:MeasureForMeasure;
    lit:wrote lit:Othello;
    bio:livedIn geo:Stratford.
bio:AnneHathaway bio:married lit:Shakespeare.
geo:Stratford geo:isIn geo:England.
geo:Scotland geo:partOf geo:UK.
geo:England geo:partOf geo:UK.
geo:Wales geo:partOf geo:UK.
geo:NorthernIreland geo:partOf geo:UK.
geo:ChannelIslands geo:partOf geo:UK.
geo:IsleOfMan geo:partOf geo:UK.
```

The basic building block of a SPARQL query is the *triple pattern*. A triple pattern looks just like a triple, but it can have variables in place of resources in any of the three positions, subject, predicate, and object. Variables are indicated as symbols preceded by the special ? character. The following are all valid triple patterns:

```
?w lit:wrote lit:KingLear.
lit:Shakespeare ?r lit:KingLear.
lit:Shakespeare lit:wrote ?p.
```

The syntax for a triple pattern is intentionally very similar to the syntax for a triple in N3: a subject, predicate, object terminated by a period (.). Each of these patterns can be interpreted as a question in a natural way, respectively:

- Who wrote *King Lear*?

- What relationship did Shakespeare have to *King Lear*?

- What did Shakespeare write?

A SPARQL query engine, given each of these queries and the sample graph from Figure 4-2 as input, will determine the results shown in Table 4-2. Since a set of RDF triples is viewed as a graph, a more interesting query is one in which the query specifies a *graph pattern*. A graph pattern is specified as a set of triple patterns, with the stipulation that any variable that appears in two or more triple patterns must match the same resource in the graph. In SPARQL syntax, graph patterns are given as a list of triple patterns enclosed within braces ({ and }). The following are valid graph patterns in SPARQL:

```
{?person bio:married?s.
?person lit:wrote lit:KingLear.}
{?person bio:livedIn ?place.
?place geo:isIn geo:England.
?person lit:wrote lit:KingLear.}
```

We can see these graph patterns as graphs in Figure 4-3. Each triple in a graph pattern appears as an edge in the graph, just as in the case of RDF graphs. Informally, these queries ask, "Find a person who married someone and who also wrote *King Lear*" and "Find a person who lived in a place that is in England and who also wrote *King Lear*." The meaning of a graph pattern is that *all* the

Table 4-2 SPARQL Results of Various Triple Patterns on the Sample Input

Triple Pattern	SPARQL Result
?w lit:wrote lit:KingLear.	?w = lit:Shakespeare
lit:Shakespeare ?r lit:KingLear.	?r = lit:wrote
lit:Shakespeare lit:wrote ?p	?p = lit:AsYouLikeIt
	?p = lit:TwelfthNight
	?p = lit:KingLear
	?p = lit:LovesLaboursLost
	?p = lit:Hamlet
	?p = lit:TheTempest
	?p = lit:WintersTale
	?p = lit:HenryV
	?p = lit:MeasureForMeasure
	?p = lit:Othello

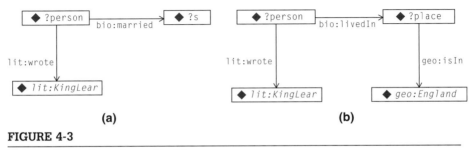

(a) (b)

FIGURE 4-3

Graph patterns shown in graphical form.

triple patterns must match, and every occurrence of a single variable must match the same resource. Table 4-3 shows the results of a SPARQL query engine for each of these graph patterns on the sample input.

The first result might seem a bit surprising; after all, Shakespeare wrote *King Lear,* and he married Anne Hathaway, right? This may well be true in the history books, but this information is not included in the sample graph. The sample graph shows only that Anne Hathaway married Shakespeare; it has no knowledge that marriage is a symmetric union and so Shakespeare must have married Anne Hathaway. We will see how to handle this sort of situation when we study the Web Ontology Language OWL in Chapter 7.

SPARQL also includes a facility for matching one triple *OR* another triple. The syntax in SPARQL is to use the keyword UNION to specify alternative graph patterns. We can use this facility to resolve the issue of who married whom in the previous example.

```
{{{?spouse1 bio:married ?spouse2}
   UNION {?spouse2 bio:married ?spouse1}}
   {?spouse1 lit:wrote lit:KingLear}}
```

The syntax gets a bit involved, but this query searches for two spouses; one has married the other (in either order), and the (arbitrarily determined) first spouse happens to have written *King Lear,* as shown in Table 4-4.

Table 4-3 SPARQL Results of Various Graph Patterns on the Sample Input

Graph Pattern	SPARQL Result
{?person bio:married ?s . ?person lit:wrote ?lit:KingLear .}	no results
{?person bio:livedIn ?place . ?place geo:isIn geo:England . ?person lit:wrote lit:KingLear . }	?person = Shakespeare ?place = Stratford

Table 4-4 Graph Pattern Built on UNION and Its Results

Graph Pattern	SPARQL Result
{{{?spouse1 bio:married ?spouse2} UNION {?spouse2 bio:married ?spouse1}} {?spouse1 lit:wrote lit:KingLear}}	?spouse1 = Shakespeare ?spouse2 = AnneHathaway

In these examples, we have shown the results of our SPARQL queries as binding lists, showing what value each variable is bound to. This mode of operation in SPARQL is called the *SELECT* form; that is, certain variables are selected from the graph pattern, and all appropriate bindings for them are returned. In the context of an RDF store, the results of the query are returned in a more standard machine-readable form. The SPARQL standard includes the SPARQL Query Results XML Format for this purpose.

The *SELECT* form in SPARQL can be thought of as converting a graph to a table; the graph pattern matches parts of the graph, and the resulting bindings are returned as a table of values for the corresponding variables. SPARQL also supports another mode of operation called the *CONSTRUCT* form. The *CONSTRUCT* form uses two graph patterns and produces a new graph built from the matches in the input graph. Variable bindings in both graph patterns must match the same resources in the graph.

As an example of the use of the CONSTRUCT mode, let's consider the reification pattern from Chapter 3, in which we represented the statement *Wikipedia says Shakespeare wrote Hamlet* with these triples:

```
q:n1 rdf:subject lit:Shakespeare;
     rdf:predicate lit:wrote;
     rdf:object lit:Hamlet.
```

Then we can express the relation of Wikipedia to this statement as follows:

```
web:Wikipedia m:says q:n1.
```

As we noted in Chapter 3, the presence of these triples does not mean that the triple

```
lit:Shakespeare lit:wrote lit:Hamlet.
```

is present, just as the statement *Wikipedia says Shakespeare wrote Hamlet* does not necessarily mean that we believe that *Shakespeare wrote Hamlet*. We can use a SPARQL construct query to pick out all of the reified statements asserted by *Wikipedia* as follows:

```
CONSTRUCT {?s ?p ?o}
WHERE {?r rdf:subject ?s.
       ?r rdf:predicate ?p.
       ?r rdf:object ?o.
       web:Wikipedia m:says ?r.}
```

This SPARQL query will construct the graph made up of all the statements that *Wikipedia* asserts. This kind of query allows an application to process reified statements according to whatever policy it wants to implement; an application that trusts *Wikipedia* can use this query to add the *Wikipedia* statements into its graph. An application that does not will refrain from using this query.

An RDF query engine is intimately tied to the RDF store. To solve a query, the engine relies on the indices and internal representations of the RDF store; the more finely tuned the store is to the query engine, the better its performance. For large-scale applications, it is preferable to have an RDF store and query engine that retain their performance even in the face of very large data sets. For smaller applications, other features (e.g., cost, ease of installation, platform, open-source status, and built-in integration with other enterprise systems) may dominate.

It is worth noting, however, that an information source other than a triple store can be queried in SPARQL (or another RDF query language). In this case, some procedural code is generally used to map the information being returned into the form required by the SPARQL query. The use of SPARQL endpoints, as such applications are known, is becoming increasingly common, and makes it possible for data resources in formats other than RDF to provide information to the Semantic Web.

Comparison to Relational Queries

In many ways, an RDF query engine is very similar to the query engine in a relational data store: It provides a standard interface to the data and defines a formalism by which data are viewed. A relational query language is based on the relational algebra of joins and foreign key references. RDF query languages look more like statements in predicate calculus. Unification variables are used to express constraints between the patterns.

A relational query describes a new data table that is formed by combining two or more source tables. An RDF query (whether in SPARQL or another RDF query language) can describe a new graph that is formed by describing a subset of a source RDF graph. That graph, in turn, may be the result of having merged together several other graphs. The inherently recursive nature of graphs simplifies a number of detailed issues that arise in table-based queries. For instance, an RDF query language like SPARQL has no need for a subquery construct; the same effect can be achieved with a single query. Similarly, there is nothing special about a "self-join" in an RDF query language.

In the special case in which an RDF store is implemented as a single table in a relational database, any graph pattern match in such a scenario will constitute a self-join on that table. Some end-developers choose to work this way in a familiar SQL environment. Oracle takes another approach to making RDF queries accessible to SQL programmers by providing its own RDF-based graph query language extension to its version of SQL, optimized for graph queries. The syntax of this language is graphlike (hence more similar to SPARQL), but it is smoothly integrated with the table/join structure of SQL.

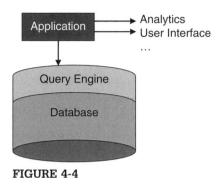

FIGURE 4-4

Application architecture for a database application.

APPLICATION CODE

Database applications include more than just a database and query engine; they also include some application code, in an application environment, that performs some analysis on or displays some information from the database. The only access the application has to the database is through the query interface, as shown in Figure 4-4.

An RDF application has a similar architecture, but it includes the RDF parser and serializer, scrapers and converters, the RDF merge functionality, and the RDF query engine. These capabilities interact with the application itself and the RDF store as shown in Figure 4-5.

The application itself can take any of several forms. Most commonly, it is written in a conventional programming language (Java, C, Python, and PERL are popular options). In this case, the RDF capabilities are provided as API bindings for that language. It is also common for an RDF store to provide a scripting language as part of the query system, which gives programmatic access to these capabilities in a way that is not unlike how advanced dialects of SQL provide scripting capabilities for relational database applications.

Regardless of the method by which the RDF store makes these functionalities available to the application, it is still the responsibility of the application to use them. Here are some examples of typical RDF applications:

- *Calendar integration*—shows appointments from different people and teams on a single calendar view

- *Map integration*—shows locations of points of interest gathered from different websites, spreadsheets, and databases all on a single map

- *Annotation*—allows a community of users to apply keywords (with URIs) to information (*tagging*) for others to consult

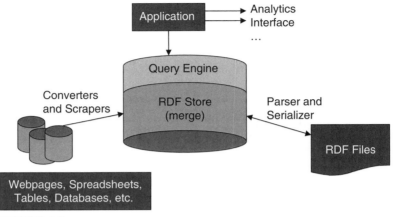

FIGURE 4-5

Application architecture for an RDF application.

- *Content management*—makes a single index of information resources (documents, webpages, databases, etc.) that are available in several content stores

The application will decide what information sources need to be scraped or converted (e.g., diary entries in XML, lists of addresses from a webpage, directory listings of content servers).

Depending on the volatility of the data, some of this process may even happen offline (e.g., the addresses of the Metro stations in Los Angeles are not likely to change for a while; this conversion could be done entirely outside the application context), whereas other data (like calendar data of team members) will have to be updated on a regular basis. Some data can remain in the RDF store itself (private information about this team); other data could be published in RDF form for other applications to use (information about the most popular documents in a repository).

Once all the required data sources have been scraped, converted, or parsed, the application uses the merge functionality of the RDF store to produce a single, federated graph of all the merged data. It is this federated graph that the application will use for all further queries. There is no need for the queries themselves to be aware of the federation strategy or schedule; the federation has already taken place when the RDF merge was performed.

From this point onward, the application behaves very like any other database application. A webpage to display the appointments of any member of a team will include a query for that information. Even if the appointments came from different sources and the information about team membership from still another source, the query is made against the federated information graph.

RDF-Backed Web Portals

When the front end of an application is a web server, the architecture (shown in Figure 4-4) is well-known for a database-backed web portal. The pages are generated using any of a number of technologies (e.g., CGI, ASP, JSP, ZOPE) that allow webpages to be constructed from the results of queries against a database. In the earliest days of the web, webpages were typically stored statically as files in a file system. The move to database-backed portals was made to allow websites to reflect the complex interrelated structure of data as it appears in a relational database.

The system architecture outlined in Figure 4-5 can be used the same way to implement a Semantic Web portal. The RDF store plays the same role that the database plays in database-backed portals. It is important to note that because of the separation between the presentation layer in both Figures 4-4 and 4-5, it is possible to use all the same technologies for the actual webpage construction for a Semantic Web portal as those used in a database-backed portal. However, because of the distributed nature of the RDF store that backs a Semantic Web portal, information on a single webpage typically comes from multiple sources. The merge capability of an RDF store supports this sort of information distribution as part of the infrastructure of the web portal. When the portal is backed by RDF, there is no difference between building a distributed web portal and one in which all the information is local. Using RDF, federated web portals are as easy as siloed portals.

DATA FEDERATION

The RDF data model was designed from the beginning with data federation in mind. Information from any source is converted into a set of triples so that data federation of any kind—spreadsheets and XML, database tables and webpages—is accomplished with a single mechanism. As shown in Figure 4-5, this strategy of federation converts information from multiple sources into a single format and then combines all the information into a single store. This is in contrast to a federation strategy, in which the application queries each source using a method corresponding to that format. RDF does not refer to a file format or a particular language for encoding data but rather to the data model of representing information in triples. It is this feature of RDF that allows data to be federated in this way. The mechanism for merging this information, and the details of the RDF data model, can be encapsulated into a piece of software—the RDF store—to be used as a building block for applications.

The strategy of federating information first and then querying the federated information store separates the concerns of data federation from the operational concerns of the application. Queries written in the application need not know where a particular triple came from. This allows a single query to seamlessly operate over multiple data sources without elaborate planning on the part of the query author. This also means that changes to the application to federate further data sources will not impact the queries in the application itself.

This feature of RDF applications forms the key to much of the discussion that follows. In our discussion of RDFS and OWL, we will assume that any federation necessary for the application has already taken place; that is, all queries and inferences will take place on the *federated graph*. The federated graph is simply the graph that includes information from all the federated data sources over which application queries will be run.

SUMMARY

The components described in this chapter—RDF parsers, serializers, stores, and query engines—are not semantic models in themselves but the components of a system that will include semantic models. Even the information represented in RDF is not necessarily a semantic model. These are the building blocks that go into making and using a semantic model. The model will be represented in RDF, to be sure. As we shall see, the semantic modeling languages of the W3C, RDFS, and OWL are built entirely in RDF, and they can be federated just like any other RDF data.

Where do semantic models fit into the application architecture of Figure 4-5? As data expressed in RDF, they will be housed in the RDF store, along with all other data. But semantic models are not simply data that will be used to answer a query, like the list of plays that Shakespeare wrote or the places where paper machines are kept. Semantic models are meta-data; they are data that help to organize other data. When we federate information from multiple sources, the RDF data model allows us to represent all the data in a single, uniform way. But it does nothing to resolve any conflicts of meaning between the sources. Do two states have the same definitions of "marriage"? Is the notion of "writing" a play the same as the notion of "writing" a song? It is the semantic models that give answers to questions like these. A semantic model acts as a sort of glue between disparate, federated data sources so we can describe how they fit together.

Just as Anyone can say Anything about Any topic, so also can anyone say anything about a model; that is, anyone can contribute to the definition and mapping between information sources. In this way, not only can a federated, RDF-based, semantic application get its information from multiple sources, but it can even get the instructions on how to combine information from multiple sources. In this way, the Semantic Web really is a web of meaning, with multiple sources describing what the information on the Web means.

Fundamental Concepts

The following fundamental concepts were introduced in this chapter:

RDF parser/serializer—A system component for reading and writing RDF in one of several file formats.

RDF store—A database that works in RDF. One of its main operations is to merge RDF stores.

RDF query engine—This provides access to an RDF store, much as an SQL engine provides access to a relational store.

SPARQL—The W3C standard query language for RDF.

SPARQL endpoint—Any application that can answer a SPARQL query, especially one where the native encoding of information is not in RDF.

Application interface—The part of the application that uses the content of an RDF store in an interaction with some user.

Scraper—A tool that extracts structured information from webpages.

Converter—A tool that converts data from some form (e.g., tables) into RDF.

RDFa and GRDDL—Proposed standards for encoding and retrieving RDF metadata from HTML pages.

RDF and Inferencing

In Chapter 1, we introduced the notion of "dumb" data and how a more connected Web infrastructure can result in behavior that lets smart applications perform to their potential. One way to make data smarter is to provide an integrated representation of information and to present information by making queries to this representation. In the Semantic Web, we have seen how RDF allows this integrated representation to be distributed over the Web. But we have also stressed the importance of modeling to making sense of this network of data. How can our Web infrastructure allow a model to help us to make sense of an integrated network of data? Let's look at another simple example of "dumb" data to show how this can work.

Suppose you hit the webpage of an online clothing retailer, and you search for "chamois" in the category of "Shirts." Your search comes up empty. You are surprised, because you were quite certain that you saw a chamois Henley in the paper catalog that landed in your mailbox. So you look up the unit number in the catalog and do another search, using that. Sure enough, there is the chamois Henley. Furthermore, you find that "Henleys" is shown as a subcategory in the broad category of "Shirts." "That's dumb," you mutter to yourself. "If it comes up under "Henleys," it should come up under "Shirts." What's the matter with this thing?"

What would it take to make this example smarter? We want any search, query, or other access to the data that references "Shirts" to also look at "Henleys." What is so special about the relationship between "Shirts" and "Henleys" to make us expect this? That is what we *mean* when we say, "'Henleys' is a subcategory of 'Shirts.'" How can we express this meaning in a way that is consistent and maintainable?

One solution to this problem is to leverage the power of the query; after all, in conventional database applications, it is in the query where relationships among data elements are elaborated. In the case of the Henley shirts, a complex query could ask, "Show me all items in category 'Shirts,' or in any subcategory of 'Shirts,' or any sub-subcategory of 'Shirts,' and so on." Depending on the syntax of any particular query language, this could be a bit cumbersome to express, but there is no essential difficulty with it. In fact, just such a solution is available using many Semantic Web tools. Just as in the relational database case, a single RDF store can be queried in different ways to create variant presentations of a single data store, ensuring information consistency across the various views. Relationships like the *subcategory* relationship in this example are represented in the query language. Systems that support this style of solution provide query languages that make this sort of query convenient so that the "and so on" doesn't require the query writer to write a program loop.

In contrast to this approach, the Semantic Web provides a model of data expression that allows for explicit representation of the relationship between various data items. In this sense, it genuinely allows a data modeler to create data that are more connected, better integrated, and, dare we say, smarter—data in which the consistency constraints on the data can be expressed *in the data itself*. It is for this reason that some people have described the Semantic Web as allowing us to model "smart data." By this we don't mean that the data are going to start curing cancer or solving complex problems, but instead that the data can describe something about the way they should be used.

As an alternative to the "smart query" approach, the Semantic Web stack includes a series of layers on top of the RDF layer to describe consistency constraints in the data. The key to these levels is the notion of *inferencing*. In the context of the Semantic Web, inferencing simply means that given some stated information, we can determine other, related information that we can also consider as if it had been stated. Inferencing is a powerful mechanism for dealing with information, and it can cover a wide range of elaborate processing. For the purposes of making our data more integrated and useful, very simple inferences are often more useful than elaborate ones. As a simple example, in Chapter 4, we saw how to write a complex query to make up for the fact that although we stated that Anne Hathaway married Shakespeare, we did not assert that Shakespeare married Anne Hathaway. It is this sort of mundane consistency completion of data that can be done with inferencing in the Semantic Web. Although inferencing of this sort seems trivial from the point of view of the natural world (after all, doesn't everyone *just know* that this is the way marriage works?), it is just this sort of correlation that is missing in dumb data applications.

INFERENCE IN THE SEMANTIC WEB

To make our data seem more connected and consistently integrated, we must be able to add relationships into the data that will constrain how the data are viewed. We want to be able to express the relationship between "Henleys" and "Shirts" that will tell us that any item in the "Henleys" category should also be in the "Shirts" category. We want to express the fact about locations that says that if a hotel chain has a hotel at a particular location, then that location is served by a hotel in that chain. We want to express the list of planets in terms of the classifications of the various bodies in the solar system.

Many of these relationships are familiar to information modelers in many paradigms. Let's take the relationship between "Henleys" and "Shirts" as an example. Taxonomists and thesaurus writers are familiar with the notion of *broader term*. "Shirts" is a broader term than "Henleys." Object-oriented programmers are accustomed to the notion of *subclasses* or *class extensions*. "Henleys" is a subclass of, or extends, the class "Shirts." In the RDF Schema language, to be described in the next chapter, we say, "Henleys" subClassOf "Shirts." It is all well and good to say these things, but what do they mean?

Thesauri and taxonomies take an informal stance on what these things mean in a number of contexts. If you use a broader term in a search, you will also find all the entries that were tagged with the narrower term. If you classify something according to a broad term, you may be offered a list of the narrower terms to choose from to focus your classification.

Many readers may be familiar with terms like *class* and *subclass* from Object-Oriented Programming (OOP). There is a close historical and technical relationship between the use of these and other terms in OOP and their use in the Semantic Web, but there are also important and subtle differences. OOP systems take a more formal, if programmatic, view of class relationships than that taken by thesauri and taxonomies. An object whose type is "Henleys" will respond to all messages defined for object of type "Shirts." Furthermore, the action associated with this call will be the same for all "Shirts," unless a more specific behavior has been defined for "Henley," and so on. The Semantic Web also takes a formal view of these relationships, but in contrast to the programmatic definition found in OOP, the Semantic Web bases the meaning of these things on the notion of *inference*.

The Semantic Web infrastructure provides a formal and elegant specification of the meaning of the various terms like subClassOf. For example, the meaning of "*B* is a SubClassOf *C*" is "Every member of class *B* is also a member of class *C*." This specification is based on the notion of inference. From the information "*x* is a member of *B*," one can derive the new information, "*x* is a member of *C*."

For the next several chapters, we will introduce terms that can be used in an RDF model, along with a statement of what each term means. This statement of meaning will always be in the form of an inference pattern: "Given some initial information, the following new information can be derived." This is how the RDF Schema language (RDFS, Chapter 6) and the Web Ontology Language (OWL, Chapter 9) work. We will take our first example from RDFS. The details of RDFS are given in a systematic fashion in Chapter 6.

The pattern for the `subClassOf` in RDFS says the following:

```
IF
?A rdfs:subClassOf ?B .
AND
?x rdf:type ?A .
THEN
?x rdf:type ?B .
```

In plain English, this says that if one class A is a subclass of another class B, and there is any individual (x) that belongs to class A (where "belongs to" means it is related by the predicate `rdf:type`), then that individual x also belongs to class B. This simple statement is the entire definition of the meaning of `subClassOf` in the RDF Schema language. We will refer to this rule for the rest of this chapter as the *type propagation* rule. This definition is consistent with the informal notion of a broader term in a thesaurus or taxonomy, since it is natural to think that any individual listed under "Henleys" should also be listed under "Shirts."

The Semantic Web definition of `subClassOf` is consistent to some extent with the definition of subclass or extension in Object Oriented Programming (OOP). In OOP, an instance of some class responds to the same methods in the same way as instances of its superclass. In Semantic Web terms, this is because that instance is also a member of the superclass, and thus must behave like any such member. For example, the reason why an instance of class "Henleys" responds to methods defined in "Shirts" is because the instance actually *is* also a member of class "Shirts."

This consistency is misleading when, in the OOP system, the subclass defines an override for a method defined in the superclass. In Semantic Web terms, the instances of "Henleys" are still instance of "Shirts" and should respond accordingly. But in most OOP semantics, this is not the case; the definitions at "Henleys" take precedence over those at "Shirts," and thus "Henleys" need not actually behave like "Shirts" at all. In the logic of the Semantic Web, this is not allowed.

Virtues of Inference-Based Semantics

Inference patterns constitute an elegant way to define the meaning of a data construct. But is this approach really useful? Why is it a particularly effective way to define the meaning of constructs in the Semantic Web?

Since our data is living in the Web, a major concern for making our data more useful is to have they behave in a consistent way when they are combined with data from multiple sources. The strategy of basing the meaning of our constraint terms on inferencing provides a robust solution to understanding the meaning of novel combinations of terms. Taking `subClassOf` as an example, it is not out of the question for a single class to be specified as `subClassOf` two other classes. What does this mean?

In an informal thesaurus setting, the meaning of such a construct is decided informally: What do we *want* such an expression to mean? Since we have a clear but informal notion of what *broader term* means, we can use that intuition to argue for a number of positions, including but not limited to, deciding that such a situation should not be allowed, to defining search behavior for all terms involved. When the meaning of a construct like *broader term* is defined informally, the interpretation of novel combinations must be resolved by consensus or authoritative proclamation.

> OOP also faces the issue of deciding an appropriate interpretation for a single sub-class of two distinct classes. The issue is known as *multiple inheritance,* and it is much discussed in OOP circles. Indeed, each OOP modeling system has a response to this issue, ranging from a refusal to allow it (C#), a distinction between different types of inheritance (*interface* vs. *implementation* inheritance, e.g., Java), to complex systems for defining such things (e.g., the Meta-Object Protocol of the Common Lisp Object System). Each of these provides an answer to the multiple inheritance question, and each is responsive to particular design considerations that are important for the respective programming language.

In an inference-based system like the Semantic Web, the answer to this question (for better or worse) is defined by the interaction of the basic inference patterns. How does multiple inheritance work in the RDF Schema Language? Just apply the rule twice. If A is `subClassOf` B and A is also `subClassOf` C, then any individual x that is a member of A will also be a member of B and of C. No discussion is needed, no design decisions. The meaning of `subClassOf`, in any context, is given elegant expression in a single simple rule: the type propagation rule. This feature of inference systems is particularly suited to a Semantic Web context, in which novel combinations of relationships are bound to occur as data from multiple sources are merged.

WHERE ARE THE SMARTS?

An inference-based system for describing the meaning of Semantic Web constructs is elegant and useful in a distributed setting, but how does it help us make our data more useful? For our application to behave differently, we will need a new component in our deployment architecture, something that will respond to queries based not only on the triples that have been asserted but also on the triples

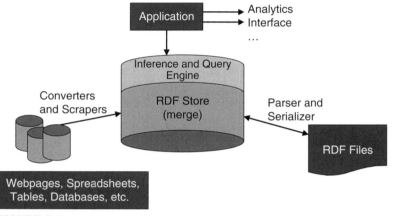

FIGURE 5-1

Semantic Web architecture with inferencing.

that can be inferred based on the rules of inference. This architecture is shown in Figure 5-1, and it is very similar to the RDF query architecture shown in Figure 4-4.

The new item in this architecture is an inferencing component that stands with the query component between the application and the RDF data store. The power of the inferencing query engine is determined by the set of inferences that it supports. An RDFS inference query engine supports a small set of inferences defined in the RDFS standard; an OWL inference query engine supports the larger set of OWL inferences. (Note that there are alternative formulations where the data is preprocessed by an inferencing engine and then queried directly. We discuss this later in this chapter.)

Example — Simple RDFS Query

Suppose we have an RDFS inference query engine working over an RDF store that contains only these two triples:

```
shop:Henleys rdfs:subClassOf shop:Shirts .
shop:ChamoisHenley rdf:type shop:Henleys .
```

Suppose we have a SPARQL triple pattern that we use to examine these triples, thus:

```
?x rdf:type shop:Shirts .
```

In a plain RDF query situation, this pattern will match no triples because there is no triple with predicate `rdf:type` and object `shop:Shirts`. However, since the RDFS inference standard includes the type propagation rule just listed, with an RDFS inferencing query engine, the following single result will be returned:

```
?x = shop:ChamoisHenley
```

Asserted Triples versus Inferred Triples

It is often convenient to think about inferencing and queries as separate processes, in which an inference engine produces all the possible inferred triples, based on a particular set of inference rules. Then, in a separate pass, an ordinary SPARQL query engine runs over the resulting augmented triple store. It then becomes meaningful to speak of *asserted triples* versus *inferred triples*.

Asserted triples, as the name suggests, are the triples that were asserted in the original RDF store. In the case where the store was populated by merging triples from many sources, all the triples are asserted. Inferred triples are the additional triples that are inferred by one of the inference rules that govern a particular inference engine. It is, of course, possible for the inference engine to infer a triple that has already been asserted. In this case, we still consider the triple to have been asserted. It is important to note that the distinction between inferred and asserted triples is a distinction for rhetorical and pedagogical purposes only; the inference engine will draw exactly the same conclusions from an inferred triple as it would have done, had that same triple been asserted.

Example **Asserted versus Inferred Triples**

Even with a single inference rule like the type propagation rule, we can show the distinction of asserted vs. inferred triples. Suppose we have the following triples in a triple store:

```
shop:Henleys rdfs:subClassOf shop:Shirts.
shop:Shirts rdfs:subClassOf shop:MensWear.
shop:Blouses rdfs:subClassOf shop:WomensWear.
shop:Oxfords rdfs:subClassOf shop:Shirts.
shop:Tshirts rdfs:subClassOf shop:Shirts.
shop:ChamoisHenley rdf:type shop:Henleys.
shop:ClassicOxford rdf:type shop:Oxfords.
shop:ClassicOxford rdf:type shop:Shirts.
shop:BikerT rdf:type shop:Tshirts.
shop:BikerT rdf:type shop:MensWear.
```

These triples are shown graphically in Figure 5-2.

An inferencing query engine that enforces just the type propagation rule will draw the following inferences:

```
shop:ChamoisHenley rdf:type shop:Shirts.
shop:ChamoisHenley rdf:type shop:MensWear.
shop:ClassicOxford rdf:type shop:Shirts.
shop:ClassicOxford rdf:type shop:MensWear.
shop:BikerT rdf:type shop:Shirts.
shop:BikerT rdf:type shop:MensWear.
```

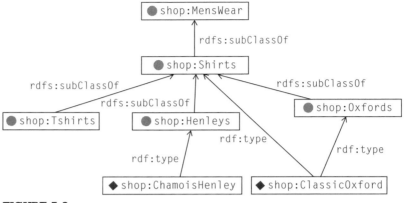

FIGURE 5-2

Asserted triples in the catalogue model.

Some of these triples were also asserted; the complete set of triples over which queries will take place is as follows, with inferred triples in italics:

```
shop:Henleys rdfs:subClassOf shop:Shirts.
shop:Shirts rdfs:subClassOf shop:MensWear.
shop:Blouses rdfs:subClassOf shop:WomensWear.
shop:Oxfords rdfs:subClassOf shop:Shirts.
shop:TShirts rdfs:subClassOf shop:Shirts.
shop:ChamoisHenley rdf:type shop:Henleys.
shop:ChamoisHenley rdf:type shop:Shirts.
shop:ChamoisHenley rdf:type shop:MensWear.
shop:ClassicOxford rdf:type shop:Oxfords.
shop:ClassicOxford rdf:type shop:Shirts.
shop:ClassicOxford rdf:type shop:MensWear.
shop:BikerT rdf:type shop:Tshirts.
shop:BikerT rdf:type shop:Shirts.
shop:BikerT rdf:type shop:MensWear.
```

All triples in the model, both asserted and inferred, are shown in Figure 5-3. We use the convention that asserted triples are printed with unbroken lines, and inferred triples are printed with dashed lines. This convention is used throughout the book.

The situation can become a bit more subtle when we begin to merge information from multiple sources in which each source itself is a system that includes an inference engine. Most RDF implementations provide a capability by which new triples can be asserted directly in the triple store. This makes it quite straightforward for an application to assert any or all inferred triples. If those triples are then serialized (say, in RDF/XML) and shared on the Web,

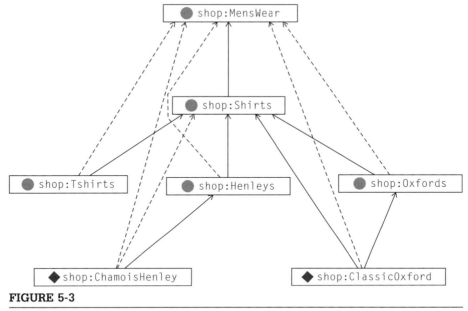

FIGURE 5-3

All triples in the catalogue model. Inferred triples are shown as dashed lines.

another application could merge them with other sources and draw further inferences. In complex situations like this, the simple distinction of *asserted* versus *inferred* might be too coarse to be a useful description of what is happening in the system.

When Does Inferencing Happen?

The RDFS and OWL standards define what inferences are valid, given certain patterns of triples. But *when* does inferencing happen? Where and how are inferred triples stored, if at all? How many of them are there?

These questions are properly outside the range of the definitions of RDFS and OWL, but they are clearly important for any implementation that conforms to these standards. It should, therefore, come as no surprise that the answers to these questions can differ from one implementation to another. The simplest approach is to store all triples in a single store, regardless of whether they are asserted or inferred. As soon as pattern is identified, any inferred triples are inserted into the store. This approach is quite simple to describe and implement but risks an explosion of triples in the triple store. At the other extreme, an implementation could instead never actually store any inferred triples in any persistent store at all. Inferencing is done in response to queries only. The query responses are produced in such a way as to respect all the appropriate inferences, but no inferred triple is retained. This method risks duplicating inference work, but it is parsimonious in terms of persistent storage.

These different approaches have an important impact in terms of change management. What happens if a data source changes—that is, a new triple is added to some data store or a triple is removed? A strategy that persistently saves inferences will have to decide which inferred triples must also be removed. This presents a difficult problem, since it is possible that there could be many ways for a triple to be inferred. Just because one inference has been undermined by the removal of a triple, does that mean that it is appropriate to remove that triple? An approach that recomputes all inferences whenever a query is made need not face this issue.

Although these are important issues in a Semantic Web deployment, they do not have a major impact on modeling decisions in the Semantic Web. For this reason, in this book, we will speak in terms of what triples can be inferred, without any commitment to the implementation choices for how they will be represented or stored.

Inferencing as Glue

Inferencing is the glue that holds the Semantic Web together. When Anyone says Anything about Any topic, and someone else says something else, inferencing is the way we make these two pieces of information fit together to provide conclusions that go beyond the facts expressed by the individuals. Even with the single inferencing pattern we have seen so far, we can see an example of how this can work.

Suppose that one source of information provides a list of members of the class "Henleys," and another source provides a list of members of the class "Oxfords." Suppose further that we know that "Henleys" and "Oxfords" are both types of "Shirts." How can we find a list of all "Shirts"?

As we have seen, we can determine that all "Henleys" are also "Shirts" by using a simple inference rule for subClassOf. Using this rule again for "Oxfords," we can determine that all "Oxfords" are also "Shirts." The merged graph now looks exactly the same as the one shown in Figure 5-3, and the inferencing determines that both the ClassicOxford and the ChamoisHenley are in fact members of the class "Shirts."

There are two fundamental components in this simple data integration example. First, there is a *model* that expresses the relationship between the two data sources; in this case, the model consists simply of a single class ("Shirts") that has both of the classes to be integrated as subclasses; this is represented with the single concept of subClassOf. Second, there is the notion of inferencing. It is the process of inferencing that applies the model to the two data sources to produce a single, integrated answer. In subsequent chapters, we will see a variety of ways in which the inferencing standards of the Semantic Web can be used to integrate data. But the two components of model and inferencing are the same for all the examples.

When data seems disconnected, it is often because some apparently simple consistency is conspicuous by its absence. This is why simple inferences are important; the simpler the missing connection, the "dumber" the data seem. The inference systems of the Semantic Web may seem quite simple (even simplistic) from the point of view of problem solving, but they are very useful for making data more consistent and connected.

SUMMARY

RDF provides a consistent way to represent data so that information from multiple sources can be brought together and treated as if they came from a single source. But when we want to use that data, the differences in those sources comes out. For instance, we'd like to be able to write a single query that can fetch related data from all the integrated data sources.

The Semantic Web approach to this problem uses a modeling language in which the relationship between the sources can be described. The meaning of the modeling language is specified by inferencing. A modeling construct's meaning is given by the pattern of inferences that can be drawn from it. Information integration is achieved by invoking inferencing before or during the query process; a query returns not only the asserted data but also inferred information. This inferred information can draw on more than one data source.

We have seen how even very simple inferencing can provide value for data integration. But just exactly what kind of inferencing is needed? There isn't a single universal answer to this question. The Semantic Web standards identify a number of different inferencing modes, intended for different levels of sophistication of data integration over the Semantic Web.

In the following chapters, we will explore three particular inferencing modes. They differ only in terms of the inferences that each of the languages allow. RDFS (Chapter 6) is a recommendation defined and maintained by the W3C. It operates on a small number of inference rules that deal mostly with relating classes to subclasses and properties to classes. RDFS-PLUS (Chapter 7) is a mode that we have defined for this book. We have found a particular set of inference patterns to be helpful both pedagogically (as a gentle introduction to the more complex inference patterns of OWL) and practically (as a useful integration tool in its own right). RDFS-PLUS builds on top of RDFS to include constraints on properties and notions of equality. OWL (Chapters 9 and 10) is a recommendation defined and maintained by the W3C, which builds further to include rules for describing classes based on allowed values for properties. All of these standards use the notion of inferencing to describe the meaning of a model; they differ in the inferencing that they support.

Fundamental Concepts

The following fundamental concepts were introduced in this chapter.

Inferencing—The process by which new triples are systematically added to a graph based on patterns in existing triples.

Asserted triples—The triples in a graph that were provided by some data source.

Inferred triples—Triples that were added to a model based on systematic inference patterns.

Inference rules—Systematic patterns defining which of the triples should be inferred.

Inference engine—A program that performs inferences according to some inference rules. It is often integrated with a query engine.

RDF Schema | 6

Just as Semantic Web modeling in RDF is about graphs, Semantic Web modeling in the RDF Schema Language (RDFS) is about sets. Some aspects of set membership can be modeled in RDF alone, as we have seen with the `rdf:type` built-in property. But RDF itself simply creates a graph structure to represent data. RDFS provides some guidelines about how to use this graph structure in a disciplined way. It provides a way to talk about the vocabulary that will be used in an RDF graph. Which individuals are related to one another, and how? How are the properties we use to define our individuals related to other sets of individuals and, indeed, to one another? RDFS provides a way for an information modeler to express the answers to these sorts of questions as they pertain to particular data modeling and integration needs.

As such, RDFS is like other schema languages: It provides information about the ways in which we describe our data. But RDFS differs from other schema languages in important ways.

SCHEMA LANGUAGES AND THEIR FUNCTIONS

RDFS is the schema language for RDF. But what is a schema language in the first place? There are a number of successful schema languages for familiar technologies, but the role that each of these languages plays in the management of information is closely tied to the particular language or system.

Let's consider document modeling systems as an example. For such a system, a schema language allows one to express the set of allowed formats for a document. For a given schema, it is possible to determine (often automatically) whether a particular document conforms to that schema. This is the major capability provided by XML Schema definitions. XML parsers can automatically determine whether a particular XML document conforms to a given schema.

Other schema languages help us to interpret particular data. For example, a database schema provides header and key information for tables in a relational database. There is neither anything in the table itself to indicate the meaning **91** of the information in a particular column nor anything to indicate which column is to be used as an index for the table. This information is appropriately included in the database schema, since it does not change from one data record to the next.

For Object Oriented Programming Systems, the class structure plays an organizing role for information as well. But in object-oriented programming, the class diagram does more than describe data. It determines, according to the inheritance policy of the particular language, what methods are available for a particular instance and how they are implemented. This stands in stark contrast to relational databases and XML, in that it does not interpret information but instead provides a systematic way for someone to describe information and available transformations for that information.

Given this variety of understandings of how schema information can be used in different modeling paradigms, one might wonder whether calling something a schema language actually tells us anything at all! But there is something in common among all these notions of a schema. In all cases, the schema tells us something about the information that is expressed in the system. The schema is information about the data.

How then can we understand the notion of schema in RDF? What might we want to say about RDF data? And how might we want to say it? The key idea of the schema in RDF is that it should help provide some sense of *meaning* to the data. The mechanism by which it does this is, again, the concept of *inference*.

The basic idea of inference is that it is possible to know more about a set of data than what is explicitly expressed in the data. By making this extra information explicit, we explicate (in a small way) the meaning of the original data. The additional information is based in a systematic way on patterns in the original data. This idea is not completely unfamiliar for schema languages. In the case of XML Schema, the validation process provides more than just a yes/no answer, but it also provides type information for the parsed data. RDFS builds on and formalizes this idea by providing detailed axioms that express exactly what inferences can be drawn from particular data patterns.

In most modeling systems, there is a clear division between the data and its schema. The schema for a relational database is not typically expressed in a table in the database; the object model of an object-oriented system is not expressed as objects, and an XML DTD is not a valid XML document. But in many cases, modern versions of such systems do model the schema in the same form as the data; the meta-object protocol of Common Lisp and the introspection API of Java represent the object models as objects themselves. The XML Stylesheet Definition defines XML Styles in an XML language.

In the case of RDF, the schema language was defined in RDF from the very beginning. That is, all schema information in RDFS is defined with RDF triples. The relationship between "plain" resources in RDF and schema resources is made with triples, just like relationships between any other resources. This elegance of design makes it particularly easy to provide a formal description of the semantics of RDFS, simply by providing inference rules that work over patterns of triples. While this is good engineering practice (in some sense, the RDF standards committee learned a lesson from the issues that the XML standards had with DTDs), its significance goes well beyond its value as good engineering. In RDF, everything is expressed as triples. The meaning of asserted triples is expressed in new (inferred) triples. The structures that drive these inferences, that describe the meaning of our data, are also in triples. This means that this process can continue as far as it needs to; the schema information that provides context for information on the Semantic Web can itself be distributed on the Semantic Web.

We can see this in action by showing how a set is defined in RDFS. The basic construct for specifying a set in RDFS is called an `rdfs:Class`. Since RDFS is expressed in RDF, the way we express that something is a class is with a triple—in particular, a triple in which the predicate is `rdf:type`, and the object is `rdfs:Class`. Here are some examples that we will use in the following discussion:

```
:AllStarPlayer rdf:type rdfs:Class.
:MajorLeaguePlayer rdf:type rdfs:Class.
:Surgeon rdf:type rdfs:Class.
:Staff rdf:type rdfs:Class.
:Physician rdf:type rdfs:Class.
```

These are triples in RDF just like any other; the only way we know that they refer to the schema rather than the data is because of the use of the term in the `rdfs:` namespace, `rdfs:Class`. But what is new here? In Chapter 3, we already discussed the notion of `rdf:type`, which we used to specify that something was a member of a set. What do we gain by specifying explicitly that something is a set? We gain a description of the meaning of membership in a set. In RDF, the only "meaning" we had for set membership was given by the results of some query; `rdf:type` actually didn't behave any differently from any other (even user-defined) property. How can we specify what we *mean* by set membership? In RDFS, we express meaning through the mechanism of inference.

WHAT DOES IT MEAN? SEMANTICS AS INFERENCE

RDFS "extends" RDF by introducing a set of distinguished resources into the language. This is similar to the way in which a traditional programming language can be extended by defining new language-defined keywords. But there is an important difference: In RDF, we already had the capability to use any resource in any triple (Anyone can say Anything about Any topic). So by identifying certain specific resources as "new keywords," we haven't actually extended the language at all! We have simply identified certain triples as having a special meaning, as defined by a standard.

How can we define the "meaning" of a distinguished resource? Reiterating what we said in Chapter 5, in RDFS, meaning is expressed by specifying inferences that can be drawn when the resource is used in a certain way. Throughout the rest of this section, whenever we introduce a new RDFS resource, we will answer the question "What does it mean?" with an answer of the form "In these circumstances (defined by some pattern of triples), you can add (infer) the following new triples." We demonstrate this principle using a simple example of the meaning of one of the most fundamental terms in RDFS: `rdfs:subClassOf`.

EXAMPLE   **Type Propagation through** `rdfs:subClassOf`

In the previous chapter, we saw the type propagation rule as an example of inferencing in the Semantic Web. The type propagation rule applies when we use `rdf:type` and `rdfs:subClassOf` in a particular pattern. But how does this kind of inference tell us anything about what it means to be a member of a class? In RDFS, membership in a class is only given meaning when there are several (well, at least more than one) classes involved, and some relation between those classes is known. What does it mean for something to be a member of a class? It means that it is also a member of any superclass. This meaning is expressed in RDFS in general through inferencing and, in particular, with the type propagation rule. The type propagation rule is just one of many rules in RDFS. When taken together, these rules provide a way to express a variety of relations between classes and properties. Such a collection of classes and properties can provide a rudimentary definition of a vocabulary for RDF data. That is, it defines set of elements and the relationship of those sets to the properties that describe the elements.

We begin with a simple example of the type propagation rule. We will combine this with other rules later on to show how `rdfs:subClassOf` forms the basis of a vocabulary definition.

Suppose we define a vocabulary that says that an `AllStarPlayer` is a `MajorLeaguePlayer` and that *Kaneda* is an `AllStarPlayer`. Our ordinary understanding of how terminology works tells us that we should be able to infer that *Kaneda* is a `MajorLeaguePlayer`.

One of the challenges in vocabulary modeling in general (and RDFS in particular) is to differentiate the two uses of the words *is a* in the example. When we say that "`AllStarPlayer` is a `MajorLeaguePlayer`," we are relating two types to one another; but when we say "*Kaneda* is an `AllStarPlayer`," we are giving type information about a particular individual—that is, relating an individual to a type. We already know how to provide individual type information from RDF; in N3, this latter statement appears as

```
:Kaneda rdf:type :AllStarPlayer.
```

RDFS provides a new resource, `rdfs:subClassOf`, to express the *is a* relationship between types. In N3, our statement about types of players appears as

```
:AllStarPlayer rdfs:subClassOf :MajorLeaguePlayer.
```

RDFS provides a meaning for `rdfs:subClassOf` in this situation, which states that we may infer that the type information for *Kaneda* propagates in the expected way:

```
:Kaneda rdf:type :MajorLeaguePlayer.
```

Inferred triples have the same status as triples that we asserted; that is, they can be used again in other rules to produce more inferred triples.

In general, the pattern for `rdfs:subClassOf` states that if we have triples of the form

```
A rdfs:subClassOf B.
r rdf:type A.
```

then we can infer

```
r rdf:type B.
```

This very simple interpretation of the subclass relationship makes it a workhorse for RDFS modeling (and also for OWL modeling, as described in subsequent chapters). It corresponds to a great degree to the IF/THEN construct of programming languages: IF something is a member of the subclass, THEN it is a member of the superclass. It should come as no surprise that this has a large number of modeling applications. In RDFS, there is no construct that corresponds to the ELSE clause that is present in most conventional programming languages; you can infer things from asserted membership of resources in classes, but you cannot infer things from the lack of asserted membership.

THE RDF SCHEMA LANGUAGE

There's a lot more to the RDF Schema Language (RDFS) than just the type propagation rule of `rdfs:subClassOf`. RDFS consists of a small number of inference patterns, each one of which can provide type information for individuals in a variety of circumstances. We will go through these patterns in turn, showing examples of their use.

Relationship Propagation through `rdfs:subPropertyOf`

We have just seen how RDFS provides a means by which classes can be related to one another by the subclass relationship and the inferences that define the meaning of this construct. This allows a modeler who is using RDFS to describe (using the notion of sets) relationships among the elements that are described in a collection of RDF triples. But if we want to give meaning to our data, we need to do more than just talk about the elements; we need to talk about the properties that link them—the predicates of the triples. RDFS provides a simple mechanism for doing just that. The mechanism works in a way very similar to the type propagation rule. The mechanism is, of course, based on an inference pattern, which is defined using the resource (keyword) `rdfs:subPropertyOf`.

The basic intuition behind the use of `rdfs:subPropertyOf` is that terminology includes verbs as well as nouns, and many of the same requirements for mapping nouns from one source to another will apply to relationships. Simple examples abound in ordinary parlance. The relationship *brother* is more specific than the relationship *sibling*; if someone is my brother, then he is also my sibling. This is formalized in RDFS for `rdfs:subPropertyOf` using an inference rule that is almost as simple as the one for `rdfs:subClassOf`.

For two properties P and R, we can assert that

    P rdfs:subPropertyOf R.

What does this mean? As always, the meaning of this statement will be given in terms of the inferences that it allows to be drawn. In particular, these inferences are that whenever we have the triple

    A P B.

We can infer the triple

    A R B.

EXAMPLE   **Employment**

A large firm engages a number of people in various capacities and has a variety of ways to administer these relationships. Some people are directly employed by the firm, whereas others are contractors. Among these contractors, some of them are directly contracted to the company on a freelance basis, others on a long-term retainer, and still others contract through an intermediate firm. All of these people could be said to work for the firm.

How can we model this situation in RDFS? First, we need to consider the inferences we wish to be able to draw and under what circumstances. There are a number of relationships that can hold between a person and the firm; we can call them `contractsTo`, `freeLancesTo`, `indirectlyContractsTo`, `isEmployedBy`, and `worksFor`.

If we assert any of these statements about some person, then we would like to infer that that person `worksFor` the firm. Furthermore, there are intermediate conclusions we can draw—for instance, both a freelancer and an indirect contractor contract to the firm and indeed work for the firm.

All these relationships can be expressed in RDFS using the `rdfs:subPropertyOf` relation:

    :freeLancesTo rdfs:subPropertyOf contractsTo.
    :indirectlyContractsTo rdfs:subPropertyOf contractsTo.

```
:isEmployedBy rdfs:subPropertyOf worksFor.
:contractsTo rdfs:subPropertyOf worksFor.
```

The discussion will be easier to follow if we represent this as a diagram, where the arrows denote, rdfs:subPropertyOf (see Figure 6-1).

To see what inferences can be drawn, we will need some instance data:

```
Goldman isEmployedBy TheFirm.
Spence freeLancesTo TheFirm.
Long indirectlyContractsTo TheFirm.
```

The rule that defines the meaning of rdfs:subPropertyOf implies a new triple, replacing any subproperty with its superproperty. So, since

```
isEmployedBy rdfs:subPropertyOf worksFor.
```

we can infer that

```
Goldman worksFor TheFirm.
```

And because of the assertions about freelancing and indirect contracts, we can infer that

```
Spence contractsTo TheFirm.
Long contractsTo TheFirm.
```

And finally, since, like asserted triples, inferred triples can be used to make further inferences, we can further infer that

```
Spence worksFor TheFirm.
Long worksFor TheFirm.
```

In general, rdfs:subPropertyOf allows a modeler to describe a hierarchy of related properties. Just as in class hierarchies, specific properties are at the bottom of the tree, and more general properties are higher up in the tree. Whenever any property in the tree holds between two entities, so does every property above it.

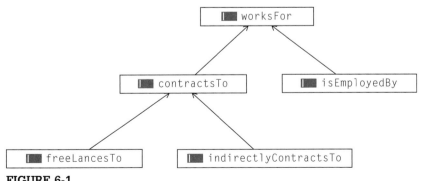

FIGURE 6-1

rdfs:subPropertyOf relations for workers in the firm.

The construct `rdfs:subPropertyOf` has no direct analog in object-oriented programming, where properties are not first-class entities (i.e., they cannot be related to one another, independent of the class in which they are defined). For this reason, unlike the case of `rdfs:subClassOf`, object-oriented programmers have no conflict with a similar known concept. The only source of confusion is that subproperty diagrams like the preceding one are sometimes mistaken for class diagrams.

Typing Data by Usage—`rdfs:domain` and `rdfs:range`

We have seen how inferences around `rdfs:subPropertyOf` can be used to describe how two properties relate to each other. But when we describe the usage of terms in our data, we would also like to represent how a property is used relative to the defined classes. In particular, we might want to say that when a property is used, the triple subject comes from (i.e., has `rdf:type`) a certain class and that the object comes from some other type. These two stipulations are expressed in RDFS with the resources (keywords) `rdfs:domain` and `rdfs:range`, respectively.

In mathematics, the words *domain* and *range* are used to refer to how a function (or more generally, a relation) can be used. The domain of a function is the set of values for which it is defined, and the range is the set of values it can take. In Real Analysis, for instance, the relation *squareroot* has the positive numbers as the domain (since negative numbers don't have square roots in the reals), and all reals as the range (since there are both positive and negative square roots).

In RDFS, the properties `rdfs:domain` and `rdfs:range` have meanings inspired by the mathematical uses of these words. A property P can have an `rdfs:domain` and/or an `rdfs:range`. These are specified, as is everything in RDF, via triples:

```
P rdfs:domain D.
P rdfs:range R.
```

The informal interpretation of this is that the relation P relates values from the class D to values from the class R. D and R need not be disjoint, or even distinct.

The meaning of these terms is defined by the inferences that can be drawn from them. RDFS inferencing interprets domain with the inference rule:

```
IF
P rdfs:domain D.
and
x P y.
THEN
x rdf:type D.
```

Similarly, range is defined with the rule

```
IF
P rdfs:range R.
and
x P y.
THEN
y rdf:type R.
```

In RDFS, domain and range give some information about how the property P is to be used; domain refers to the subject of any triple that uses P as its predicate, and range refers to the object of any such triple. When we assert that property P has domain D (respectively, range R), we are saying that whenever we use the property P, we can infer that the subject (respectively object) of that triple is a member of the class D (respectively R). In short, domain and range tell us how P is to be used. Rather than signaling an error if P is used in a way that is apparently inconsistent with this declaration, RDFS will infer the necessary type information to bring P into compliance with its domain and range declarations.

In RDFS, there is no way to assert that a particular individual is not a member of a particular class (contrast with OWL, Chapter 10). In fact, in RDFS, there is no notion of an incorrect or inconsistent inference. This means that, unlike the case of XML Schema, an RDF Schema will never proclaim an input as invalid; it will simply infer appropriate type information. In this way, RDFS behaves much more like a database schema, which declares what joins are possible but makes no statement about the validity of the joined data.

Combination of Domain and Range with rdfs:subClassOf

So far, we have seen inference patterns for some resources in the *rdfs* namespace: rdfs:domain, rdfs:range, rdfs:subPropertyOf, and rdfs:subClassOf. We have seen how the inference patterns work on sample triples. But the inference patterns can also interact with one another in interesting ways. We can already see this happening with the three patterns we have seen so far. We will show the interaction between rdfs:subClassOf and rdfs:domain by starting with an example.

Suppose we have a very simple class tree that includes just two classes, Woman and MarriedWoman, in the usual subclass relation:

```
:MarriedWoman rdfs:subClassOf :Woman.
```

Suppose we have a property called maidenName, whose domain is MarriedWoman:

```
:maidenName rdfs:domain :MarriedWoman.
```

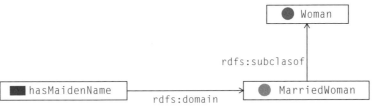

FIGURE 6-2

Domain and subClassOf triples for maidenName.

Figure 6-2 shows how this looks in diagram form.

This unsurprising model holds some subtlety; let's examine closely what it says. If we assert the maidenName of anything (even if we don't know that it is a Woman!), the rule for rdfs:domain allows us to infer that it is a MarriedWoman. So, for instance, if someone asserts

    :Karen :maidenName "Stephens".

We can infer

    :Karen rdf:type :MarriedWoman.

But we can make further inferences based on the rdfs:subClassOf relationship between the classes—namely, that

    :Karen rdf:type :Woman.

There was nothing in this example that was particular to Karen; in fact, if we learn of any resource at all that it has a maidenName, then we will infer that it is a Woman. That is, we know that for any resource X, if we have a triple of the form

    X :maidenName Y.

we can infer

    X rdf:type :Woman.

But this is exactly the definition of rdfs:domain; that is, we have just seen that

    :maidenName rdfs:domain :Woman.

This is a different way to use the definition of rdfs:domain from what we have encountered so far. Until now, we applied the inference pattern whenever a triple using rdfs:domain was asserted or inferred. Now we are inferring an rdfs:domain triple whenever we can prove that the inference pattern holds. That is, we view the inference pattern as the definition of what it means for rdfs:domain to hold.

We can generalize this result to form a new inference pattern as follows:

```
IF
P rdfs:domain D.
and
D rdfs:subClassOf C.
THEN
P rdfs:domain C.
```

That is, whenever we specify the `rdfs:domain` of a property to be some class, we can also infer that the property also has any superclass as `rdfs:domain`. The same conclusion holds for `rdfs:range`, using the same argument.

These simple definitions of `domain` and `range` are actually quite aggressive; we can draw conclusions about the type of any element based simply on its use in a single triple whenever we have domain or range information about the predicate. As we shall see in later examples, this can result in some surprising inferences. The definitions of `domain` and `range` in RDFS are the most common problem areas for modelers with experience in another data modeling paradigm. It is unusual to have such a strong interpretation for very common concepts.

The interaction between `rdfs:domain` and `rdfs:subClassOf` can seem particularly counterintuitive when viewed in comparison to Object-Oriented Programming. One of the basic mechanisms for organizing code in OOP is called inheritance. There are a number of different schemes for defining *inheritance*, but they typically work by propagating information down the class tree; that is, something (e.g., a method or a variable) that is defined at one class is also available at its subclasses.

When they first begin working with RDFS, there is a tendency for OO programmers to expect inheritance to work the same way. This tendency results from an "obvious" mapping from RDFS to OOP in which an `rdfs:Class` corresponds to a Class in OOP, a property in RDFS corresponds to a variable in OOP, and in which the assertion

```
P rdfs:domain C.
```

corresponds to the definition of the variable corresponding to P being defined at class C. From this "obvious" mapping comes an expectation that these definitions should inherit in the same way that variable definitions inherit in OOP.

But in RDFS, there is no notion of inheritance per se; the only mechanism at work in RDFS is inference. The inference rule in RDFS that most closely corresponds to the OO notion of inheritance is the subclass propagation rule: that the members of a subclass are also members of a class. The ramifications of this rule for instance correspond to what one would expect from inheritance. Since an instance of a subclass is also an instance of the parent class, then anything we say about

(Continued)

members of the parent class will necessarily hold for all instances of the subclass; this is consistent with usual notions of inheritance.

The interaction between `rdfs:domain` and `rdfs:subClassOf`, on the other hand, is more problematic. Using to the "obvious" interpretation, we asserted that the variable `maidenName` was defined at `MarriedWoman` and then inferred that it was defined at a class higher in the tree—namely, `Woman`. Seen from an OO point of view, this interaction seems like inheritance up the tree—in other words, just the opposite of what is normally expected of inheritance in OOP.

The fallacy in this conclusion comes from the "obvious" mapping of `rdfs:domain` as defining a variable relative to a class. In the Semantic Web, because of the AAA slogan, a property can be used anywhere, and it must be independent of any class. The property `maidenName` was, by design, always available for any resource in the universe (including members of the class `Woman`); the assertion or inference of `rdfs:domain` made no change in that respect. That is, it is never accurate in the Semantic Web to say that a property is "defined for a class." A property is defined independently of any class, and the RDFS relations specify which inferences can be correctly made about it in particular contexts.

RDFS MODELING COMBINATIONS AND PATTERNS

The inference rules for RDFS are few in number and quite simple. Nevertheless, their effect can be quite subtle in the context of shared information in the Semantic Web. In this section, we outline a number of patterns of use of the basic RDFS features, illustrating each one with a simple example.

Set Intersection

It is not uncommon for someone modeling in RDFS to ask whether some familiar notions from logic are available. "Can I model set intersection in RDFS?" is a common question. The technically correct answer to this question is simply "no." There is no explicit modeling construct in RDFS for set intersection (or for set union). However, when someone wants to model intersections (or unions), they don't always need to model them explicitly. They often only need certain particular inferences that are supported by these logical relations. Sometimes these inferences are indeed available in RDFS through particular design patterns that combine the familiar RDFS primitives in specific ways.

In the case of intersection in particular, one of the inferences someone might like to draw is that if a resource x is in C, then it is also in both A and B. Expressed formally, the relationship they are expressing is that $C \subseteq A \cap B$. This inference can be supported by making C a common subclass of both A and B, as follows:

```
C rdfs:subClassOf A.
C rdfs:subClassOf B.
```

How does this support an intersection-like conclusion? From the inference rule governing `rdfs:subClassOf`, it is evident that from the triple

```
x rdf:type C.
```

We can infer

```
x rdf:type B.
x rdf:type A.
```

as desired. Notice that we can only draw the inferences in one direction; from membership in C, we can infer membership in A and B. But from membership in A and B, we cannot infer membership in C. That is, we cannot express $A \cap B \subseteq C$. This is the sense in which RDFS cannot actually express set intersection; it can only approximate it by supporting the inferencing in one direction.

EXAMPLE   ### Hospital Skills

Suppose we are describing the staff at a hospital. There are a number of different jobs and people who fill them, including nurses, doctors, surgeons, administrators, orderlies, volunteers, and so on. A very specialized role in the hospital is the Surgeon. Among the things we know about surgeons is that they are members of the hospital staff. They are also qualified physicians. Logically, we would say that $Surgeon \subseteq Staff \cap Physician$—that is, *Surgeon* is a subset of those people who are both staff members and physicians.

Notice that we don't want to say that *every* staff physician is a surgeon, so the set inclusion goes only one way. From this statement, we want to be able to infer that if Kildare is a surgeon, then he is also a member of the staff, and he is a physician. If we say

```
:Surgeon rdfs:subClassOf :Staff.
:Surgeon rdfs:subClassOf :Physician.
:Kildare rdf:type :Surgeon.
```

then we can infer that

```
:Kildare rdf:type :Staff.
:Kildare rdf:type :Physician.
```

We cannot make the inference the other way; that is, if we were to assert that Kildare is a physician and member of the staff, no RDFS rules are applicable, and no inferences are drawn. This is appropriate; consider the case in which Kildare is a psychiatrist. As such, he is both a member of the staff and a physician, but it is inappropriate to conclude that he must be a surgeon. (OWL, Chapter 10, provides means for making it so that this conclusion would hold, but RDFS does not.)

Property Intersection

In RDFS, properties are treated in a way analogous to the treatment of classes, and all the same operations and limitations apply. Even though it might seem unfamiliar to think of a property as a set, we can still use the set combination terms (intersection, union) to describe the functionality supported for properties. As was the case for Class intersections and unions, RDFS cannot express these things exactly, but it is possible to approximate these notions with judicious use of `subPropertyOf`.

One of the inferences we can express using `subPropertyOf` is that one property is an intersection of two others, $P \subseteq R \cap S$. That is, if we know that two resources x and y are related by property P,

```
x P y.
```

we want to be able to infer both

```
x R y.
x S y.
```

EXAMPLE | **Patients in Hospital Rooms**

Suppose we are describing patients in a hospital. When a patient is assigned to a particular room, we can infer a number of things about the patient: We know that they are on the duty roster for that room and that their insurance will be billed for that room. How do we express that both of these inferences come from the single assignment of a patient to a room?

```
:lodgedIn rdfs:subPropertyOf :billedFor.
:logdedIn rdfs:subPropertyOf :assignedTo.
```

Now if patient `Marcus` is `lodgedIn` *Room101*,

```
:Marcus :lodgedIn :Room101.
```

we can infer the billing and duty roster properties as well:

```
:Marcus :billedFor :Room101.
:Marcus :assignedTo :Room101.
```

Notice that we cannot make the inference in the other direction; that is, if we were to assert that `Marcus` is `billedFor` *Room101* and `assignedTo` *Room101*, no RDFS rules are applicable, and no inferences can be drawn.

Set Union

Using a pattern similar to the one we used for set intersection, we can also express certain things about set unions in RDFS. In particular, we can express that $A \cap B \subseteq C$. We do this by making C a common superclass of A and B, thus:

```
A rdfs:subClassOf C.
B rdfs:subClassOf C.
```

Any instance x that is a member of either A or B is inferred to be also a member of C; that is,

```
x rdf:type A.
```

or

```
x rdf:type B.
```

implies

```
x rdf:type C.
```

EXAMPLE **All-Stars**

In determining the candidates for a season's All Stars, a league's rules could state that they will select among all the players who have been named Most Valuable Player (MVP), as well as among those who have been top scorers (TopScorer) in their league. We can model this in RDFS by making AllStarCandidate a common superclass of MVP and TopScorer as follows:

```
:MVP rdfs:subClassOf :AllStarCandidate.
:TopScorer rdfs:subClassOf :AllStarCandidate.
```

Now, if we know that *Reilly* was named MVP and *Kaneda* was a TopScorer:

```
:Reilly rdf:type :MVP.
:Kaneda rdf:type :TopScorer.
```

then we can infer that both of them are AllStarCandidates

```
:Reilly rdf:type :AllStarCandidate.
:Kaneda rdf:type :AllStarCandidate.
```

as desired. Notice that as in the case of intersection, we can only draw the inference in one direction—that is, we can infer that AllStarCandidate $\supseteq$ MVP $\cap$ TopScorer, but not the other way around.

In summary, we can use rdfs:subClassOf to represent statements about intersection and union as follows:

- $C \subseteq A \cap B$ (by making C rdfs:subClassOf both A and B)
- $C \supseteq A \cap B$ (by making both A and B rdfs:subClassOf C).

Property Union

One can use `rdfs:subPropertyOf` to combine properties from different sources in a way that is analogous to the way in which `rdfs:subClassOf` can be used to combine classes as a union. If two different sources use properties P and Q in similar ways, then a single amalgamated property R can be defined with `rdfs:subPropertyOf` as follows:

```
P rdfs:subPropertyOf R.
Q rdfs:subPropertyOf R.
```

For any pair of resources x and y related by P or by Q

```
x P y.
```

or

```
x Q y.
```

we can infer that

```
x R y.
```

EXAMPLE   **Merging Library Records**

Suppose one library has a table in which it keeps lists of patrons and the books they have borrowed. It uses a property called *borrows* to indicate that a patron has borrowed a book. Another library uses `checkedOut` to indicate the same relationship.

Just as in the case of classes, there are a number of ways to handle this situation. If we are sure that the two properties have exactly the same meaning, we can make one property equivalent to another with a creative use of `rdfs:subPropertyOf` as follows:

```
Library1:borrows rdfs:subPropertyOf Library2:checkedOut.
Library2:checkedOut rdfs:subPropertyOf Library1:borrows.
```

Then any relationship that is expressed by one library will be inferred to hold for the other. In such a case, both properties are essentially equivalent.

If we aren't sure that the two properties are used in exactly the same way, but we have an application that we do know wants to treat them as the same, then we use the Union pattern to create a common superproperty of both, as follows:

```
Library1:borrows rdfs:subPropertyOf :hasPossession.
Library2:checkedOut rdfs:subPropertyOf :hasPossession.
```

Using these triples, all patrons and books from both libraries will be related by the property `hasPossession`, thus merging information from the two sources.

Property Transfer

When modeling the relationship between information that comes from multiple sources, a common requirement is to state that if two entities are related by some relationship in one source, the same entities should be related by a corresponding relationship in the other source. This can be accomplished quite easily in RDFS with a single triple. That is, if we have a property P in one source and property Q in another source, and we wish to state that all uses of P should be considered as uses of Q, we can simply assert that

```
P rdfs:subPropertyOf Q.
```

Now, if we have any triple of the form

```
X P Y.
```

then we can infer that

```
X Q Y.
```

It may seem strange to have a design pattern that consists of a single triple, but this use of `rdfs:subPropertyOf` is so pervasive that it really merits being called out as a pattern in its own right.

EXAMPLE   **Terminology Reconciliation**

There are a growing number of standard information representation schemes being published in RDFS form. Information that has been developed in advance of these standards (or in a silo away from them) needs to be retargeted to be compliant with the standard. This process can involve a costly and error-prone search-and-replace process through all the data sources. When the data are represented in RDF, there is often an easier option available, using the Property Transfer pattern.

As a particular example, the *Dublin Core* is a set of standard attributes used to describe bibliographic information for library systems. One of the most frequently used Dublin Core terms is `dc:creator`, which indicates an individual (person or organization) that is responsible for having created a published artifact.

Suppose that a particular legacy bibliography system uses the term *author* to denote the person who created a book. This has worked fine for this system because it was not intended to classify books that were created without an author, such as compilations (which instead have an editor).

How can we make this data conformant to the Dublin Core without performing a costly and error-prone process to copy-and-replace *author* with `dc:creator`? This can be achieved in RDFS with the single triple

```
:author rdfs:subPropertyOf dc:creator.
```

Now any individual for which the author property has been defined will now have the same value defined for the (standard) `dc:creator` property. The work is done by the RDFS inference engine instead of by an off-line editing process. In particular, this means that legacy applications that are using the *author* property can continue to operate without modification, while newer, Dublin Core–compliant applications can use the inferred data to operate in a standard fashion.

CHALLENGES

Each of the preceding patterns demonstrates the utility of combining one or more RDFS constructs to achieve a particular modeling goal. In this section, we outline a number of modeling scenarios that can be addressed with these patterns and show how they can be applied to address these challenges.

Term Reconciliation

One of the most common challenges in terminology management is the resolution of terms used by different agents who want to use their descriptions together in a single federated application. For example, suppose that one agent uses the word *analyst,* and another uses the word *researcher.* There are a number of relationships that can hold between these two usages; we will examine a number of common relations as a series of challenges.

Challenge 2 How do we then enforce the assertion that any member of the one class will automatically be treated as a member of the other? There are a number of approaches to this situation, depending on the details of the situation. All of them can be implemented using the patterns we have identified so far.

SOLUTION

Let's first take the case in which we determine that a particular term in one vocabulary is fully subsumed by a term in another. For example, we determine that a *researcher* is actually a special case of an *analyst*. How can we represent this fact in RDFS?

First, we examine the inferences we want RDFS to draw, given this information. If a researcher is a special case of an analyst, then all researchers are also analysts. We can express this sort of "IF/THEN" relationship with a single `rdfs:subClassOf` relationship, thus:

```
:Researcher rdfs:subClassOf :Analyst.
```

Now any resource that is a `Researcher`, such as

```
:Wenger rdf:type :Researcher.
```

will be inferred to be an `Analyst` as well:

```
:Wenger rdf:type :Analyst.
```

If the relationship happens to go the other way around (that is, all analysts are researchers), the `rdfs:subClassOf` triple can be reversed accordingly.

Challenge 3 What if the relationship is more subtle? Suppose there is considerable semantic overlap between the two concepts *analyst* and *researcher,* but neither concept is defined in a sharp, formal way. It seems that there could be some analysts who are not researchers, and vice versa. Nevertheless, for the purposes of the federated application, we want to treat these two entities as the same. What can we do?

SOLUTION

In such a case, we can use the Union pattern outlined previously. We can define a new term (for the federated domain) that is not defined in either of the sources, such as *investigator.* Then we effectively define *investigator* as the union of *researcher* and *analyst*, using the common superproperty idiom:

```
:Analyst rdfs:subClassOf :Investigator.
:Researcher rdfs:subClassOf :Investigator.
```

Described this way, we have made no commitment to a direct relationship between *analyst* and *researcher*, but we have provided a federated handle for speaking of the general class of these entities.

Challenge 4 At the other extreme, suppose that we determine that the two classes really are identical in every way—that these two terms really are just two words for the same thing. In terms of inference, we would like any member of one class to be a member of the other, and vice versa.

SOLUTION

RDFS does not provide a primitive statement of class equivalence, but the same result can be achieved with creative use of `rdfs:subClassOf`:

```
:Analyst rdfs:subClassOf :Researcher.
:Researcher rdfs:subClassOf :Analyst.
```

This may seem a bit paradoxical, especially to someone who is accustomed to object-oriented programming, but the conclusions based on RDFS inferencing are clear. For example, if we know that

```
:Reilly rdf:type :Researcher.
:Kaneda rdf:type :Analyst.
```

then we can infer the other statements:

```
:Reilly rdf:type :Analyst.
:Kaneda rdf:type :Researcher.
```

In effect, the two `rdfs:subClassOf` triples together (or, indeed, any cycle of `rdfs:subClassOf` triples) assert the equivalence of the two classes.

Instance-Level Data Integration

Suppose you have contributions to a single question coming from multiple sources. In the case where the question determines which instances are of interest, there is a simple way to integrate them using `rdfs:subClassOf`. We will give an example from a simplified military domain.

A Command-and-Control Mission Planner wants to determine where ordnance can be targeted or, more specifically, where it cannot be targeted. There are a number of different sources of information that contribute to this decision. One source provides a list of targets and their types, some of which must never be targeted (civilian facilities like churches, schools, and hospitals). Another source provides descriptions of airspaces, some of which are off-limits (e.g., politically defined no-fly zones). A target is determined to be off-limits if it is excluded on the grounds of either of these data sources.

Challenge 5   Define a single class whose contents will includes all the individuals from all of these data sources (and any new ones that are subsequently discovered).

SOLUTION

The solution is to use the Union construction to join together the two information sources into a single, federated class.

```
fc:CivilianFacility rdfs:subClassOf cc:OffLimits.
space:NoFlyZone rdfs:subClassOf cc:OffLimits.
```

Now any instance from either the facility descriptions or the airspace descriptions that have been identified as restricted will be inferred to have `cc:OffLimitsTarget`.

Readable Labels with `rdfs:label`

Resources on the Semantic Web are specified by URIs, which provide a globally scoped unique identifier for the resource. But URIs are not particularly attractive or meaningful to people. RDFS provides a built-in property, `rdfs:label`, whose intended use is to provide a printable name for any resource. This provides a standard way for presentation engines (e.g., webpages or desktop applications) to display the print name of a resource.

Depending on the source of the RDF data that are being displayed, there might be another source for human-readable names for any resource. One solution would be to change the display agent to use a particular display property for each resource. A simpler solution can be done entirely using the semantics of RDFS, through a combination of the property union and property transfer patterns.

Suppose we have imported RDF information from an external form, such as a database or spreadsheet. There are two classes of individuals defined by the import: `Person` and `Movie`. For `Person`, a property called `personName` is defined that gives the name by which that person is professionally known. For `Movie`, the property called `movieTitle` gives the title under which the movie was released. Some sample data from this import might be as follows:

```
:Person1 :personName "James Dean".
:Person2 :personName "Elizabeth Taylor".
:Person3 :personName "Rock Hudson".
:Movie1 :movieTitle "Rebel Without a Cause".
:Movie2 :movieTitle "Giant".
:Movie3 :movieTitle "East of Eden".
```

Challenge 6   We would like to use a generic display mechanism, which uses the standard property `rdfs:label` to display information about these people and movies. How can we use RDFS to achieve this?

SOLUTION

The answer is to define each of these properties as subproperties of `rdfs:label` as follows:

```
:personName rdfs:subPropertyOf rdfs:label.
:movieTitle rdfs:subPropertyOf rdfs:label.
```

When the presentation engine queries for `rdfs:label` of any resource, by the rules of RDFS inferencing, it will find the value of `personName` or `movieTitle`, depending on which one is defined for a particular individual. There is no need for the presentation engine to include any code that understands the (domain-specific) distinction between `Person` and `Movie`.

Data Typing Based on Use

Suppose a shipping company has a fleet of vessels that it manages. The fleet includes new vessels that are under construction, vessels that are being repaired, vessels that are currently in service, and vessels that have been retired from service. The information that the company keeps about its ships might include the information in Table 6-1.

The information in the table can be expressed in RDF triples in the manner outlined in Chapter 3. Each row corresponds to a resource of type `ship:Vessel`;

Table 6-1 Ships

Name	Maiden Voyage	Next Departure	Decommission Date	Destruction Date	Commander
Berengaria	June 16, 1913		1938		Johnson
QEII	May 2, 1969	March 4, 2010			Warwick
Titanic	April 10, 1912			April 14, 1912	Smith
Constitution	July 22, 1798	January 12, 2009			Preble

triples express the information that appears in the body of the table, such as the following:

```
ship:Berengaria ship:maidenVoyage "Dec. 16, 1946".
ship:QEII ship:nextDeparture "Mar 4, 2010".
```

In addition to the class `ship:Vessel`, we can have subclasses that correspond to the status of the ships, such as the following:

```
ship:DeployedVessel rdfs:subClassOf ship:Vessel.
ship:InServiceVessel rdfs:subClassOf ship:Vessel.
ship:OutOfServiceVessel rdfs:subClassOf ship:Vessel.
```

A `DeployedVessel` is one that has been deployed sometime in its lifetime; an `InServiceVessel` is one that is currently in service; and an `OutOfServiceVessel` is one that is currently out of service (for any reason, including retired ships and ships that have not been deployed).

Challenge 7 How can we automatically classify each vessel into more specific subclasses, depending on the information we have about it in Table 6-1? For instance, if a vessel has had a maiden voyage, then it is a `ship:DeployedVessel`. If its next departure is set, then it is an `ship:InServiceVessel`. If it has a decommission date or a destruction date, then it is an `ship:OutOfServiceVessel`.

SOLUTION

We can enforce these inferences using rdfs:domain as follows:

```
ship:maidenVoyage rdfs:domain ship:DeployedVessel.
ship:nextDeparture rdfs:domain ship:InServiceVessel.
```

```
ship:decommissionedDate rdfs:domain ship:OutOfServiceVessel.
ship:destructionDate rdfs:domain ship:OutOfServiceVessel.
```

The whole structure is shown in Figure 6-3. *Vessel* has three subclasses: DeployedVessel, InServiceVessel, and OutOfServiceVessel. Each of these is in the domain of one or more of the properties maidenVoyage, nextDeparture, decommissionedDate, and destructionDate, as shown in the preceding triples and in Figure 6-3. Four instances are shown; maidenVoyage is specified for all four of them, so all of them have been classified as DeployedVessel. *QEII* and *Constitution* have nextDeparture dates specified, so these two are classified as InServiceVessel. The remaining two vessels, *Titanic* and *Berengaria*, have specified destructionDate and decommissionedDate, respectively, and thus are classified as OutOfServiceVessel.

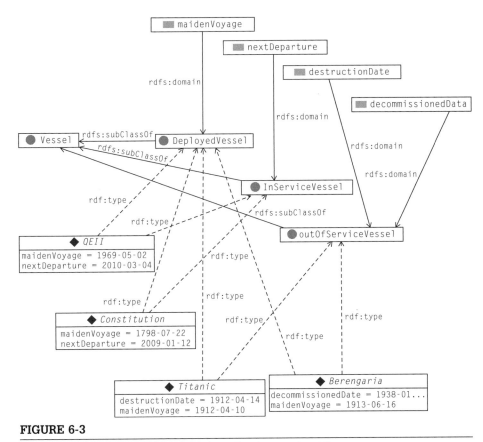

FIGURE 6-3

Inferring classes of vessels from the information known about them.

Challenge 8   All of these inferences concern the subject of the rows, that is, the vessels themselves. It is also possible to draw inferences about the entities in the other table cells.

How can we express the fact that the commander of a ship has the rank of `Captain`?

SOLUTION

We express ranks as classes, as follows:

```
ship:Captain rdfs:subClassOf ship:Officer.
ship:Commander rdfs:subClassOf ship:Officer.
ship:LieutenantCommander rdfs:subClassOf ship:Officer.
ship:Lieutenant rdfs:subClassOf ship:Officer.
ship:Ensign rdfs:subClassOf ship:Officer.
```

Now we can express the fact that a ship's commander has rank *Captain* with `rdfs:range`, as follows:

```
ship:hasCommander rdfs:range ship:Captain.
```

From the information in Table 6-1, we can infer that all of `Johnson`, `Warwick`, `Black`, and **Montgomery** are members of the class `ship:Captain`. These inferences, as well as the triples that led to them, can be seen in Figure 6-4.

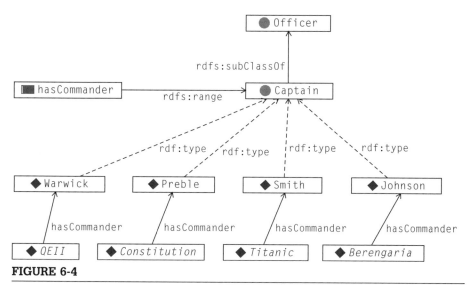

FIGURE 6-4

Inferring that the commanders of the ships have rank "Captain."

Filtering Undefined Data

A related challenge is to sort out individuals based on the information that is defined for them. The set of individuals for which a particular value is defined should be made available for future processing; those for which it is undefined should not be processed.

Challenge 9 In the preceding example, the set of vessels for which `nextDeparture` is defined could be used as input to a scheduling system that plans group tours. Ships for which no `nextDeparture` is known should not be considered.

SOLUTION

It is easy to define the set of vessels that have `nextDeparture` specified by using `rdfs:domain`. First, define a class of `DepartingVessels` that will have these vessels as its members. Then define this to be the domain of `nextDeparture`:

```
ship:DepartingVessel rdf:type rdfs:Class.
ship:nextDeparture rdfs:domain ship:DepartingVessel.
```

From Table 6-1, only the *Constitution* and the *QEII* are members of the class `ship:DepartingVessels` and can be used by a scheduling program (see Figure 6-5).

RDFS and Knowledge Discovery

The use of `rdfs:domain` and `rdfs:range` differs dramatically from similar notions in other modeling paradigms. Because of the inference-based semantics

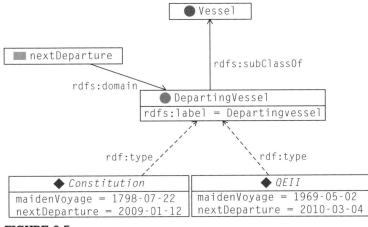

FIGURE 6-5

Ships with a `nextDeparture` specified are `DepartingVessels`.

of RDFS (and OWL), domains and ranges are not used to validate information (as is the case, for example, in OO modeling and XML) but instead are used to determine new information based on old information. We have just seen how this unique aspect of `rdfs:domain` and `rdfs:range` support particular uses of filtering and classifying information.

These definitions are among the most difficult for beginning Semantic Web modelers to come to terms with. It is common for beginning modelers to find these tools clumsy and difficult to use. This difficulty can be ameliorated to some extent by understanding that RDFS in general, and `domain` and `range` in particular, are best understood as tools for knowledge discovery rather than knowledge description. On the Semantic Web, we don't know in advance how information from somewhere else on the Web should be interpreted in a new context. The RDFS definitions of `domain` and `range` allow us to discover new things about our data based on its use.

What does this mean for the skillful use of `domain` and `range` in RDFS? They are not to be used lightly—that is, merely as a way to bundle together several properties around a class. Filtering results such as those shown in these challenge problems are the result of the use of `domain` and `range`. Proper use of `domain` and `range` must take these results into account. Recommended use of `domain` and `range` goes one step further; its use is in one of these patterns, where some particular knowledge filtering or discovery pattern is intended. When used in this way (e.g., using `domain` to describe which of the ships are departing), it is guaranteed that the meaning of `domain` and `range` will be appropriate even in a web setting.

MODELING WITH DOMAINS AND RANGES

Although RDFS has considerable applicability in data amalgamation, and the simplicity of its small number of axioms makes it compact and easy to implement, there are some confusions that arise even in very simple modeling situations when using RDFS.

Multiple Domains/Ranges

In our shipping example, we had two definitions for the of `nextDeparture` domain:

```
ship:nextDeparture rdfs:domain DepartingVessel.
ship:nextDeparture rdfs:domain InServiceVessel.
```

What is the interpretation of these two statements? Is the `nextDeparture` domain `DepartingVessel`, `InServiceVessel`, or both? What does this sort of construction mean?

The right way to understand what a statement or set of statements means in RDFS is to understand what inferences can be drawn from them. Let's consider the case of the *QEII*, for which we have the following asserted triples:

```
ship:QEII ship:maidenVoyage "May 2, 1969".
ship:QEII ship:nextDeparture "Mar 4, 2010".
ship:QEII ship:hasCommander Warwick.
```

The rules of inference for `rdfs:domain` allow us to draw the following conclusions:

```
ship:QEII rdf:type ship:DepartingVessel .
ship:QEII rdf:type ship:InServiceVessel.
```

Each of these conclusions is drawn from the definition of `rdfs:domain`, as applied, respectively, to each of the domain declarations just given. This behavior is not a result of a discussion of "what will happen when there are multiple domain statements?" but rather a simple logical conclusion based on the definition of `rdfs:domain`.

How can we interpret these results? Any vessel for which a `nextDeparture` is specified will be inferred to be a member (i.e., `rdf:type`) of both `Departing Vessel` and `InServiceVessel` classes. Effectively, any such vessel will be inferred to be in the *intersection* of the two classes specified in the domain statements. This is something that many people find counterintuitive, even though it is "correct" in RDFS.

In object-oriented modeling, when one asserts that a property (or field, or variable, or slot) is associated with a class (as is done by `rdfs:domain`), the intuition is that "it is now permissible to use this property to describe members of this class." If there are two such statements, then the intuitive interpretation is that "it is now permissible to use this property with members of either of these classes." Effectively, multiple domain declarations are interpreted in the sense of set union: You may now use this property to describe any item in the *union* of the two specified domains. For someone coming in with this sort of expectation, the *intersection* behavior of RDFS can be something of a surprise.

This interaction makes it necessary to exercise some care when modeling information with the expectation that it will be merged with other information. Let's suppose we have another modeling context in which a company is managing a team of traveling salespeople. Each salesperson has a schedule of business trips. Some of the triples that define this model are as follows:

```
sales:SalesPerson rdfs:subClassOf foaf:Person.
sales:sells rdfs:domain sales:SalesPerson.
sales:sells rdfs:range sales:ProductLine.
sales:nextDeparture rdfs:domain sales:SalesPerson.
```

That is, we have a sales force that covers certain `ProductLines`; each member travels on a regular basis, and it is useful for us to track the date of the next departure of any particular `SalesPerson`.

Suppose we were to merge the information for our sales force management with the schedules of the oceanliners. This merge becomes interesting if we map some of the items in one model to items in another. An obvious candidate for such a mapping is between `sales:nextDeparture` and `ship:nextDeparture`. Both refer to dates, and the intuition is that they specify the next departure date of something or someone. So a simple connection to make between the two models would be to link these two properties, such as the following:

```
sales:nextDeparture rdfs:subPropertyOf ship:nextDeparture.
ship:nextDeparture rdfs:subPropertyOf sales:nextDeparture.
```

using the mutual `subPropertyOf` pattern. The intuition here is that the two uses of `nextDeparture`, one for ships and the other for sales, are in fact the same.

But wait! Let's see what inferences are drawn from this merger. Suppose we have a triple that describes a member of the sales force:

```
sales:Johannes sales:nextDeparture "May 31, 2008".
```

and we already have the triple about the *QEII*:

```
ship:QEII ship:nextDeparture "Mar 4, 2010".
```

What inferences can we draw from these two triples? Using `rdfs:subPropertyOf` inferences first, then `rdfs:domain` inferences, and finally using the `rdfs:subClassOf` triple with `foaf:Person`, we get the following inferred triples:

```
sales:Johannes ship:nextDeparture "May 31, 2008" .
ship:QEII sales:nextDeparture "Mar 4, 2010".
sales:Johannes rdf:type ship:DepartingVessel.
ship:QEII rdf:type sales:SalesPerson.
ship:QEII rdf:type foaf:Person.
```

These inferences start off innocently enough, but they become more and more counterintuitive as they go on, and eventually (when the *QEII* is classified as a `foaf:Person`) become completely outrageous (or perhaps dangerously misleading, especially given that the Monarch herself might actually be a `foaf:Person`, causing the inferences to confuse the Monarch with the ship named after her). The asserted triples, and the inferences that can be drawn from them, are shown in Figure 6-6.

It is easy to lay blame for this unfortunate behavior at the feet of the definition of `rdfs:domain`, but to do so would throw out the baby with the bathwater. The real issue in this example is that we have made a modeling error. The error resulted from the overzealous urge to jump to the conclusion that two properties should be mapped so closely to each other. The ramifications of using `subPropertyOf` (or any other RDFS construct) can be subtle and far-reaching.

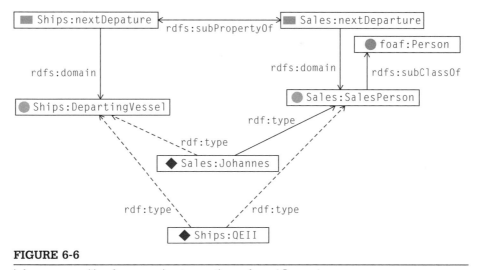

FIGURE 6-6

Inferences resulting from merging two notions of `nextDeparture`.

In particular, when each of these models stated its respective domain and range statements about `sales:nextDeparture` and `ship:nextDeparture`, respectively, it was saying, "Whenever you see any individual described by `sales:nextDeparture` (resp. `ship:nextDeparture`), that individual is known to be of type `sales:SalesPerson` (resp. `ship:DepartingVessel`)." This is quite a strong statement, and it should be treated as such. In particular, it would be surprising if two properties defined so specifically would not have extreme ramifications when merged.

So what is the solution? Should we refrain from merging properties? This is hardly a solution in the spirit of the Semantic Web. Should we avoid making strong statements about properties? This will not help us to make useful models. Should we change the RDFS standard so we can't make these statements? This is a bit extreme, but as we shall see, OWL does provide some more subtle constructs for property definitions that allow for finer-grained modeling. Rather, the solution lies in understanding the source of the modeling error that is at the heart of this example: We should refrain from merging things, like the two notions of `nextDeparture`, whose meanings have important differences.

Using the idioms and patterns of RDFS shown in this chapter, there are more things we can do, depending on our motivation for the merger. In particular, we can still merge these two properties but without making such a strong statement about their equivalence.

If, for instance, we just want to merge the two notions of `nextDeparture` to drive a calendar application that shows all the departure dates for the sales force and the ocean liner fleet, then what we really want is a single property that will provide us the information we need (as we did in the property union pattern). Rather than mapping the properties from one domain to another, instead we map both properties to a third, domain-neutral property, thus:

```
ship:nextDeparture rdfs:subPropertyOf cal:nextDeparture.
sales:nextDeparture rdfs:subPropertyOf cal:nextDeparture.
```

Notice that the amalgamating property `cal:nextDeparture` doesn't need any domain information at all. After all, we don't need to make any (further) inferences about the types of the entities that it is used to describe. Now we can infer that

```
sales:Johannes cal:nextDeparture "May 31, 2008" .
ship:QEII cal:nextDeparture "Mar 4, 2010".
```

A single calendar display, sorted by the property `cal:nextDeparture`, will show these two dates, but no further inference can be made. In particular, no inferences will be made about considering the *QEII* as a member of the sales force or *Johannes* as a sailing vessel.

What can we take from this example into our general Semantic Web modeling practice? Even with a small number of primitives, RDFS provides considerable subtlety for modeling relationships between different data sources. But with this power comes the ability to make subtle and misleading errors. The way to understand the meaning of modeling connections is by tracing the inferences. The ramifications of any modeling mapping can be worked through by following the simple inference rules of RDFS.

NONMODELING PROPERTIES IN RDFS

In addition to the properties described so far, RDFS also provides a handful of properties that have no defined inference semantics—that is, there are no inferences that derive from them. We already saw one example of such a property, `rdfs:label`. No inferences are drawn from `rdfs:label`, so in that sense it has no semantics. Nevertheless, it does by convention have an operational semantics in that it describes the ways in which display agents interact with the model.

Cross-Referencing Files: rdfs:seeAlso

Every resource in a Semantic Web model is specified by a URI that can also be dereferenced and used as a URL. In the case where this URL resolves to a real document, this provides a place where defining information about a resource can be stored.

In some contexts, it is useful to include some supplementary information about a resource for its use in a certain context. This is usually meant to be other documents that might help explain the entity—for example, we might include a pointer to a Wikipedia entry, or a pointer to related data (e.g., if the resource corresponds to a table from a database, the supplementary information could be the other tables from the same database) or even to another RDF or RDFS file that contains linked information. For such cases, `rdfs:seeAlso` provides a way to specify the web location of this supplementary information (i.e. it should be a URI, not a human-readable property). `rdfs:seeAlso` has no formal semantics, so the precise behavior of any processor when it encounters `rdfs:seeAlso` is not specified. A common behavior of tools that encounter `rdfs:seeAlso` links is to expose those links in a browser or application interface through which the RDFS document is being used.

Organizing Vocabularies: rdfs:isDefinedBy

Just as `rdfs:seeAlso` can provide supplementary information about a resource, `rdfs:isDefinedBy` provides a link to the primary source of information about a resource. This allows modelers to specify where the definitional description of a resource can be found. `rdfs:isDefinedBy` is defined in RDF to be a `rdfs:subPropertyOf` of `rdfs:seeAlso`.

Model Documentation: rdfs:comment

Just as in any computer language (modeling languages, markup languages, or programming languages), sometimes it is helpful if a document author can leave natural language comments about a model for future readers to see. Since RDFS is implemented entirely in RDF, the comment feature is also implemented in RDF. To make a comment on some part of a model, simply assert a triple using the property `rdfs:comment` as a predicate. For example:

```
sales:nextDeparture rdfs:comment "This indicates the next
    planned departure date for a salesperson."
```

SUMMARY

RDFS is the schema language for RDF; it describes constructs for types of objects (`Classes`), relating types to one another (`subClasses`), properties that describe objects (`Properties`), and relationships between them (`subProperty`). The Class system in RDFS includes a simple and elegant notion of inheritance, based on set inclusion; one class is a subclass of another means that instances of the one are also instances of the other.

The RDFS language benefits from the distributed nature of RDF by being expressed in RDF itself. All schema information (classes, subclasses, subproperties, domain, range, etc.) is expressed in RDF triples. In particular, this makes schema information, as well as data, subject to the AAA slogan: Anyone can say Anything about Any topic—even about the schema.

The semantics of RDFS is expressed through the mechanism of inferencing; that is, the meaning of any construct in RDFS is given by the inferences that can be inferred from it. For example, it is this simple but powerful mechanism for specifying semantics that allows for the short and elegant definition of subclass and subproperty.

RDFS also includes the constructs `rdfs:domain` and `rdfs:range` to describe the relationship between properties and classes. The meanings of these constructs are given by very simple rules, but these rules have subtle and far-reaching impact. The rules may be simple, but the statements are powerful.

Even with its small set of constructs and simple rules, RDFS allows for the resolution of a wide variety of integration issues. Whenever you might think of doing a global find-and-replace in a set of structured data, consider using `rdfs:subPropertyOf` or `rdfs:subClassOf` instead. It may seem trivial to say that one should merge only entities from multiple sources that don't have important differences. Using the inference mechanism of RDFS, we can determine just what happens when we do merge things and judge whether the results are desirable or dangerous. Although RDFS does not provide logical primitives like union and intersection, it is often possible to achieve desired inferences by using specific patterns of `subClassOf` and `subPropertyOf`. RDFS provides a framework through which information can flow; we can think of `subClassOf` and `subPropertyOf` as the IF/THEN facility of semantic modeling. This utility persists even when we move on to modeling in OWL. In fact, using `subClassOf` in this way provides a cornerstone of OWL modeling.

When used in careful combination, the constructs of RDFS are particularly effective at defining how differently structured information can be used together in a uniform way.

Fundamental Concepts

The following fundamental concepts were introduced in this chapter.

rdfs:subClassOf—Relation between classes, that the members of one class are included in the members of the other.

rdfs:subPropertyOf—Relation between properties, that the pairs related by one property are included in the other.

rdfs:domain and rdfs:range—Description of a property that determines class membership of individuals related by that property.

Logical operations (Union, Intersection, etc.) in RDFS—RDFS constructs can be used to simulate certain logical combinations of sets and properties.

RDFS-Plus | 7

RDFS provides a very limited set of inference capabilities that, as we have seen, have considerable utility in a Semantic Web setting for merging information from multiple sources. In this chapter, we take the first step toward the Web Ontology Language OWL, in which more elaborate constraints on how information is to be merged can be specified. We have selected a particular set of OWL constructs to present at this stage. This set was selected to satisfy a number of goals:

- Pedagogically, these constructs constitute a gentle addition to the constructs that are already familiar from RDFS, increasing the power of the language without making a large conceptual leap from RDFS.

- Practically, we have found that this set of OWL constructs has considerable utility in the information integration projects we have done. In fact, it is much easier to find and describe case studies using RDFS plus this set of OWL constructs than it is to find case studies that use RDFS by itself.

- Computationally, this subset of OWL can be implemented using a wide variety of inferencing technologies, lessening the dependency between the Semantic Web and any particular technology.

For these reasons, we feel that this particular subset will have value beyond the pedagogical value in this book. We call this subset of OWL *RDFS-Plus*, because we see a trend among vendors of Semantic Web tools and Web applications designers for determining a subset of OWL that is at the same time useful and can be implemented quickly. We have identified this particular subset via an informal poll of cutting-edge vendors, and from our own experience with early adopters of Semantic Web technology.

Just as was the case for RDFS, RDFS-Plus is expressed entirely in RDF. The only distinction is that there are a number of resources, all in the namespace *owl*. The meaning of these resources is specified, as before, by the rules that govern the inferences that can be made from them.

In the case of RDFS, we saw how the actions of an inference engine could be used to combine various features of the schema language in novel ways. This **123** trend will continue for RDFS-Plus, but as you might expect, the more constructs we have to begin with, the more opportunity we have for useful and novel combinations.

INVERSE

The names of many of the OWL constructs come from corresponding names in mathematics. Despite their mathematical names, they also have a more common, everyday interpretation. The idea `owl:inverseOf` is a prime example; if a relationship—say, `hasParent`—is interesting enough to mention in a model, then it's a good bet that another relationship—say, `hasChild`—is also interesting. Because of the evocative names `hasParent` and `hasChild`, you can guess the relationship between them, but of course the computer can't. The OWL construct `owl:inverseOf` makes the relationship between `hasParent` and `hasChild` explicit, and describes precisely what it means.

In mathematics, the inverse of a function f (usually written as f^{-1}) is the function that satisfies the property that if $f(x) = y$, then $f^{-1}(y) = x$. Similarly in OWL, the inverse of a property is another property that reverses its direction.

To be specific, we look at the meaning of `owl:inverseOf`. In OWL, as in RDFS, the meaning of any construct is given by the inferences that can be drawn from it. If we have the following triples:

```
P owl:inverseOf Q .
x P y .
```

then we can infer that

```
y Q x .
```

In the examples in the book, we have already seen a number of possibilities for inverses, though we haven't used them so far. In our Shakespeare examples, we have the triples

```
lit:Shakespeare lit:wrote lit:Macbeth .
lit:Macbeth lit:setIn geo:Scotland .
```

If, in addition to these triples, we also state some inverses, such as:

```
lit:wrote owl:inverseOf lit:writtenBy .
lit:settingFor owl:inverseOf lit:setIn .
```

then we can infer that

```
lit:Macbeth lit:writtenBy lit:Shakespeare .
geo:Scotland lit:setingFor lit:Macbeth .
```

Although the meaning of `owl:inverseOf` is not difficult to describe, what is the utility of such a construct in a modeling language? After all, the effect of `inverseOf` can be achieved just as easily by writing the query differently. For instance, if we want to know all the plays that are `setIn` Scotland, we can use the inverse property `settingFor` in our query pattern, such as

```
{geo:Scotland lit:settingfor ?play . }
```

Because of the semantics of the inverse property, this will give us all plays that were `setIn` Scotland.

But we could have avoided the use of the inverse property and simply written the query as

```
{?play lit:setIn geo:Scotland . }
```

We get the same answers, and we don't need an extra construct in the modeling language.

While this is true, `owl:inverseOf` nevertheless does have considerable utility in modeling, based on how it can interact with other modeling constructs. In the next challenge, we'll see how the Property Union challenge can be extended using inverses.

Challenge: Integrating Data that Do Not Want to Be Integrated

In the Property Union challenge, we had two properties, `borrows` and `checked-Out`. We were able to combine them under a single property by making them both `rdfs:subPropertyOf` the same parent property, `hasPosession`. We were fortunate that the two sources of data happened to link a *Patron* as the subject to a *Book* as the object (i.e., they had the same domain and range). Suppose instead that the second source was an index of books, and for each book there was a field specifying the patron the book was `signedTo` (i.e., the domain and range are reversed).

Challenge 10   How can we merge `signedTo` and `borrows` in a way analogous to how we merged `borrows` and `checkedOut`, given that `signedTo` and `borrows` don't share good domains and ranges?

SOLUTION

The solution involves a simple use of `owl:inverseOf` to specify two properties for which the domain and range do match, as required for the merge. We define a new property—say, `signedOut`—as the inverse of `signedTo`, as follows:

```
:signedTo owl:inverseOf :signedOut .
```

Now we can use the original Property Union pattern to merge `signedOut` and `borrows` into the single `hasPossession` property:

```
:signedOut rdfs:subPropertyOf :hasPossession .
:borrows rdfs:subPropertyOf :hasPossession .
```

So if we have some data expressed using `signedTo`, along with data expressed with `borrows`, as follows:

```
:Amit :borrows :MobyDick .
:Marie :borrows :Orlando .
:LeavesOfGrass :signedTo :Jim .
:WutheringHeights :signedTo :Yoshi .
```

then with the rule for `inverseOf`, we have the additional triples

```
:Jim :signedOut :LeavesOfGrass .
:Yoshi :signedOut :WutheringHeights .
```

and with subPropertyOf, we have

```
:Amit :hasPossession :MobyDick .
:Marie :hasPossession :Orlando .
:Jim :hasPossession :LeavesOfGrass .
:Yoshi :hasPossession :WutheringHeights .
```

as desired.

SOLUTION (ALTERNATIVE)

There is a certain asymmetry in this solution; the choice to specify an inverse for `signedTo` rather than for `hasPossession` was somewhat arbitrary. Another solution that also uses `owl:inverseOf` and `rdfs:subPropertyOf` and is just as viable as the first is the following:

```
:signedTo :rdfs:subPropertyOf :possessedBy .
:borrows rdfs:subPropertyOf :hasPossession .
:possessedBy owl:inverseOf :hasPossession .
```

These statements use the same rules for `owl:inverseOf` and `rdfs:subPropertyOf` but in a different order, resulting in the same `hasPossession` triples. Which solution is better in what situations? How can we tell which to use?

If all we were concerned with was making sure that the inferences about `hasPossession` will be supported, then there would be no reason to prefer one solution over the other. But modeling in the Semantic Web is not just about supporting desired inferences but also about supporting reuse. What if someone else wants to use this model in a slightly different way? A future query is just as likely to be interested in `hasPossession` as `possessedBy`. Furthermore, we might in the future wish to combine `hasPossession` (or `possessedBy`) with another property. For this reason, one might choose to use both solutions together by using both `inverseOf` and `subPropertyOf` in a systematic way—that is, by

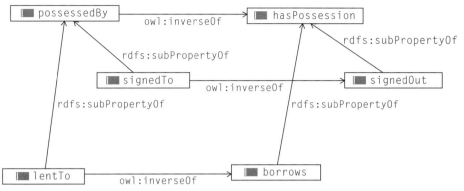

FIGURE 7-1

Systematic combination of `inverseOf` and `subPropertyOf`.

specifying inverses for every property, regardless of the `subPropertyOf` level. In this case, this results in

```
:signedTo owl:inverseOf :signedOut .
:signedTo rdfs:subPropertyOf :possessedBy .
:signedOut rdfs:subPropertyOf :hasPossession .
:lentTo owl:inverseOf :borrows .
:lentTo rdfs:subPropertyOf :possessedBy .
:borrows rdfs:subPropertyOf :hasPossession .
:possessedBy owl:inverseOf :hasPossession .
```

The systematicity of this structure can be more readily seen in Figure 7-1. The attentive reader might have one more concern about the systematicity of Figure 7-1—in particular, the selection of which properties are the subject of `owl:inverseOf` and which are the object (in the diagram, which ones go on the left or on the right of the diagram) is arbitrary. Shouldn't there be three more `owl:inverseOf` triples, pointing from right to left? Indeed, there should be, but there is no need to assert these triples, as we shall see in the next challenge.

Challenge: Using the Modeling Language to Extend the Modeling Language

It is not unusual for beginning modelers to look at the list of constructs defined in OWL and say, "There is a feature of the OWL language I would like to use that is very similar to the ones that are included. Why did they leave it out? I would prefer to build my model using a different set of primitives." In many cases, the extra language feature that they desire is actually already supported by OWL as a combination of other features. It is a simple matter of using these features in combination.

Challenge 11   For example, RDFS allows you to specify that one class is a `subClassOf` another, but you might like to think of it the other way around (perhaps because of the structure of some legacy data you want to work with) and specify that something is `superClassOf` something else. That is, you want the parent class to be the subject of all the definitional triples. Using your own namespace `myowl:` for this desired relation, you would like to have the triples look like this:

```
:Food myowl:superClassOf :BakedGood;
    myowl:superClassOf :Confectionary;
    myowl:superClassOf :PackagedFood;
    myowl:superClassOf :PreparedFood;
    myowl:superClassOf :ProcessedFood .
```

If we instead use `rdfs:subClassOf`, all the triples go the other way around; *Food* will be the object of each triple, and all the types of *Food* will be the subjects.

Since OWL does not provide a `superClassOf` resource (or to speak more correctly, OWL does not define any inference rules that will provide any semantics for a `superClassOf` resource), what can we do?

SOLUTION

What do we want `myowl:superClassOf` to mean? For every triple of the form

```
P myowl:superClassOf Q .
```

we want to be able to infer that

```
Q rdfs:subClassOf P .
```

This can be accomplished simply by declaring an inverse

```
myowl:superClassOf owl:inverseOf rdfs:subClassOf .
```

It is a simple application of the rule for `owl:inverseOf` to see that this accomplishes the desired effect. Nevertheless, this is not a solution that many beginning modelers think of. It seems to them that they have no right to modify or extend the meaning of the OWL language or to make statements about the OWL and RDFS resources (like `rdfs:subClassOf`). But remember the AAA slogan of RDF: *Anyone can say Anything about Any topic.* In particular, a modeler can say things about the resources defined in the standard.

In fact, we can take this slogan so far as to allow a modeler to say

```
rdfs:subClassOf owl:inverseOf rdfs:superClassOf .
```

This differs from the previous triple in that the subject is a resource in the (standard) RDFS namespace. The RDF slogan allows a modeler to say this, and indeed, there is nothing in the standards that will prevent it. However, referring to a resource in the RDFS namespace is likely to suggest to human readers of the model that this relationship is part of the RDFS standard. Since one purpose of a model is to communicate to other human beings, it is generally not a good idea to make statements that are likely to be misleading, so we do not endorse this practice.

Selecting namespaces for resources that extend the capabilities of the OWL language is a delicate matter; in the next chapter, we will examine a case study in which this has been done in a careful way.

Challenge: The Marriage of Shakespeare

In a previous chapter, we lamented that even though we had asserted that Anne Hathaway had married Shakespeare, we did not know that Shakespeare had married Anne Hathaway. We are now in a position to remedy that.

Challenge 12   How can we infer marriages in the reverse direction from which they are asserted?

SOLUTION

We could do this by simply declaring `bio:married` to be its own inverse, thus:

```
bio:married owl:inverseOf bio:married .
```

Now any triple that used `bio:married` would automatically be inferred to hold in the other direction. In particular, if we asserted

```
bio:AnneHathaway bio:married lit:Shakespeare .
```

we could infer that

```
lit:Shakespeare bio:married bio:AnneHathaway .
```

This pattern of self-inverses is so common that it has been built into OWL using a special construct called `owl:SymmetricProperty`.

SYMMETRIC PROPERTIES

`owl:inverseOf` relates one property to another. The special case in which these two properties are the same (as was the case for `bio:married` for the Shakespeare example) is common enough that the OWL language provides a special name for it: `owl:SymmetricProperty`. Unlike `owl:inverseOf`, which is a property that relates two other properties, `owl:SymmetricProperty` is just an aspect of a single property and is expressed in OWL as a Class. We express that a property is symmetric in the same way as we express membership in any class—in other words:

```
P rdf:type owl:SymmetricProperty .
```

As usual, the meaning of this statement is given by the inferences that can be drawn from it. From this triple, we can infer that

```
P owl:inverseOf P .
```

So in the case of the marriage of Shakespeare, we can assert that

```
bio:married rdf:type owl:SymmetricProperty .
```

Using OWL to Extend OWL

As we describe more and more of the power of the OWL modeling language, there will be more and more opportunities to define at least some aspects of a new construct in terms of previously defined constructs. We can use this method to streamline our presentation of the OWL language. We have seen a need for this already in figure Figure 7-1, in which all of our inverses are expressed in one direction but we really need to have them go both ways, as shown in Figure 7-2.

We asserted the triples from left to right—namely:

```
:possessedBy owl:inverseOf :hasPossession .
:signedTo owl:inverseOf :signedOut .
:lentTo owl:inverseOf :borrows .
```

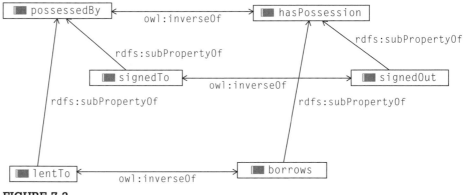

FIGURE 7-2

Systematic combination of `inverseOf` and `subPropertyOf`. Contrast this with Figure 7-1, with one-directional inverses.

But we would like to be able to infer the triples from right to left—namely:

```
:hasPossession owl:inverseOf :possessedBy.
:signedOut owl:inverseOf :signedTo.
:borrows owl:inverseOf :lentTo.
```

Challenge 13   How can we infer all of these triples without having to assert them?

SOLUTION

Since we want `owl:inverseOf` to work in both directions, this can be done easily by asserting that `owl:inverseOf` is its own inverse, thus:

```
owl:inverseOf owl:inverseOf owl:inverseOf .
```

You might have done a double take when you read that `owl:inverseOf` is its own inverse. Fortunately, we now have a more readable and somewhat more understandable way to say this—namely:

```
owl:inverseOf rdf:type owl:SymmetricProperty .
```

In either case, we get the inferences we desire for Figure 7-2, in which the inverses point both ways. This also means that all the inferences in both directions will always be found.

TRANSITIVITY

In mathematics, a relation *R* is said to be *transitive* if *R(a,b)* and *R(b,c)* implies *R(a,c)*. The same idea is used for the OWL construct `owl:Transitive-Property`. Just like `owl:SymmetricProperty`, `owl:TransitiveProperty` is a class of properties, so a model can assert that a property is a member of the class

```
P rdf:type owl:TransitiveProperty .
```

The meaning of this is given by a somewhat more elaborate rule than we have seen so far in this chapter. Namely, if we have two triples of the form

```
X P Y .
Y P Z .
```

then we can infer that

```
X P Z .
```

Notice that there is no need for even more elaborate rules like

```
A P B .
B P C .
C P D .
```

implies

```
A P D .
```

since this conclusion can be reached by applying the simple rule over and over again.

Some typical examples of transitive properties include ancestor/descendant (if Victoria is an ancestor of Edward, and Edward is an ancestor of Elizabeth, then Victoria is an ancestor of Elizabeth) and geographical containment (if Osaka is in Japan, and Japan is in Asia, then Osaka is in Asia).

Challenge: Relating Parents to Ancestors

A model of genealogy will typically include notions of parents as well as ancestors, and we'd like them to fit together. But parents are not transitive (my parents' parents are not my parents), whereas ancestors are.

Challenge 14   How can we allow a model to maintain consistent ancestry information, given parentage information.

SOLUTION

Start by defining the parent property to be a `subPropertyOf` the ancestor property, thus:

```
:hasParent rdfs:subPropertyOf :hasAncestor .
```

Then declare ancestor (only) to be a transitive property:

```
:hasAncestor rdf:type owl:TransitiveProperty .
```

Let's see how this works on some examples.

```
:Alexia :hasParent :WillemAlexander .
:WillemAlexander :hasParent :Beatrix .
:Beatrix :hasParent :Wilhelmina .
```

Because of the `subPropertyOf` relation between `hasParent` and `hasAncestor` and the fact that `hasAncestor` is a `TransitiveProperty`, we can infer that

```
:Alexia :hasAncestor :WillemAlexander.
:WillemAlexander :hasAncestor :Beatrix.
:Alexia :hasAncestor :Beatrix.
:WillemAlexander :hasAncestor :Wilhelmina.
:Alexia :hasAncestor :Wilhelmina.
```

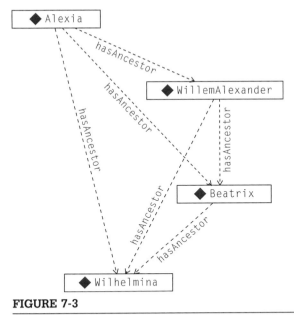

FIGURE 7-3

Inferences from transitive properties.

Information about the heritage is integrated, regardless of whether it originated with `hasParent` or `hasAncestor`. Information about `hasParent`, on the other hand, is only available as it was directly asserted because it was not declared to be transitive. The results of this inference are shown in Figure 7-3.

Challenge: Layers of Relationships

Sometimes it can be somewhat controversial whether a property is transitive or not. For instance, the relationship that is often expressed by the words "part of" in English is sometimes transitive (a piston is part of the engine, and the engine is part of the car; is the piston part of the car?) and sometimes not (Mick Jagger's thumb is part of Mick Jagger, and Mick Jagger is part of the Rolling Stones; is Mick Jagger's thumb part of the Rolling Stones?). In the spirit of anticipating possible uses of a model, it is worthwhile to support both points of view whenever there is any chance that controversy might arise.

Challenge 15 How can we simultaneously maintain transitive and nontransitive versions of the `partOf` information?

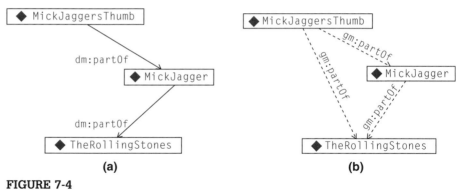

FIGURE 7-4

Different interpretations of partOf.

SOLUTION

We can define two versions of the partOf property in different namespaces (or with different names) with one a subPropertyOf the other, and with the super-property declared as transitive:

```
dm:partOf rdfs:subPropertyOf gm:partOf .
gm:partOf rdf:type owl:TransitiveProperty .
```

Depending on which interpretation of partOf any particular application needs, it can query the appropriate property. For those who prefer to think that Mick Jagger's thumb is not part of the Rolling Stones, the original dm:partOf property is useful. For those who instead consider that Mick Jagger's thumb is part of the Rolling Stones, the transitive superproperty gm:partOf is appropriate (see Figure 7-4).

Managing Networks of Dependencies

The same modeling patterns we have been using to manage relationships (like ancestry), or set containment (like part of) can be used just as well in a very different setting—namely, to manage networks of dependencies. In the series of challenges that follow, we will see how the familiar constructs of rdfs:subPropertyOf, owl:inverseOf, and owl:TransitiveProperty can be combined in novel ways to model important aspects of such networks.

A common application of this idea is in workflow management. In a complex working situation, a variety of tasks must be repeatedly performed in a set sequence. The idea of workflow management is that the sequence can be represented explicitly and the progress of each task tracked in that sequence. Why would someone want to model workflow in a Semantic Web? The answer is for the same reason one wants to put anything on the web: so that parts of the workflow can be shared with others, encouraging reuse, review, and publication of work fragments.

Real workflow specifications are far too detailed to serve as examples in a book, so we will use a simple example to show how it works. Let's make some ice cream, using the following recipe:

> Slice a vanilla bean lengthwise, and scrape the contents into 1 cup of heavy cream. Bring the mixture to a simmer, but do not boil.

> While the cream is heating, separate three eggs. Add 1/2 cup white sugar, and beat until fluffy. Gradually add the warm cream, beating constantly. Return the custard mixture to medium heat, and cook until mixture leaves a heavy coat on the back of a spatula. Chill well. Combine custard with 1 cup whole milk, and turn in ice cream freezer according to manufacturer's instructions.

First, let's use a property `dependsOn` to represent the dependencies between the steps and define its inverse `enables`, since each step enables the next in the correct execution of the workflow:

```
:dependsOn owl:inverseOf :enables .
```

Now we can define the dependency structure of the recipe steps:

```
:SliceBean :enables :HeatCream .
:SeparateEggs :enables :AddSugar .
:AddSugar :enables :BeatEggs .
:BeatEggs :enables :GraduallyMix .
:HeatCream :enables :GraduallyMix .
:GraduallyMix :enables :CookCustard .
:CookCustard :enables :Chill .
:Chill :enables :AddMilk .
:AddMilk :enables :TurnInFreezer .
```

Because of the `inverseOf`, we can view these steps either in enabling order as asserted or in dependency order, as show in Figure 7-5.

Challenge 16 For any particular step in the process, we might want to know all the steps it depends on or all the steps that depend on it. How can we do this, using the patterns we already know?

SOLUTION

We can use the `subPropertyOf/TransitiveProperty` pattern for each of `dependsOn` and `enables` as follows:

```
:dependsOn rdfs:subPropertyOf :hasPrerequisite .
:hasPrerequisite rdf:type owl:TransitiveProperty .
:enables rdfs:subPropertyOf :prerequisiteFor .
:prerequisiteFor rdf:type owl:TransitiveProperty .
```

These relationships can be seen graphically in Figure 7-6.

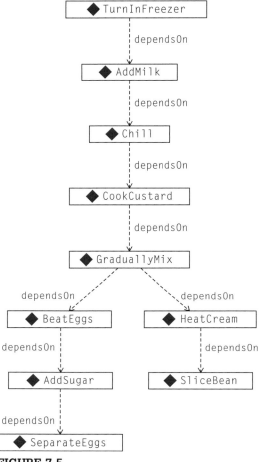

FIGURE 7-5

Dependencies for homemade ice cream.

From these triples, for instance, we can infer that `GraduallyMix` has five prerequisites—namely:

```
:GraduallyMix :hasPrerequisite :AddSugar ;
   :hasPrerequisite :SeparateEggs ;
   :hasPrerequisite :SliceBean ;
   :hasPrerequisite :HeatCream ;
   :hasPrerequisite :BeatEggs .
```

Challenge 17   In a more realistic workflow management setting, we wouldn't just be managing a single process (corresponding to a single recipe). We would be managing several processes that interact in complex ways. We could even

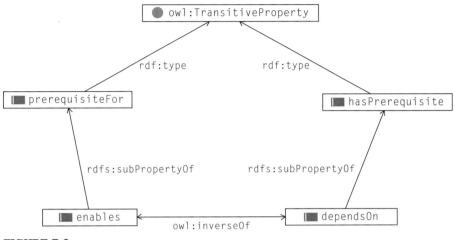

FIGURE 7-6

Transitive properties `hasPrerequisite` and `prerequisiteFor` defined in terms of `dependsOn` and `enables`.

lose track of which steps are in the same procedure. Is there a way to find out, given a particular step, what the other steps in the same process are? In our recipe example, can we model the relationship between steps so that we can connect steps in the same recipe together?

SOLUTION

First, we combine together both of our fundamental relationships (`enables` and `dependsOn`) as common `subPropertyOf` a single unifying property (`neighbor-Step`). We then, in turn, make that a `subPropertyOf` of a transitive property (`inSameRecipe`), shown here in N3 and in Figure 7-7(a).

```
:dependsOn rdfs:subPropertyOf :neighborStep .
:enables rdfs:subPropertyOf :neighborStep .
:neighborStep rdfs:subPropertyOf :inSameRecipe .
:inSameRecipe rdf:type owl:TransitiveProperty .
```

What inferences can we draw from these triples for the instance `GraduallyMix`? Any directly related step (related by either `dependsOn` or `enables`) becomes a `neighborStep`, and any combination of neighbors is rolled up with `inSame-Recipe`. A few selected inferences are shown here:

```
:GraduallyMix :neighborStep :BeatEggs ;
              :neighborStep :HeatCream ;
              :neighborStep :CookCustard .
              :CookCustard  :neighborStep :Chill ;
              :neighborStep :GraduallyMix .
```

```
:GraduallyMix :inSameRecipe :BeatEggs ;
              :inSameRecipe :HeatCream ;
              :inSameRecipe :CookCustard .
              :CookCustard  :inSameRecipe :Chill ;
              :inSameRecipe :GraduallyMix .
...
:GraduallyMix :inSameRecipe :AddMilk ;
              :inSameRecipe :CookCustard ;
              :inSameRecipe :TurnInFreezer ;
              :inSameRecipe :AddSugar ;
              :inSameRecipe :SeparateEggs ;
              :inSameRecipe :SliceBean ;
              :inSameRecipe :HeatCream ;
              :inSameRecipe :GraduallyMix ;
              :inSameRecipe :Chill ;
              :inSameRecipe :BeatEggs .
```

All the steps in this recipe have been gathered up with inSameRecipe, as desired. In fact, any two steps in this recipe will be related to one another by inSameRecipe, including relating each step to itself. In particular, the triple

```
:GraduallyMix :inSameRecipe :GraduallyMix .
```

has been inferred. Although this is, strictly speaking, correct (after all, indeed GraduallyMix is in the same recipe as GraduallyMix), it might not be what we actually wanted to know.

Challenge 18   How can we define a property that will relate a recipe step only to the other steps in the same recipe?

SOLUTION

Earlier we defined two properties, hasPrerequisite and prerequisiteFor, one looking "downstream" along the dependencies and one looking "upstream."

```
:dependsOn rdfs:subPropertyOf :hasPrerequisite .
:hasPrerequisite rdf:type owl:TransitiveProperty .
:enables rdfs:subPropertyOf :prerequisiteFor .
:prerequisiteFor rdf:type owl:TransitiveProperty .
```

If we join these two together under a common superproperty that is not transitive, we get the following:

```
:hasPrerequisite rdfs:subPropertyOf :otherStep .
:prerequisiteFor rdfs:subPropertyOf :otherStep .
```

These relationships are shown diagrammatically in Figure 7-7(b).

We track the inferences separately for each property. For hasPrerequisite, we have already seen that we can infer the following:

```
:GraduallyMix :hasPrerequisite :AddSugar ;
    :hasPrerequisite :SeparateEggs ;
    :hasPrerequisite :SliceBean ;
    :hasPrerequisite :HeatCream ;
    :hasPrerequisite :BeatEggs .
```

For prerequisiteOf, we get the following inferences:

```
:GraduallyMix :prerequisiteFor :AddMilk ;
    :prerequisiteFor :CookCustard ;
    :prerequisiteFor :TurnInFreezer ;
    :prerequisiteFor :Chill .
```

Now, for otherStep, we get the combination of these two. Notice that neither list includes GraduallyMix itself, so it does not appear in this list either.

```
:GraduallyMix :otherStep :AddMilk ;
    :otherStep :CookCustard ;
    :otherStep :TurnInFreezer ;
    :otherStep :AddSugar ;
    :otherStep :SeparateEggs ;
    :otherStep :SliceBean ;
    :otherStep :HeatCream ;
    :otherStep :Chill ;
    :otherStep :BeatEggs .
```

Figure 7-7 shows the two patterns. For inSameRecipe, we have a single transitive property at the top of a subPropertyOf tree; both primitive properties (enables and dependsOn) are brought together, and any combinations of the resulting property (neighborStep) are chained together as a TransitiveProperty (inSameRecipe). For otherStep, the top-level property itself is *not* transitive but is a simple combination (via two subPropertyOf links) of two transitive properties (hasPrerequisite and prerequisiteFor). Inference for each of these transitive properties is done separately from the other, and the results combined (without any more transitive interaction). Hence, for inSameRecipe, the reflexive triples like

```
:GraduallyMix :inSameRecipe :GraduallyMix .
```

are included, whereas for otherStep, they are not.

EQUIVALENCE

RDF provides a global notion of identity that has validity across data sources; that global identity is the URI. This makes it possible to refer to a single entity

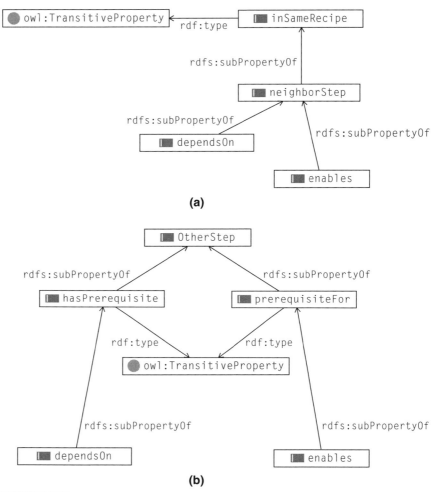

(a)

(b)

FIGURE 7-7

Contrast patterns for inSameRecipe (includes self) and otherStep (excludes self). Both patterns work from the same input properties dependsOn and enables but yield different results.

in a distributed way. But when we want to merge information from multiple sources controlled by multiple stakeholders, it is not necessarily the case that any two stakeholders will use the same URI to refer to the same entity. Thus, in a federated information setting, it is useful to be able to stipulate that two URIs actually refer to the same entity. But there are different ways in which two entities can be the same. Some are more equal than others. RDFS-Plus provides a variety of notions of equivalence. As with other constructs in OWL, these different constructs are defined by the inferences they entail.

Equivalent Classes

We previously used a simple idiom to express that one class had the same elements as another; in particular, we asserted two triples

```
:Analyst rdf:subClassOf :Researcher .
:Researcher rdf:subClassOf :Analyst .
```

to indicate that every *Analyst* is a *Researcher* and every *Researcher* is an *Analyst*. As we saw, the rule for rdf:subClassOf can be applied in each direction to support the necessary inferences to make every *Analyst* a *Researcher* and vice versa. When two classes are known to always have the same members, we say that the classes are *equivalent*. The preceding pattern allows us to express class equivalence in RDFS, if in a somewhat unintuitive way.

RDFS-Plus provides a more intuitive expression of class equivalence, using the construct owl:equivalentClass. A single triple expresses class equivalence in the obvious way:

```
:Analyst owl:equivalentClass :Researcher .
```

As with any other construct in RDFS or OWL, the precise meaning of owl:equivalentClass is given by the inferences that can be drawn. In particular, if we know that

```
A owl:equivalentClass B .
r rdf:type A .
```

then we can infer that

```
r rdf:type B .
```

So far, this is just the type propagation rule that we used to define the meaning of rdf:subClassOf in Chapter 6. But owl:equivalentClass has another rule as well—given

```
A rdf:subClassOf B .
r rdf:type B .
```

then we can infer that

```
r rdf:type A .
```

That is, the two classes A and B have exactly the same members.

It seems a bit of a shame that something as simple as equivalence requires two rules to express, especially when the rules are so similar. In fact, this isn't necessary; if we observe that

```
owl:equivalentClass rdfs:type owl:SymmetricProperty .
```

then there is no need for the second rule; we can infer it from the first rule and the symmetry of equivalentClass.

In fact, we don't actually need any rules at all; if we also assert that

```
owl:equivalentClass rdfs:subPropertyOf rdfs:subClassOf .
```

we can use the rules for `subPropertyOf` and `subClassOf` to infer everything about `equivalentClass`! Let's see how the rules for OWL, which we have already learned work for `owl:equivalentClass`, in the case of the *Analyst* and the *Researcher*.

From the rule about `rdfs:subClassOf` and the statement of equivalence of *Analyst* and *Researcher*, we can infer that

```
:Analyst rdfs:subClassOf :Researcher .
```

But since `owl:equivalentClass` is symmetric, we can also infer that

```
:Researcher owl:equivalentClass :Analyst .
```

and by applying the rule for `rdfs:subClassOf` once again, we get

```
:Researcher rdfs:subClassOf :Analyst .
```

That is, simply by applying what we already know about `rdfs:subClassOf` and `owl:SymmetricProperty`, we can infer both `rdfs:subClassOf` triples from the single `owl:equivalentClass` triple.

Notice that when two classes are equivalent, it only means that the two classes have the same members. Other properties of the classes are not shared; for example, each class keeps its own `rdfs:label`. This means that if these classes have been merged from two different applications, each of these applications will still display the class by the original print name; only the members of the class will change.

Equivalent Properties

We have seen how to use `rdfs:subPropertyOf` to make two properties behave in the same way; the trick we used there was very similar to the double `subClassOf` trick. We use `rdfs:subPropertyOf` twice to indicate that two properties are equivalent.

```
:borrows rdfs:subPropertyOf :checkedOut .
:checkedOut rdfs:subPropertyOf :borrows .
```

RDFS-Plus also provides a more intuitive way to express property equivalence, using `owl:equivalentProperty`, as follows:

```
:borrows owl:equivalentProperty :checkedOut .
```

When two properties are equivalent, we expect that in any triple that uses one as a predicate, the other can be substituted—that is, for any triple

```
A borrows B .
```

we can infer that

```
A checkedOut B .
```

and vice versa. We can accomplish this in a manner analogous to the method used for `owl:equivalentClass`. We define `owl:equivalentProperty` in terms of other RDFS-Plus constructs.

```
owl:equivalentProperty rdfs:subPropertyOf rdfs:subPropertyOf.
owl:equivalentProperty rdf:type owl:SymmetricProperty .
```

Starting with the asserted equivalence of *borrows* and checkedOut, using these triples, and the rules for `rdfs:subPropertyOf` and `owl:SymmetricProperty`, we can infer that

```
:borrows rdfs:subPropertyOf checkedOut .
:checkedOut owl:equivalentProperty borrows .
:checkedOut rdfs:subPropertyOf borrows .
```

Once we have inferred that borrows and checkedOut are `rdfs:subPropertyOf` one another, we can make all the appropriate inferences.

When we express new constructs (like `owl:equivalentProperty` in this section) to constructs we already know (`rdfs:subPropertyOf` and `owl:Symmetric-Property`), we explicitly describe how the various parts of the language fit together. That is, rather than just noticing that the rule governing `owl:equivalent Property` is the same rule as the one that governs `rdfs:subPropertyOf` (except that it works both ways!), we can actually model these facts. By making `owl:equivalentProperty` a subproperty of `rdfs:subPropertyOf`, we explicitly assert that they are governed by the same rule. By making `owl:equivalentProperty` a `owl:SymmetricProperty`, we assert the fact that this rule works in both direct ions. This makes the relationship between the parts of the OWL language explicit and, in fact, models them in OWL.

Same Individuals

Class equivalence—that is, `owl:equivalentClass`—and property equivalence (`own:equivalentProperty`) provide intuitive ways to express relationships that were already expressible in RDFS. In this sense, neither of these constructs have increased the expressive power of RDFS-Plus beyond what was already available in RDFS. They have just made it easier to express and clearer to read. These constructs refer respectively to classes of things and the properties that relate them.

But when we are describing things in the world, we aren't only describing classes and properties; we are describing the things themselves. These are the members of the classes. We refer to these as *individuals*. We have encountered a number of individuals in our examples so far—Wenger the Analyst, *Twelfth Night* the Play, Shakespeare the Playwright, Kildare the Surgeon, Kaneda the

All-Star Player—and any number of things whose class membership has not been specified—Wales, The Firm, and *Moby Dick*. But remember the non-unique naming assumption: Often, our information comes from multiple sources that might not have done any coordination in their reference to individuals. How do we handle the situation in which we determine that two individuals that we originally thought of separately are in fact the same individual?

In RDFS-Plus, this is done with the single construct `owl:sameAs`. Our old friend William Shakespeare will provide us with an example of how `owl:sameAs` works. From Chapter 3, we have the following triples about the literary career of William Shakespeare:

```
lit:Shakespeare lit:wrote lit:AsYouLikeIt ;
    lit:wrote lit:HenryV ;
    lit:wrote lit:LovesLaboursLost ;
    lit:wrote lit:MeasureForMeasure ;
    lit:wrote lit:TwelfthNight ;
    lit:wrote lit:WintersTale ;
    lit:wrote lit:Hamlet ;
    lit:wrote lit:Othello .
```

Suppose we have at our disposal information from the Stratford Parish Register, which lists the following information from some baptisms that occurred there. We will use `spr:` as the namespace identifier for URIs from the Stratford Parish Register.

```
spr:Gulielmus spr:hasFather spr:JohannesShakspere .
spr:Susanna spr:hasFather spr:WilliamShakspere .
spr:Hamnet spr:hasFather spr:WilliamShakspere .
spr:Judeth spr:hasFather spr:WilliamShakspere .
```

Suppose that our research determines that, indeed, the resources mentioned here as `spr:Gulielmus`, `spr:WilliamShakspere` and `lit:Shakespeare` all refer to the same individual, so the answer to the question "Did Hamnet's father write *Hamlet*?" would be "yes." If we had known that all of these things refer to the same person in advance of having represented the Stratford Parish Register in RDF, we could have used the same URI (e.g., `lit:Shakespeare`) for each occurrence of the Bard. But now it is too late; the URIs from each data source have already been chosen. What is to be done?

First, let's think about how to pose the question "Did Hamnet's father write *Hamlet*?" We can write this as a graph pattern in SPARQL as follows:

```
{spr:Hamnet spr:hasFather ?d .
?d lit:wrote lit:Hamlet . }
```

that is, we are looking for a single resource that links Hamnet to *Hamlet* via the two links `spr:hasFather` and `lit:wrote`.

In RDFS-Plus, we have the option of asserting the sameness of two resources. Let's start with just one:

```
spr:WilliamShakspere owl:sameAs lit:Shakespeare .
```

The meaning of this triple, as always in RDFS-Plus, is expressed by the inferences that can be drawn. The rule for `owl:sameAs` is quite intuitive; it says that if A `owl:sameAs` B, then in any triple where we see A, we can infer the same triple, with A replaced by B. So for our *Shakespeare* example, we have that for any triple of the form

```
spr:WilliamShakespere P O .
```

we can infer that

```
lit:Shakespeare P O .
```

Similarly, for any triple of the form

```
S P spr:WilliamShakespere .
```

we can infer that

```
S P lit:Shakespeare .
```

Also, as we did for `owl:equivalentClass` and `owl:equivalentProperty`, we assert that `owl:sameAs` is a `owl:SymmetricProperty` :

```
owl:sameAs rdf:type owl:SymmetricProperty .
```

This allows us to infer that

```
lit:Shakespeare owl:sameAs spr:WilliamShakspere.
```

so that we can replace any occurrence of `lit:Shakespeare` with `spr:William-Shakspere` as well.

Let's see how this works with the triples we know from literary history and the Register. We list all triples, with asserted triples in Roman and inferred triples in *italics*. Among the inferred triples, we begin by replacing `lit:Shakespeare` with `spr:WilliamShakspere`, then continue by replacing `spr:WilliamShakspere` with `lit:Shakespeare`:

```
lit:Shakespeare lit:wrote lit:AsYouLikeIt ;
    lit:wrote lit:HenryV ;
    lit:wrote lit:LovesLaboursLost ;
    lit:wrote lit:MeasureForMeasure ;
    lit:wrote lit:TwelfthNight ;
    lit:wrote lit:WintersTale ;
    lit:wrote lit:Hamlet ;
    lit:wrote lit:Othello .
spr:Gulielmus spr:hasFather spr:JohannesShakspere .
spr:Susanna spr:hasFather spr:WilliamShakspere .
```

```
spr:Hamnet spr:hasFather spr:WilliamShakspere .
spr:Judeth spr:hasFather spr:WilliamShakspere .
spr:WilliamShakspere
    lit:wrote lit:AsYouLikeIt ;
    lit:wrote lit:HenryV ;
    lit:wrote lit:LovesLaboursLost ;
    lit:wrote lit:MeasureForMeasure ;
    lit:wrote lit:TwelfthNight ;
    lit:wrote lit:WintersTale ;
    lit:wrote lit:Hamlet ;
    lit:wrote lit:Othello .
spr:Susanna spr:hasFather lit:Shakespeare .
spr:Hamnet spr:hasFather lit:Shakespeare .
spr:Judeth spr:hasFather lit:Shakespeare .
```

Now the answer to the query "Did Hamnet's father write *Hamlet?*" is "yes," since there is a binding for the variable *?d* in the preceding SPARQL graph pattern. In fact, there are two possible bindings: *?d* = lit:Shakespeare and *?d* = spr:Shakspere.

Challenge: Merging Data from Different Databases

We have seen how to interpret information in a table as RDF triples. Each row in the table became a single individual, and each cell in the table became a triple. The subject of the triple is the individual corresponding to the row that the cell is in; the predicate is made up from the table name and the field name; and the object is the cell contents. Table 7-1 (from Table 3-10) shows 63 triples for the 7 fields and 9 rows. Let's look at just the triples having to do with the Manufacture_Location.

```
mfg:Product1 mfg:Product_Manufacture_Location Sacramento .
mfg:Product2 mfg:Product_Manufacture_Location Sacramento .
mfg:Product3 mfg:Product_Manufacture_Location Sacramento .
mfg:Product4 mfg:Product_Manufacture_Location Elizabeth .
mfg:Product5 mfg:Product_Manufacture_Location Elizabeth .
mfg:Product6 mfg:Product_Manufacture_Location Seoul .
mfg:Product7 mfg:Product_Manufacture_Location Hong Kong .
mfg:Product8 mfg:Product_Manufacture_Location Cleveland .
mfg:Product9 mfg:Product_Manufacture_Location Cleveland .
```

Suppose that another division in the company keeps its own table of the products with information that is useful for that division's business activities—namely, it describes the sort of facility that is required to produce the part. Table 7-2 shows some products and the facilities they require. Some of the products in Table 7-2 also appeared in Table 7-1, and some did not. It is not uncommon for different databases to overlap in such an inexact way.

Table 7-1 Sample Tabular Data for Triples

			Product			
ID	Model Number	Division	Product Line	Manufacture Location	SKU	Available
1	ZX-3	Manufacturing Support	Paper Machine	Sacramento	FB3524	23
2	ZX-3P	Manufacturing Support	Paper Machine	Sacramento	KD5243	4
3	ZX-3S	Manufacturing Support	Paper Machine	Sacramento	IL4028	34
4	B-1430	Control Engineering	Feedback Line	Elizabeth	KS4520	23
5	B-1430X	Control Engineering	Feedback Line	Elizabeth	CL5934	14
6	B-1431	Control Engineering	Active Sensor	Seoul	KK3945	0
7	DBB-12	Accessories	Monitor	Hong Kong	ND5520	100
8	SP-1234	Safety	Safety Valve	Cleveland	HI4554	4
9	SPX-1234	Safety	Safety Valve	Cleveland	OP5333	14

Table 7-2 Sample Data: Parts and the Facilities Required to Produce Them

	Product	
ID	Model Number	Facility
1	B-1430	Assembly Center
2	B-1431	Assembly Center
3	M13-P	Assembly Center
4	ZX-3S	Assembly Center
5	ZX-3	Factory
6	TC-43	Factory
7	B-1430X	Machine Shop
8	SP-1234	Machine Shop
9	1180-M	Machine Shop

Challenge 19 Using the products that appear in both tables, how can we write a federated query that will cross-reference cities with the facilities that are required for the production that takes place there?

SOLUTION

If these two tables had been in a single database, then there could have been a foreign-key reference from one table to the other, and we could have joined the two tables together. Since the tables come from two different databases, there is no such common reference.

When we turn both tables into triples, the individuals corresponding to each row are assigned global identifiers. Suppose that we use the namespace p: for this second database; when we turn Table 7-2 into triples, we get 27 triples, for the 9 rows and 3 fields. The triples corresponding to the required facilities are as follows:

```
p:Product1 p:Product_Facility "Assembly Center" .
p:Product2 p:Product_Facility "Assembly Center" .
p:Product3 p:Product_Facility "Assembly Center" .
p:Product4 p:Product_Facility "Assembly Center" .
p:Product5 p:Product_Facility "Factory" .
p:Product6 p:Product_Facility "Factory" .
p:Product7 p:Product_Facility "Machine Shop" .
p:Product8 p:Product_Facility "Machine Shop" .
p:Product9 p:Product_Facility "Machine Shop" .
```

Although we have global identifiers for individuals in these tables, those identifiers are not the same. For instance, p:Product1 is the same as mfg:Product4 (both correspond to model number B-1430). How can we cross-reference from one table to the other? The answer is to use a series of owl:sameAs triples, as follows:

```
p:Product1 owl:sameAs mfg:Product4 .
p:Product2 owl:sameAs mfg:Product6 .
p:Product4 owl:sameAs mfg:Product3 .
p:Product5 owl:sameAs mfg:Product1 .
p:Product7 owl:sameAs mfg:Product5 .
p:Product8 owl:sameAs mfg:Product8 .
```

Now if we match the following SPARQL graph pattern:

```
{?p p:Product_Facility ?facility .
 ?p mfg:Product_Manufacture_Location ?location .}
```

and display *?facility* and *?location,* we get the results in Table 7-3.

Table 7-3 Locations Cross-Referenced with Facilities, Computed via Products

?location	?facility
Elizabeth	Assembly Center
Seoul	Assembly Center
Sacramento	Assembly Center
Sacramento	Factory
Elizabeth	Machine Shop
Cleveland	Machine Shop

This solution has addressed the challenge for the particular data in the example, but the solution relied on the fact that we knew which product from one table matched with which product from another table. But `owl:sameAs` only solves part of the problem. In real data situations, in which the data in the tables change frequently, it is not practical to assert all the `owl:sameAs` triples by hand. In the next section, we will see how RDFS-Plus provides a solution to the rest of the challenge.

COMPUTING SAMENESS—FUNCTIONAL PROPERTIES

Functional Properties in OWL get their name from a concept in mathematics, but like most of the OWL constructs, they have a natural interpretation in everyday life. A function property is one for which there can be just one value. Examples of such properties are quite common: `hasMother` (since a person has just one biological mother), `hasBirthplace` (someone was born in just one place), and `birthdate` (just one) are a few simple examples.

In mathematics, a *function* is a mapping that gives one value for any particular input, so x^2 is a function, since for any value of x, there is exactly one value for x^2. Another way to say this is that if $x = y$, then $x^2 = y^2$. To solve the previous challenge problem, we have to have constructs in RDFS-Plus that have this same sort of behavior; that is, we want to describe something as being able to refer to only a single value.

The next two constructs, `FunctionalProperty` and `InverseFunctionalProperty`, we describe use this idea to determine when two resources refer to the same individual, thereby providing the OWL modeler with a means for describing how information from multiple sources are to be considered as a distributed web of information. These constructs provide an important semantic framework for using RDFS-Plus in the Semantic Web setting.

Functional Properties

RDFS-Plus borrows the name *functional* to describe a property that, like a mathematical function, can only take one value for any particular individual. The precise details of the meaning of `owl:FunctionalProperty` is given, as usual, as an inference pattern. If we have the following triples:

```
P rdf:type owl:FunctionalProperty .
X P A .
X P B .
```

then we can infer that

```
A owl:sameAs B .
```

This definition of `owl:FunctionalProperty` is analogous to the mathematical situation in which we know that x^2 has a single unambiguous value. More precisely, if we know that $x^2 = a$ and $x^2 = b$, then we may conclude that $a = b$. In RDFS-Plus, this looks as follows, in which the first three triples are asserted and the fourth is inferred:

```
math:hasSquare rdf:type owl:FunctionalProperty .
x math:hasSquare A .
x math:hasSquare B .
A owl:sameAs B .
```

Functional properties are important in RDFS-Plus because they allow sameness to be inferred. For instance, suppose that in the Stratford Parish Registry we have an entry that tells us

```
lit:Shakespeare fam:hasFather bio:JohannesShakspere .
```

and that from Shakespeare's grave we learn that

```
lit:Shakespeare fam:hasFather bio:JohnShakespeare .
```

We would like to conclude that John and Johannes are in fact the same person. If we know from a background model of family relationships that

```
fam:hasFather rdf:type owl:FunctionalProperty .
```

then we can conclude, from the definition of `owl:FunctionalProperty`, that

```
bio:JohannesShakspere owl:sameAs bio:JohnShakespeare .
```

as desired.

Although `owl:FunctionalProperty` provides us with a means of concluding that two resources are the same, this is not the usual pattern for determining that two entities are the same in most real data. Much more common is the closely related notion of `owl:InverseFunctionalProperty`, which we treat next.

Inverse Functional Properties

Some people consider `owl:InverseFunctionalProperty` to be the most important modeling construct in RDFS-Plus, especially in situations in which a model is being used to manage data from multiple sources. Whether or not this is true, it is certainly true that it has the most difficult name with respect to its utility of any construct.

The name `owl:InverseFunctionalProperty` was chosen to be consistent with the closely related `owl:FunctionalProperty`, and in fact one can think of an `owl:InverseFunctionalProperty` simply as the inverse of an `owl:Functional Property`. So if `math:hasSquare` is a functional property, then its inverse, `math: hasSquareRoot`, is an inverse functional property.

What exactly does this mean in terms of inferences that can be drawn? The rule looks very similar to the rule for `owl:FunctionalProperty`. If we know that

```
P rdf:type owl:InverseFunctionalProperty .
A P X .
B P X .
```

then we can infer that

```
A owl:sameAs B .
```

For example, if we define a property `buriedAt` to be sufficiently specific that we cannot have two people buried at the same location, then we can declare it to be an `owl:InverseFunctionalProperty`. If we were then to have two triples that assert

```
spr:Shakespere buriedAt :TrinityChancel .
lit:Shakespeare buriedAt :TrinityChancel .
```

then we could infer that

```
spr:Shakespere owl:sameAs lit:Shakespeare .
```

An `owl:InverseFunctionalProperty` plays the role of a key field in a relational database. A single value of the property cannot be shared by two entities, just as a key field may not be duplicated in more than one row. Unlike the case of a relational database, RDFS-Plus does not signal an error if two entities are found to share a value for an inverse functional property. Instead, RDFS-Plus infers that the two entities must be the same. Because of the nonunique naming assumption, we cannot tell that two entities are distinct just by looking at their URIs.

Examples of inverse functional properties are fairly commonplace; any identifying number (Social Security number, employee number, driver's license number, serial number, etc.) is an inverse functional property. In some cases, full names are inverse functional properties, though in most applications, name duplications (is it the same John Smith?) are common enough that full names are not inverse functional properties. In an application at the Boston Children's

Hospital, it was necessary to find an inverse functional property that would uniquely identify a baby (since newborns don't always have their Social Security numbers assigned yet). The added catch was that it had to be a property that the mother was certain, or at least extremely likely, to remember. Although babies are born at any time of day in a busy hospital, it is sufficiently unusual for two babies to be born at exactly the same minute that time of birth could be used as an inverse functional property. And every mother was able to remember when her baby was born.

Now that we have inverse functional properties, we are able to continue the solution to the challenge. Previously, we merged information from two databases by matching the global URIs of individuals from two databases with the following series of `owl:sameAs` triples:

```
p:Product1 owl:sameAs mfg:Product4 .
p:Product2 owl:sameAs mfg:Product6 .
p:Product4 owl:sameAs mfg:Product3 .
p:Product5 owl:sameAs mfg:Product1 .
p:Product7 owl:sameAs mfg:Product5 .
p:Product8 owl:sameAs mfg:Product8 .
```

Once we had these triples, we were able to cross-reference cities with facilities, using products as an intermediary. But we had to create these triples by hand.

Challenge 20   How can we infer the appropriate `owl:sameAs` triples from the data that have already been asserted?

SOLUTION

The approach we will take to this challenge is to find an inverse functional property that is present in both data sets that we can use to bridge between them. When we examine Tables 7-1 and 7-2, we see that they both have a field called `ModelNo` , which refers to the identifying model number of the product. As is typical for such identifying numbers, if two products have the same model number, they are the same product. So we want to declare `ModelNo` to be an inverse functional property, thus:

```
mfg:Product_ModelNo rdf:type owl:InverseFunctionalProperty .
```

This almost works, but there is still a catch: Each database has its own `ModelNo` property. The one in this triple came from the database in Chapter 3; in this chapter, there is another property, `p:Product_ModelNo` . So it seems that we still have more integration to do. Fortunately, we already have the tool we need to do this; we simply have to assert that these two properties are equivalent, thus:

```
p:Product_ModelNo owl:equivalentProperty mfg:Product_ModelNo .
```

It really doesn't matter in which order we do any of these things. Since `owl:equivalentProperty` is symmetric, we can write this triple with the subject and object reversed, and it will make no difference to the inferences.

Let's see how these inferences roll out. We begin with the asserted triples from both data sources and proceed with inferred triples:

```
p:Product1 p:Product_ModelNo "B-1430" .
p:Product2 p:Product_ModelNo "B-1431" .
p:Product3 p:Product_ModelNo "M13-P" .
p:Product4 p:Product_ModelNo "ZX-3S" .
p:Product5 p:Product_ModelNo "ZX-3" .
p:Product6 p:Product_ModelNo "TC-43" .
p:Product7 p:Product_ModelNo "B-1430X" .
p:Product8 p:Product_ModelNo "SP-1234" .
p:Product9 p:Product_ModelNo "1180-M" .
mfg:Product1 mfg:Product_ModelNo "ZX-3" .
mfg:Product2 mfg:Product_ModelNo "ZX-3P" .
mfg:Product3 mfg:Product_ModelNo "ZX-3S" .
mfg:Product4 mfg:Product_ModelNo "B-1430" .
mfg:Product5 mfg:Product_ModelNo "B-1430X" .
mfg:Product6 mfg:Product_ModelNo "B-1431" .
mfg:Product7 mfg:Product_ModelNo "DBB-12" .
mfg:Product8 mfg:Product_ModelNo "SP-1234" .
mfg:Product9 mfg:Product_ModelNo "SPX-1234" .
p:Product1 mfg:Product_ModelNo "B-1430" .
p:Product2 mfg:Product_ModelNo "B-1431" .
p:Product3 mfg:Product_ModelNo "M13-P" .
p:Product4 mfg:Product_ModelNo "ZX-3S" .
p:Product5 mfg:Product_ModelNo "ZX-3" .
p:Product6 mfg:Product_ModelNo "TC-43" .
p:Product7 mfg:Product_ModelNo "B-1430X" .
p:Product8 mfg:Product_ModelNo "SP-1234" .
p:Product9 mfg:Product_ModelNo "1180-M" .
p:Product1 owl:sameAs mfg:Product4 .
p:Product2 owl:sameAs mfg:Product6 .
p:Product4 owl:sameAs mfg:Product3 .
p:Product5 owl:sameAs mfg:Product1 .
p:Product7 owl:sameAs mfg:Product5 .
p:Product8 owl:sameAs mfg:Product8 .
```

The last six triples are exactly the `owl:sameAs` triples that we needed to complete our challenge.

Although this use of `owl:InverseFunctionalProperty` works fine for an example like this, most real data integration situations rely on more elaborate notions of identity that include multiple properties as well as uncertainty (what about that one freak day when two babies were born the same minute and the same second at the same hospital?). This problem can often be solved by using combinations of OWL properties that we will explore later in this book, although a fully general solution remains a topic of research.

Combining Functional and Inverse Functional Properties

It is possible and often very useful for a single property to be both an `owl:FunctionalProperty` and an `owl:InverseFunctionalProperty`. When a property is in both of these classes, then it is effectively a *one-to-one* property; that is, for any one individual, there is exactly one value for the property, and vice-versa. In the case of identification numbers, it is usually desirable that the property be one-to-one, as the following challenge illustrates.

Challenge 21   Suppose we want to assign identification numbers to students at a university. These numbers will be used to assign results of classes (grades), as well as billing information for the students. Clearly no two students should share an identification number, and neither should one student be allowed to have more than one identification number. How do we model this situation in RDFS-Plus?

SOLUTION

Define a property `hasIdentityNo` that associates a number with each student so that its domain and range are defined by

```
:hasIdentityNo rdfs:domain :Student .
:hasIdentityNo rdfs:range xsd:Integer .
```

Furthermore, we can enforce the uniqueness properties by asserting that

```
:hasIdentityNo rdf:type owl:FunctionalProperty .
:hasIdentityNo rdf:type owl:InverseFunctionalProperty .
```

Now any two students who share an identity number must be the same (since it is Inverse Functional); furthermore, each student can have at most one identity number (since it is Functional).

To summarize, there are several ways we can use these properties:

Functional only—`hasMother` is a functional property only. Someone has exactly one mother, but many people can share the same mother.

Inverse Functional Only—`hasDiary` is an inverse functional property only. A person may have many diaries, but it is the nature of a diary that it is not a collaborative effort; it is authored by one person only.

Both Functional and Inverse Functional—`taxID` is both inverse functional and functional, since we want there to be exactly one `taxID` for each person and exactly one person per `taxID`.

A FEW MORE CONSTRUCTS

RDFS-Plus provides a small extension to the vocabulary beyond RDFS, but these extensions greatly increase the scope of applicability of the language. In the preceding examples, we have seen how these new features interact with the features of RDFS to provide a richer modeling environment. The inclusion of `owl:inverseOf` combines with `rdfs:subClassOf` by allowing us to align properties that might not have been expressed in compatible ways in existing data schemas. The inclusion of `owl:TransitiveProperty` combines with `rdfs:subPropertyOf` in a number of novel combinations, as seen here, allowing us to model a variety of relationships among chains of individuals.

The most applicable extensions, from a Semantic Web perspective, are those that deal with sameness of different individuals. `sameAs`, `FunctionalProperty`, and `InverseFunctionalProperty` in particular provide the OWL modeler with a means for describing how information from multiple sources is to be merged in a distributed web of information.

OWL provides a few more distinctions that, although they do not provide any semantics to a model, provide some useful discipline and provide information that many editing tools can take advantage of when displaying models. For example, when displaying what value some property takes for some subject, should the GUI display be a link to another object or a widget for a particular data type? Tools that get this right seem intuitive and easy to use; tools that don't seem awkward. So OWL provides a way to describe properties that can help a tool sort this out. This is done in OWL by distinguishing between `owl:DatatypeProperty` and `owl:ObjectProperty`.

In RDF, a triple always has a resource as its subject and predicate, but it can have either another resource as object or it can have a data item of some XML data type. We have seen plentiful examples of both of these:

```
ship:QEII ship:maidenVoyage "May 2, 1969" .
mfg:Product1 mfg:Product_SKU "FB3524" .
AnneHathaway bio:married lit:Shakespeare .
GraduallyMix inSameRecipe BeatEggs .
spr:Susanna spr:hasFather spr:WilliamShakspere .
```

Most tools that deal with OWL at this time prefer to make the distinction. In this case, `ship:maidenVoyage` and `mfg:Product_SKU` are datatype properties, while `bio:married`, `inSameRecipe`, and `spr:hasFather` are object properties. In triples, we say:

```
ship:maidenVoyage rdf:type owl:DatatypeProperty .
mfg:Product_SKU rdf:type owl:DatatypeProperty .
bio:married rdf:type owl:ObjectProperty .
inSameRecipe rdf:type owl:ObjectProperty .
spr:hasFather rdf:type owl:ObjectProperty .
```

Another distinction that is made in OWL is the difference between `rdfs:Class` and `owl:Class` .

In Chapter 6, we introduced the notion of `rdfs:Class` as the means by which schema information could be represented in RDF. Since that time, we have introduced a wide array of "schema-like" constructs like inverse, subproperty, transitivity, and so on. OWL also provides a special case of `rdfs:Class` called `owl:Class`. Since OWL is based on RDFS, it was an easy matter to make `owl:Class` backward compatible with `rdfs:Class` by saying that every member of `owl:Class` is also a member of `rdfs:Class`. This statement needn't be made in prose, since we can say it in RDFS. In particular, the OWL specification stipulates that

```
owl:Class rdfs:subClassOf rdfs:Class .
```

Most tools today insist that classes used in OWL models be declared as members of `owl:Class` . In this chapter, we have left these class declarations out, since this level of detail was not needed for the modeling examples we provided. Implicit in the examples in this chapter, are statements such as

```
:Food rdf:type owl:Class .
:BakedGood rdf:type owl:Class .
:Confectionary rdf:type owl:Class .
:PackagedFood rdf:type owl:Class .
:PreparedFood rdf:type owl:Class .
:ProcessedFood rdf:type owl:Class .
mfg:Product rdf:type owl:Class .
p:Product rdf:type owl:Class .
```

Most OWL tools today will work more consistently if classes are defined as instances of `owl:Class`; most model editors will do this automatically when a class is created. However, there are subtle distinctions that we will discuss more in Chapter 13.

SUMMARY

The constructs in RDFS-Plus are a subset of the constructs in OWL. This subset provides considerable flexibility for modeling in the Semantic Web. In the next chapter, we will see some examples of how RDFS-Plus is used in some large-scale Semantic Web projects. A summary of the constructs in this set follow.

Fundamental Concepts

rdfs:subClassOf—Members of subclass are also member of superclass.

rdfs:subPropertyOf—Relations described by subproperty also hold for superproperty.

rdfs:domain—The subject of a triple is classified into the domain of the predicate.

rdfs:range—The object of a triple is classified into the range of the predicate

Annotation Properties

rdfs:label—No inferential semantics, printable name

rdfs:comment—No inferential semantics, information for readers of the model

OWL Features: Equality

equivalentClass—Members of each class are also members of the other.

equivalentProperty—Relations that hold for each property also hold for the other.

sameAs—All statements about one instance hold for the other.

OWL Features: Property Characteristics

inverseOf—Exchange subject and object

TransitiveProperty—Chains of relationships collapse into a single relationship.

SymmetricProperty—A property that is its own inverse

FunctionalProperty—Only one value allowed (as object)

InverseFunctionalProperty—Only one value allowed (as subject)

ObjectProperty—Property can have resource as object.

DatatypeProperty—Property can have data value as object.

Using RDFS-Plus in the Wild

8

We have seen a number of examples of the use of RDFS-Plus modeling for merging information from multiple sources in a dynamic and flexible way. In this chapter, we describe two extended uses of the RDFS-Plus constructs. Both of these applications of RDFS-Plus have attracted considerable user communities in their respective fields. Both of them also make essential use of the constructs in RDFS-Plus, though often in quite different ways. These are real modeling applications built by groups who originally had no technology commitment to RDFS or OWL (though both were conceived as RDF applications).

In both cases, the projects are about setting up an infrastructure for a particular web community. The use of RDFS-Plus appears in the models that describe data in these communities, rather than in the everyday use in these communities. In this book, we are describing how modeling works in RDFS and OWL, so we focus on the community infrastructure of these projects.

The first application is called SKOS, the Simple Knowledge Organization System, and proposes a Semantic Web approach to expressing concept organization systems such as thesauri, taxonomies, and controlled vocabularies in RDF.

The second application is called FOAF, for "Friend of a Friend." FOAF is a project dedicated to creating and using machine-readable homepages that describe people, the links between them, and the things they create and do. It is based on RDF, but it originally made no commitment to RDFS or OWL.

Both of these projects were originally based on RDF because of the inherently distributed and weblike nature of the project requirements. As the projects evolved, they found a need to be able to describe the relationships between various resources in a formal way; this led both of them to RDFS and then on to RDFS-Plus.

In this chapter, we describe each of these modeling systems and show the use they have made of the RDFS-Plus constructs we introduced in previous chapters.

SKOS

SKOS (Simple Knowledge Organization System) was developed by the Institute for Learning & Research Technology to provide a means for representing **159** knowledge organization systems (including controlled vocabularies, thesauri, taxonomies, and folksonomies) in a distributed and linkable way. Given the existence of several thesaurus standards, one could well wonder why this group found it necessary to create another one. The key differentiator between SKOS and thesaurus standards is its basis in the Semantic Web. Unlike the standards, SKOS was designed from the start to allow modelers to create modular knowledge organizations that can be reused and referenced across the web. SKOS was not designed to replace any thesaurus standard but in fact to augment it by bringing the distributed nature of the Semantic Web to thesauri and controlled vocabularies. Toward this end, it was also a design goal of SKOS that it be possible to map any thesaurus standards to SKOS in a fairly straightforward way.

SKOS is organized in layers: The SKOS Core is the most mature and is the part that maps directly to the thesaurus standards. SKOS Mapping is an extension to SKOS that defines a number of specific properties for mapping thesaurus concepts from one source to another. In this section we will concentrate on describing the mature SKOS Core in terms of its usage of RDFS-Plus and the inferences that it entails.

Figure 8-1 shows a sample from a SKOS thesaurus, in which a small fragment of the UK Archival Thesaurus has been rendered in SKOS. The diagram shows seven concepts, which are related to one another by various properties that are defined in the SKOS Core. Data properties are shown within the boxes corresponding to the concepts. As we shall see, each of these properties is defined in relation to other properties, so certain useful inferences can be made.

The same information from Figure 8-1 is shown as triples in N3 here:

```
@prefix rdf: <http://www.w3.org/1999/02/22-rdf-syntax-ns#>.
@prefix rdfs: <http://www.w3.org/2000/01/rdf-schema#>.
@prefix owl: <http://www.w3.org/2002/07/owl#>.
@prefix core: <http://www.w3.org/2004/02/skos/core#>.
@prefix UKAT: <http://www.workingontologist.com/Ch8/UKAT.
  owl#>.

    UKAT:EconomicCooperation a core:Concept;
        core:altLabel "Economic co-operation";
        core:broader UKAT:EconomicPolicy;
        core:narrower UKAT:IndustrialCooperation,
                      UKAT:EconomicIntegration,
                      UKAT:EuropeanIndustrialCooperation,
                      UKAT:EuropeanEconomicCooperation;
        core:prefLabel "Economic cooperation";
        core:related UKAT:Interdependence;
        core:scopeNote "Includes cooperative measures in banking,
            trade, industry etc., between and among countries.."

    UKAT:EconomicIntegration a core:Concept;
        core:prefLabel "Economic integration."
```

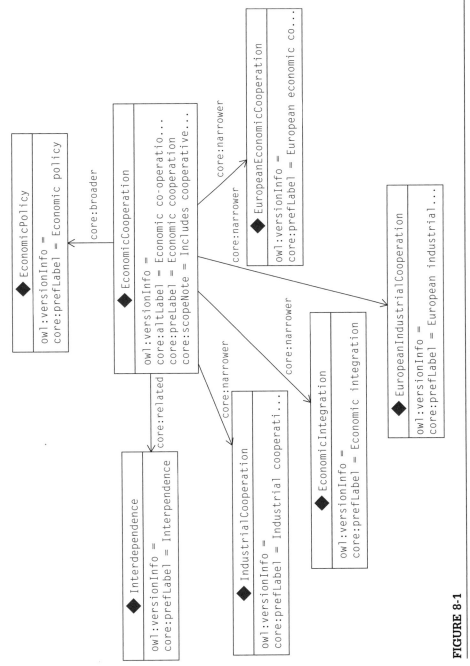

FIGURE 8-1

Sample thesaurus in SKOS. Example from W3C; data from UKAT.

```
UKAT:EconomicPolicy a core:Concept;
    core:prefLabel "Economic policy."

UKAT:EuropeanEconomicCooperation a core:Concept;
    core:prefLabel "European economic cooperation."

UKAT:EuropeanIndustrialCooperation a core:Concept;
    core:prefLabel "European industrial cooperation."

UKAT:IndustrialCooperation a core:Concept;
    core:prefLabel "Industrial cooperation."

UKAT:Interdependence a core:Concept;
    core:prefLabel "Interdependence."
```

First, let's look at the notion of labels in SKOS. As we have seen before, there is already a label resource defined in RDFS: rdfs:label. Although rdfs:label has no formal semantics defined (that is, there are no inferences that concern rdfs:label), it does have the informal meaning that it is something that can be used as the printable or human readable name of a resource. SKOS provides a more detailed notion of a concept's label, in accordance with usual thesaurus practice. In particular, it defines three different kinds of labels: a preferred label, an alternative label, and a hidden label. These are defined in SKOS with the following triples:

```
skos:prefLabel
    a rdf:Property ;
    rdfs:label "preferred label" ;
    rdfs:subPropertyOf rdfs:label .

skos:altLabel
    a rdf:Property ;
    rdfs:label "alternative label" ;
    rdfs:subPropertyOf rdfs:label .

skos:hiddenLabel
    a rdf:Property ;
    rdfs:label "hidden label" ;
    rdfs:subPropertyOf rdfs:label .
```

The SKOS definition includes a number of other triples defining these properties, but we will concentrate on these for this description.

Notice that each property has an rdfs:label, which provides a human readable version of the name of each resource. Furthermore, each of these properties is declared to be of type rdf:Property. Finally, each of these is declared to be a subproperty of rdfs:label. What does this mean in terms of RDFS-Plus?

As we have already seen, rdfs:subPropertyOf propagates triples from the subproperty to the superproperty. In the first case, from any triple using skos:prefLabel as a predicate, we can infer the same triple with rdfs:label as a predicate instead. The same is true for `skos:altLabel` and `skos:hiddenLabel`; in particular, in our UKAT example, we can infer the following triples:

```
UKAT:EconomicCooperation
     rdfs:label "Economic co-operation" .
UKAT:EconomicCooperation
     rdfs:label "Economic cooperation" .
UKAT:EconomicIntegration
     rdfs:label "Economic integration" .
UKAT:EconomicPolicy
     rdfs:label "Economic policy" .
UKAT:EuropeanEconomicCooperation
     rdfs:label "European economic cooperation" .
UKAT:EuropeanIndustrialCooperation
     rdfs:label "European industrial cooperation" .
UKAT:IndustrialCooperation
     rdfs:label "Industrial cooperation" .
UKAT:Interdependence
     rdfs:label "Interdependence" .
```

That is, every SKOS label shows up as an `rdfs:label`. In some cases (e.g., UKAT: EconomicCooperation), more than one value for `rdfs:label` can be inferred. This is perfectly legal in RDFS-Plus (after all, `rdfs:label` is not an `owl:Functional-Property`), even though its informal interpretation as the printable name of a resource is not clear.

SKOS uses this same pattern for many of the properties it defines; for each of them, the sort of inference it supports is similar. So for the seven documentation properties in SKOS, six of them are subproperties of the seventh, thus:

```
core:definition rdfs:subPropertyOf core:note .
core:scopeNote rdfs:subPropertyOf core:note .
core:example rdfs:subPropertyOf core:note .
core:historyNote rdfs:subPropertyOf core:note .
core:editorialNote rdfs:subPropertyOf core:note .
core:changeNote rdfs:subPropertyOf core:note .
```

Similarly, SKOS defines three properties having to do with symbols:

```
core:altSymbol rdfs:subPropertyOf core:symbol .
core:prefSymbol rdfs:subPropertyof core:symbol .
```

Just as was the case for the SKOS label properties, any triple using one of the symbol properties or documentation properties will entail a triple using `core:symbol` or `core:note`, respectively.

Semantic Relations in SKOS

SKOS defines three so-called Semantic Properties; these are the properties that relate concepts to one another, using the familiar terms *broader*, *narrower,* and *related* from thesaurus standards. SKOS defines some simple constraints among these properties:

```
skos:broader
    a owl:TransitiveProperty ;
    owl:inverseOf skos:narrower ;
    rdfs:comment "Broader concepts are typically rendered as
        parents in a concept hierarchy (tree)." ;
    rdfs:label "has broader" .

skos:narrower
    a owl:TransitiveProperty ;
    owl:inverseOf skos:broader ;
    rdfs:comment "Narrower concepts are typically rendered as
        children in a concept hierarchy (tree)." ;
    rdfs:label "has narrower" .

skos:related
    a owl:SymmetricProperty;
    rdfs:label "related to" ;
    rdfs:subPropertyOf rdfs:seeAlso .
```

These properties take advantage of a handful of the constructs of RDFS-Plus. We'll see how these work together in the UKAT example.

First, since `skos:narrower` is an inverse of `skos:broader`, we can make the following inferences about UKAT concepts in Figure 8-1.

```
UKAT:EconomicPolicy core:narrower UKAT:EconomicCooperation .
UKAT:IndustrialCooperation core:broader UKAT:Economic
    Cooperation .
UKAT:EconomicIntegration core:broader UKAT:Economic
    Cooperation .
UKAT:EuropeanIndustrialCooperation core:broader
    UKAT:EconomicCooperation .
UKAT:EuropeanEconomicCooperation core:broader
    UKAT:EconomicCooperation .
```

Furthermore, since each of `core:narrower` is a `owl:TransitiveProperty`, we can infer that every concept in this sample is narrower than the item at the "top" of the tree, `UKAT:EconomicPolicy`:

```
UKAT:EconomicPolicy core:narrower
    UKAT:IndustrialCooperation ,
    UKAT:EconomicIntegration ,
    UKAT:EuropeanIndustrialCooperation ,
    UKAT:EuropeanEconomicCooperation .
```

Similar triples can be inferred (swapping subject for object, as usual) for the inverse property, `core:broader`.

In the case of `core:related`, it is not defined as `owl:TransitiveProperty`, so we cannot make inferences about chains of related items. This is probably as it should be; since it is easy to imagine a chain of pairwise-related terms in which the first term is not related to the last term. However, we see that `core:related` is an `owl:SymmetricProperty`; this means that we can make the following inference. If we assert that

```
UKAT:EconomicCooperation core:related UKAT:Interdependence .
```

then we can infer that

```
UKAT:Interdependence core:related UKAT:EconomicCooperation .
```

Meaning of Semantic Relations

It is no accident that there is a considerable similarity between the definitions in SKOS of `skos:narrower` and `skos:broader` and the definitions of `rdfs:subClassOf` and `superClassOf`. Both of these pairs of properties are intended for modeling hierarchies. In both cases, it is desirable that the hierarchies could be traversed either "upward" or "downward." In both cases, the intention of the hierarchical structure is that the relationship be transitive—that is, narrower than narrower is narrower, and `subClassOf subClassOf` is `subClassOf`.

There is one definition for `subClassOf` that has no corresponding condition in SKOS; that is the semantic rule that says that if we have triples of the form

```
B rdfs:subClassOf C .
x rdf:type B .
```

then we can infer that

```
x rdf:type C .
```

Because of this rule, there is no confusion about the interpretation of `rdfs:subClassOf`. This rule makes it clear that `C` has more members (or at least, just as many) as `B`; that is, `C` is the more encompassing of the two classes.

Since we have no such rule in SKOS, there is the possibility for confusion; when we say

```
UKAT:EconomicCooperation skos:broader UKAT:EconomicPolicy .
```

should we read this (in English) as "Economic Cooperation has broader category Economic Policy," or should we read it as "Economic Cooperation is broader than Economic Policy"? There is nothing in the formal SKOS model to tell us which is which. The relationship is expressed informally in the annotations on `skos:broader` and `skos:narrower`; that is, the labels "has broader" and "has narrower" respectively indicate that the former interpretation is the intended one—economic cooperation has broader-term economic policy. It is important to keep this in mind when reading the SKOS examples that follow in this book, where we will see triples like

```
:Milk skos:broader :Dairy .
```

For many people, this interpretation of *broader* is backward from what they expect.

If there were an inference-based definition of the semantics of `skos:broader` (as there is, for example, for `rdfs:subClassOf`), then the intended direction of this statement would be explicit. There would be no need to rely on the interpretation of examples (like this one for *Milk* and *Dairy*) to communicate which way the terms are intended to be used.

Special Purpose Inference

SKOS includes a special provision for implementing Collections of concepts. Collections of terms are common in thesaurus and indexing standards. Consider the following example from the W3C SKOS Core Guide.

A term index describes agricultural products and includes several kinds of milk: cow milk, goat milk, sheep milk, and buffalo milk. There is a meaningful collection of these concepts called "milk by source animal." This practice of grouping concepts is common practice in indexing and cataloguing. It is important to notice that according to the common practice of professional cataloguers, the grouping "milk by source animal" is itself not a concept in its own right; it is simply a grouping for concepts.

SKOS uses a class called `skos:Collection` and a property called `skos:member` to express such situations, as shown in Figure 8-2. The triples for Figure 8-2 are given in N3 as

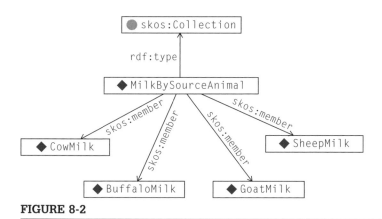

FIGURE 8-2

"Milk by source animal" is a collection of four concepts related to milk.

```
agro:MilkBySourceAnimal a skos:Collection;
  rdfs:label "Milk by source animal ;
  core:member agro:CowMilk,
    agro:BuffaloMilk,
    agro:GoatMilk,
    agro:SheepMilk .

agro:BuffaloMilk a skos:Concept;
  skos:prefLabel "Buffalo milk .

agro:CowMilk a skos:Concept;
  skos:prefLabel "Cow milk" .

agro:GoatMilk a skos:Concept;
  skos:prefLabel "Goat milk" .

agro:SheepMilk a skos:Concept;
  skos:prefLabel "Sheep milk" .
```

The interest in this example comes when we examine what inferences we can draw from such a construct. So far, we have used only `skos:narrower` to express that one term has another as a narrower term. But what would it mean to this same notion of `skos:narrower` to describe the relationship between a term and a collection? For example:

```
agro:Milk skos:narrower agro:MilkBySourceAnimal .
```

SKOS does not model the answer to this question in RDFS-Plus but instead specifies a special purpose rule as part of the SKOS specification. If we have triples of the form

```
X skos:narrower C .
C skos:member Y .
```

then we can infer the triple

```
X skos:narrower Y .
```

When we apply this rule to `agro:Milk`, we can infer that it has as a narrower term each of the kinds of milk in the collection `agro:MilkBySourceAnimal`, thus:

```
agro:Milk skos:narrower agro:BuffaloMilk .
agro:Milk skos:narrower agro:CowMilk .
agro:Milk skos:narrower agro:SheepMilk .
agro:Milk skos:narrower agro:GoatMilk .
```

SKOS represents this constraint as a rule rather than modeling it in RDFS-Plus. This is not surprising, since the constructs of RDFS-Plus are not well-suited to this problem. We shall see in Chapter 10 how further constructs in OWL can be brought to bear on situations like this one.

Published Subject Indicators

SKOS includes support for the notion of a Published Subject Indicator, or PSI. The idea of a PSI is that a community can agree on a particular publication that can act as a unique identifier for a certain concept. For traditional, generic concepts like "Milk" or "Economic Policy," it is unlikely that there will be a useful unique publication for the concept. But for the results of standards bodies, such publications are commonplace. Examples include things like CDC disease listings, technical standards, acts of governments, and so forth. For instance, if two diseases have the same CDC listing, then they are the same disease.

SKOS provides a property—`skos:subjectIndicator`—to link a `skos:Concept` to a published document. Since a PSI is intended as a unique identifier of a concept, it should not be possible for two different concepts to share the same `subjectIndicator`. This stipulation is quite simple to represent in RDFS-Plus, as we saw when we discussed `owl:InverseFunctionalProperty`. The SKOS specification includes the triple

```
skos:subjectIndicator rdf:type owl:InverseFunctionalProperty .
```

This indicates that any two concepts that share the same PSI must therefore refer to the same concept, unifying them in the knowledge organization system. For instance, suppose that the document at *http://www.usdoj.gov/foia/ privstat.htm* is the PSI for the U.S. Privacy Act of 1974. Then, if we have concepts from two different knowledge organization systems, such as the following:

```
policy:Privacy a skos:Concept;
    skos:subjectIndicator   http://www.usdoj.gov/foia/privstat.
    htm .

gov:InfoAccess a skos:Concept ;
    skos:subjectIndicator   http://www.usdoj.gov/foia/privstat.
    htm .
```

We can infer that these two concepts are indeed the same:

```
gov:InfoAccess owl:sameAs policy:Privacy .
```

Any indexing application that utilizes the thesaurus can then respond accordingly; for example, any items indexed under `gov:InfoAccess` will also be accessible under `policy:Privacy`. This illustrates how the property `skos:subjectIndicator` plays an important role in the utilization of SKOS on the Semantic Web, since it allows terms from different vocabularies to be mapped to one another.

SKOS in Action

SKOS is an example of a model on the Semantic Web; it models particular standards for how to represent thesauri. In this section, we examined what the SKOS model says about terms and concepts in a thesaurus and how they can relate to one another. But how is SKOS itself being used? What do we gain by representing a thesaurus in SKOS?

The information explosion that we are familiar with on the Web is taking place elsewhere as well. Libraries around the world are interested in indexing their materials in a way that will allow patrons to find information from all around the world. The United Nations has been quite successful with a thesaurus called AGROVOC, which provides multilingual indexing for materials concerning any aspect of agriculture. Not surprisingly, member nations have their own indices for agriculture. The National Agriculture Library (NAL) of the United States also has an extensive thesaurus (in English) for indexing agricultural materials.

When the United Nations pursued a project to map these thesauri together, they needed a representation that would allow for terms from multiple sources to be distinguished in a global way. For example, the AGROVOC word for "Ground Water" and the NAL word for "Ground Water" must be managed separately, but it also must be possible to represent the relationship between them. The use of URIs in RDF (and thus in SKOS) is ideal for this job. SKOS itself provides a set of terms as described here for familiar thesaurus relationships *broader* and *narrower*. This makes it a straightforward task to export each thesaurus in SKOS. In fact, both AGROVOC and the NAL had independently sponsored SKOS exports of their thesauri. With these SKOS representations in place, it was a straightforward matter to represent mappings between the two vocabularies in RDF.

FOAF

FOAF (Friend of a Friend) is a format for supporting distributed descriptions of people and their relationships. The name Friend of a Friend is intended to evoke the fundamental relationship that holds in social networks; you have direct knowledge of your own friends, but only through your network can you access the friends of your friends.

FOAF works in the spirit of the AAA principle: Anyone can say Anything about Any topic. In the case of FOAF, the topics that anyone is usually saying things about are people. Other things that are commonly related to what we might want to say about people, such as Organizations (that people belong to), Projects (that people work on), Documents (that people have created or that describe them), and Images (that depict people), are also included in the core FOAF description. Information about a single person is likely to be distributed across the Web and represented in different forms. On their own webpage, a person is likely to list basic information about interests, current projects, and some images. Further information will be available only on other pages; a photoset taken at a party or conference could include a picture that depicts a person who has not listed that photoset in her own webpage. A conference organizer could include information about a paper that lists its authors, even if the authors themselves might not have listed the paper on their own web site. A laboratory or office might have a page that lists all of its members. FOAF leverages the distributed nature of RDF to provide a distributed representation of this information. Social networking sites have begun to make information available in FOAF for web-scale distribution.

Given that there are a number of social networking websites available and that each one of them has a way to represent its members, information about them, and ways in which they are connected to one another, one could well ask why there is a need for yet another way to describe people and their social networks. The idea of FOAF is not to replace any of these systems but to provide a framework whereby this information can be distributed. Furthermore, using RDF, FOAF provides a framework that is extensible. Because Anyone can say Anything about Any topic, FOAF allows anyone to make novel statements about people, projects, and so on, and to relate these statements to other statements already made.

FOAF leverages the AAA principle as well as the distributed and extensible nature of RDF in an essential way. At any point in time, FOAF is a work in progress. There are vocabulary terms in FOAF whose semantics are defined only by natural language descriptions in the FOAF "standard." Other terms have definitions defined in RDFS-Plus that relate them in a formal way to the rest of the description. FOAF is designed to grow in an organic fashion, starting with a few intuitive terms and focusing their semantics as they are used. There is no need to commit early on to a set vocabulary, since we can use RDFS-Plus to connect new vocabulary and old vocabulary, once we determine the desired relationship between them.

FOAF provides a small number of classes and properties as its starting point; these use some of the basic constructs of RDFS-Plus to maintain consistency and to implement FOAF policies for information merging. FOAF is a fairly simple system for describing people, the things they create, and the projects they participate in. It is primarily organized around three classes: `foaf:Person`, `foaf:Group`, and `foaf:Document`.

People and Agents

Although FOAF is primarily about people, some of the things we want to say about people are true of other things as well: groups, companies, and so forth. So a `foaf:Person` is defined as part of a compact hierarchy under the general grouping of `foaf:Agent`:

```
foaf:Person rdfs:subClassOf foaf:Agent .
foaf:Group rdfs:subClassOf foaf:Agent .
foaf:Organization rdfs:subClassOf foaf:Agent .
```

Many things we might say about a `foaf:Person` can hold for any `foaf:Agent`. In fact, FOAF is quite liberal in this regard; most of the properties we describe here for people hold for agents in general. Details of exactly which properties are used for which classes are available in the FOAF Vocabulary Specification at *http://xmlns.com/foaf/0.1/.*

Names in FOAF

Probably the most essential thing we know about a person is that person's name. FOAF provides a number of vocabulary terms to describe the name of a person. Even something as simple as a person's name can be quite complex. FOAF begins with a simple notion of name, which it sensibly calls `foaf:name`.

```
foaf:name rdfs:domain owl:Thing .
foaf:name rdfs:subPropertyOf rdfs:label .
```

That is, anything in the world can have a name (including a `foaf:Person`), and that name is also used as the printable label for that thing. For a `foaf:Person`, the name is typically the full name of the person, like "William Shakespeare" or "Anne Hathaway."

Although the full name of a person is quite useful, parts of a person's name are needed in some circumstances. `foaf:firstName`, `foaf:givenname`, `foaf:family_name`, and `foaf:surname` are four properties relating to names of people that are defined in FOAF. Each of them has an intuitive meaning, but there are no formal semantics; the meaning is given only in prose descriptions and by evolving conventions of use. As FOAF evolves, it will need to encompass different cultures and their use of names. Does the given name always come first? Is a family name always the surname? How do culture-specific names (for example, the "Christian name" that is still used in some cultures) relate to other names?

One of the advantages to basing FOAF on RDF is that it is not necessary to resolve all of these issues to begin the project of marking up data using the FOAF vocabulary. The strategy taken by FOAF is to begin by annotating a person's name while providing other naming vocabulary such as *surname, firstname, givenname,* and so on. Usage patterns will dictate which of these will turn out to be useful. If it turns out that, say, two properties are used in exactly the same way, then this observation can be cast by describing the relationship in OWL. For example:

```
foaf:surname owl:equivalentProperty foaf:family_name .
```

Nicknames and Online Names

Since FOAF is primarily used on the Web, it is expected that many of the people FOAF will be used to describe will be active in various internet communities. For instance, it is likely that a FOAF Person will have a screen name on some online chat service. FOAF identifies `foaf:aimChatID`, `foaf:icqChatID`, `foaf:msnChatID`, and `foaf:yahooChatID` currently. A recent addition includes `foaf:jabberID` as well. In the spirit of extensibility of FOAF, new ID properties can be added on an as-needed basis. Although some part of the semantics of these properties is given by their natural language descriptions (which connect `foaf:yahooChatID` to the chat service Yahoo!), FOAF also makes a formal connection between these properties. In particular, all of them are subproperties of a single property, `foaf:nick`:

```
foaf:aimChatID rdfs:subPropertyOf foaf:nick .
foaf:icqChatID rdfs:subPropertyOf foaf:nick .
foaf:msnChatID rdfs:subPropertyOf foaf:nick .
foaf:yahooChatID rdfs:subPropertyOf foaf:nick .
foaf:jabberID rdfs:subPropertyOf foaf:nick .
```

Following the rules of `rdfs:subPropertyOf` from Chapter 6, this means that any `foaf:Person` who is active in chat spaces is likely to have multiple values for the property `foaf:nick`—that is, to have multiple nicknames. They can, of course, have further nicknames as well. For instance, when William Shakespeare became active in Internet chat rooms, from a FOAF point of view, all those screen names are also nicknames:

```
lit:Shakespeare foaf:aimChatID "Willie1564" .
lit:Shakespeare foaf:msnChatID "TempestMan" .
lit:Shakespeare foaf:nick "Willie1564" .
lit:Shakespeare foaf:nick "TempestMan" .
```

Of course, we can still assert a nickname for the poet and playwright, even if he doesn't use it as a screen name anywhere:

```
lit:Shakespeare foaf:nick "The Bard of Avon" .
```

Online Persona

The Internet provides a number of ways for a person to express himself, and FOAF is under constant revision to provide properties to describe these things. A person is likely to have an electronic mailbox, and FOAF provides a property `foaf:mbox` for this purpose. Many people maintain a number of webpages describing parts of their lives. Some have personal homepages, some have homepages at their workplace or school, and some may even have both. Even their workplaces can have homepages. FOAF uses the same strategy for these properties as it does for names: It provides a wide array of properties, defined informally (by natural language descriptions).

foaf:homepage—relates a person to their primary homepage. This property applies to anything in FOAF, not just to people.

foaf:workplaceHomepage—the homepage of the workplace of a person. Anything can have a homepage (even an employer), but only a `foaf:Person` can have a `workplaceHomepage`.

foaf:workInfoHomepage—the homepage of a person at their workplace. Such a page is usually hosted by a person's employer, but it is about the person's own work there.

foaf:schoolHomepage—the homepage of the school that a `foaf:Person` attended.

As the Internet provides new means of expression, FOAF keeps up:

foaf:weblog—the address of the web blog of a person.

All of these properties specify instances of the class `foaf:Document`—that is, a webpage is a `foaf:Document`, a weblog is a `foaf:Document`, and so on.

Groups of People

One of the interesting things about people is the groups they belong to. FOAF provides a class called `foaf:Group` to define these groups. A group is connected to its members via a property called, appropriately enough, `foaf:member`. A `foaf:Group` is defined quite loosely; any grouping of people can be described this way. For instance, we could define a group called English Monarchy as follows:

```
:English_Monarchy
   a foaf:Group ;
   foaf:name "English Monarchy" ;
   foaf:homepage "http://www.monarchy.com/" ;
   foaf:member :William_I, :Henry_I, :Henry_II,
      :Elizabeth_I, :Elizabeth_II .
```

A group in FOAF is an individual of type `foaf:Group`. As such, there are a number of properties that can describe it, like `foaf:name` (as we see here). In fact, a `foaf:Group` has a lot in common with a `foaf:Person`; it can have a chat ID, a nickname, an e-mail box, a homepage, or even a blog.

It is also useful to consider the members of a group as instances of a class—that is, to relate the instance of `foaf:Group` to an `rdfs:Class`. For this purpose, FOAF provides a link from a group to a class, called `foaf:membershipClass`. Suppose that the membership class for `English_Monarchy` is called *Monarch*; this connection is expressed in FOAF with the triple

```
:English_Monarchy foaf:membershipClass :Monarch .
```

The members of the group `English_Monarchy` all have type *Monarch*:

```
:William_I a :Monarch .
:Henry_I a :Monarch .
:Henry_II a :Monarch .
:Elizabeth_I a :Monarch .
:Elizabeth_II a :Monarch .
```

Ideally, all of these triples should be maintained automatically; that is, any individual of type *Monarch* should appear as a member of the group `English_Monarchy` and every member of the group `English_Monarchy` should have *Monarch* as a type. This stipulation is state explicitly as part of the FOAF description. We will see in Chapter 9 how to use the capabilities of OWL to build a model from which we can infer these triples. The distinction between the instance `English_Monarchy` and the class *Monarch* is a subtle one: The class *Monarch* is a type in RDFS, and as such, it refers to schematic things about monarchs—property domains, subclasses, and so on. `English_Monarchy`, on the other hand, refers to the institution of the monarchy itself, which refers to things like this history of the monarchy, webpages and books about the monarchy, and so on.

In our examples so far, we have been kept the world of classes separate from the world of instances. The only relationship between an instance and a class has been the `rdf:type` property. The intuition behind `foaf:membershipClass` is that it indicates a class, whose instances are exactly the same as the members of the group. The expression of this kind of relationship, in which we sometimes wish to view something as an instance (e.g., `English_Monarchy`, an instance of the class `foaf:Group`) and sometimes as a class (e.g., the class *Monarch*, representing all the instances that are `foaf:member` of that group), is an example of a practice called *meta-modeling*. We will see more about meta-modeling when we learn about the rest of the OWL language, and we will see how we can use meta-modeling constructs in OWL to formalize the relationship between a `foaf:Group` and its `foaf:membershipClass`.

Things People Make and Do

Interesting people create things. They write books, publish webpages, create works of art, found companies, and start organizations. FOAF provides two properties to relate people to their creations: `foaf:made` and `foaf:maker`. They are inverses of one another, and they relate a `foaf:Agent` to an `owl:Thing` as follows:

```
foaf:made rdfs:domain foaf:Agent .
foaf:made rdfs:range owl:Thing .
foaf:maker rdfs:domain owl:Thing .
foaf:maker rdfs:range foaf:Agent .
foaf:made owl:inverseOf foaf:maker .
```

That is, anything in the describable universe is fair game for being made by some agent. Even another agent could have a `foaf:maker`!

If a person is an author, then he is likely to have publications to his credit. The property `foaf:publications` relates a `foaf:Person` to any `foaf:Document` published. Interestingly, FOAF does not specify that a person has `foaf:made` **any of their** `foaf:publications`. In the spirit of the AAA principle, if we were to decide to make such a statement, we could do so simply by saying

```
foaf:publications rdfs:subPropertyOf foaf:made .
```

Identity in FOAF

The main goal of FOAF is to apply the AAA principle to describing networks of people; anyone can contribute descriptions about anyone. But this leads to a problem: It is easy enough for me to describe myself; I can publish a document that says whatever I wish to make known. If someone else wants to contribute information about me (say, for example, that the publisher of this book wants to add the information that I am an author), how will that person refer to me? Or if I have several profiles on different sites that I would like to merge together, how can I link them to describe the one thing that is "me"?

The RDF answer to this question is quite simple but not really adequate for the uses of FOAF. RDF uses URIs to denote the things it describes; that means that I should have a URI that denotes me, and anyone who wants to make a comment about me can make it using that URI. This is a simple, elegant, and standard solution to this problem.

The problem arises in the adoption of FOAF. When someone makes their first FOAF page, how do they determine their own URI? Do they just make it up? It just isn't very common on the Web for people to have their own personal URIs to describe themselves. In order to lower the barriers to adopting FOAF, there must be a way people can refer to one another that uses some part of the Internet infrastructure that is already ubiquitous and familiar. FOAF needs to utilize some preexisting way to identify individuals. Is there any identifying marker that everyone on the Internet already has and is already familiar with?

The clearest answer to this puzzle is e-mail. Just about anyone who is described on the Web in any way at all has an e-mail address. Furthermore, it is quite rare that two people share the same e-mail address. It is so rare that for the purposes of FOAF, e-mail can serve as a unique identifier for people on the Web. Notice that it isn't a problem if someone has two or more e-mail addresses or if one e-mail address is valid only for a limited period of time. All FOAF requires of the e-mail address is that another person doesn't share it (either simultaneously or later on).

We can express this constraint in plain language by saying simply that two people who share the same e-mail address are in fact not two distinct people at all but instead are the same person. As we have already seen, RDFS-PLUS has a way to formalize this relationship. When a property uniquely identifies an individual, we say that the property is an `owl:InverseFunctionalProperty`. So in FOAF, we can express the central role that `foaf:mbox` plays in identifying individuals with the single triple

```
foaf:mbox rdf:type owl:InverseFunctionalProperty .
```

Once we identify `foaf:mbox` as an `owl:InverseFunctionalProperty`, we realize that a similar statement can be made about a number of the properties we use to describe people; it is unusual for two people to share a `yahooChatID` or an `aimChatID`. In fact, all of the following properties in FOAF are `owl:InverseFunctionalProperties`:

```
foaf:aimChatID rdf:type owl:InverseFunctionalProperty .
foaf:homepage rdf:type owl:InverseFunctionalProperty .
foaf:icqChatID rdf:type owl:InverseFunctionalProperty .
foaf:jabberID rdf:type owl:InverseFunctionalProperty .
foaf:mbox rdf:type owl:InverseFunctionalProperty .
foaf:msnChatID rdf:type owl:InverseFunctionalProperty .
foaf:weblog rdf:type owl:InverseFunctionalProperty .
foaf:yahooChatID rdf:type owl:InverseFunctionalProperty .
```

Using the `foaf:mbox` (and similar properties) as identifiers of individuals solves the technical problem of identifying individuals by some preexisting identification, but it raises another problem: Publishing someone's e-mail address is considered a violation of privacy, since e-mail addresses (and chat IDs) can be used to pester or even attack someone by sending unwanted, offensive, or just bulky mail. So if we want to apply the AAA principle to William Shakespeare, and we know that he uses the e-mail address `Shakespeare@gmail.com`, we can refer to him as "the person with e-mail '`Shakespeare@gmail.com`'" (using a blank node, as we did for Shakespeare's inspiration):

```
[ foaf:mbox "Shakespeare@gmail.com"]
```

When we do this, we publish his e-mail address in plain text for information vandals to steal and use. This isn't a very polite thing to do to someone we know and respect. For this reason, FOAF also offers an obfuscated version of `foaf:mbox`, called `foaf:mbox_sha1sum`. It indicates the result of applying a hashing function called SHA-1 to the e-mail address. The SHA-1 function is publicly available but very difficult to reverse. To get the obfuscated string—`f964f2dfd4784fe9d68ada960099e0b592e16a95`—we apply the algorithm to Shakespeare's e-mail address. Now we can refer to him using this value:

```
[ foaf:mbox_sha1sum "f964f2dfd4784fe9d68ada960099e0b592e16a95" ]
```

without compromising his privacy. Unfortunately, FOAF does not provide a standard way to obfuscate the other identifying properties such as `foaf:aimChatID`, `foaf:yahooChatID`, and so forth.

It's Not What You Know, It's Who You Know

The key to FOAF as a social networking system is the ability to link one person to another. FOAF provides a single, high-level property for this relationship, called `foaf:knows`. The idea behind `foaf:knows` is simple: One person knows another one, who knows more people, and so on, forming a network of people who know people. There isn't a lot of inferencing going on with `foaf:knows`; the only triples defined for it are

```
foaf:knows rdfs:domain foaf:Person .
foaf:knows rdfs:range foaf:Person .
```

that is, `foaf:knows` just links one `foaf:Person` to another.

The lack of inferencing over `foaf:knows` is by design; the `foaf:knows` design is intentionally vague, to indicate some relationship between people. Such a relationship could be concluded informally from other information—for instance, coauthors can usually be assumed to know one another. And while it is usual to think that if one person knows another that the relationship is mutual, the FOAF designers intentionally left out the assertion of `foaf:knows` as an `owl:SymmetricProperty`, since there might even be some disagreement about whether one person knows another. Despite its vague definition, `foaf:knows` provides the infrastructure for using FOAF for social networking, as it links one person to the next and then to the next and so on.

SUMMARY

SKOS and FOAF demonstrate how a fairly simple set of modeling constructs can be used to create extensible, distributed information networks. They both take advantage of the distributed nature of RDF to allow extension to a network of information to be distributed across the web. Both of them rely on the inferencing structure of RDFS-Plus to add completeness to their information structure. Both of them use `owl:InverseFunctionalProperty` to determine identity of key elements.

Although they are similar in these ways, FOAF and SKOS are organized very differently in terms of how they support extension by their expected user communities. FOAF takes something of an evolutionary approach to information extension. Many concepts have a broad number of terms (like the several variants of "name" that we examined). FOAF can be extended as new features are needed. For instance, `foaf:weblog` was not as important before blogging became fashionable, but recently, it has almost surpassed the more classical `foaf:homepage` in importance.

SKOS, in contrast, takes a much more orderly approach to extension. SKOS comes in three parts: the SKOS Core, which has been described here; SKOS Mapping, which includes vocabulary for mapping vocabularies from different sources; and the SKOS Extensions, for particular vertical applications of SKOS. The SKOS Core is intended to be a sort of interlingua for thesauri, and it has been designed by a small committee in an attempt to consolidate the fundamentals of other thesaurus systems into a single Semantic Web model. The other two documents import the Core and build further semantics on top of it.

The difference in these two approaches becomes more apparent when we think about how they will be extended. FOAF takes very seriously the AAA slogan, to the point that the actual preferred parts of the representation will be determined to a large extent by its use. SKOS, on the other hand, has a fairly stable core, which has been designed by an informed committee who have performed a detailed commonality/variability analysis of extant vocabulary systems. The architecture of SKOS has been determined and published, and it serves as a roadmap for its development.

The technical structure of RDF supports both of these modes. The free extension style of FOAF and the orderly layering of SKOS are accomplished using the same graph overlay mechanism of RDF. The difference is in how the overlay is organized and governed. Neither approach is inherently superior to the other; each of them accomplishes certain goals that are of importance to each of these projects.

The SKOS and FOAF efforts are similar in many ways to standards efforts. Each of them is maintained by a committee who makes and publishes policy decisions about them. But they differ from standards in an important way. Neither of them is intended as a complete work that will provide prescriptive advice to someone who is designing a vocabulary control system or a social networking system. Their role is to provide an exchange mechanism on the Web for sharing this sort of information. This is the power of a model on the Semantic Web; it does not prescribe how to represent things, but it provides a means of transfer from one representation to another. Each of these efforts provides an example of how a model can play this sort of mediating role.

Fundamental Concepts

The following fundamental concepts were introduced in this chapter.

foaf—Namespace for a system of representation of social network information; short for "friend of a friend."

SKOS—Namespace for a system of representation for information management. SKOS stands for "Simple Knowledge Organization System."

Meta-modeling—Generally speaking, the craft of building a model that describes another model. A specific example is the practice of representing a class in a model as an individual member of another class. FOAF does this explicitly with the `foaf:membershipClass` property that links an individual of type `foaf:Group` to the Class of all members of the group.

UKAT—The UK Archival Thesaurus. See *http://www.ukat.org.uk/*.

Basic OWL

9

In previous chapters, we saw how RDFS-Plus as a modeling system provides considerable support for distributed information and federation of information. Simple constructs in RDFS-Plus can be combined in various ways to match properties, classes, and individuals. We saw its utility in application to social networking (FOAF) and knowledge organization (SKOS); although RDFS-Plus has provided considerable and valuable infrastructure for these projects, we also identified capabilities required by these systems that RDFS-Plus cannot provide. In this chapter, we go further into the modeling capabilities of OWL, beyond RDFS-Plus, which provides a systematic treatment of information description. OWL provides constructs for describing information structure that will satisfy many of the outstanding requirements of FOAF and SKOS, as well as a number of more general information integration issues.

We continue our presentation of OWL with a treatment of `owl:Restriction`. This single construct opens up the representational power of OWL by allowing us to describe classes in terms of other things we have already modeled. As we shall see, this opens up whole new vistas in modeling capabilities.

RESTRICTIONS

Suppose we have defined in RDFS a class we call `BaseballTeam`, with a particular subclass called `MajorLeagueTeam`, and another class we call `BaseballPlayer`. The roster for any particular season would be represented as a property `playsFor` that relates a `BaseballPlayer` to a `BaseballTeam`. Certain players are special in that they play for a `MajorLeagueTeam`. We'd like to define that class and call it `MajorLeaguePlayers`. If we are interested in the fiscal side of baseball, we could also be interested in the class of Agents who represent Major League Players, and then the bank accounts controlled by the Agents who represent Major League Players and so on.

One of the great powers of the Semantic Web is that information that has been specified by one person in one context can be reused either by that **179** person or by others in different contexts. There is no expectation that the same source who defined the roster of players will be the one that defines the role of the agents or of the bank accounts. If we want to use information from multiple sources together, we need a way to express concepts from one context in terms of concepts from the other. In OWL, this is achieved by having a facility with which we can describe new classes in terms of classes that have already been defined. This facility can also be used to model more complex constructs than the ones we've discussed so far.

We have already seen how to define simple classes and relationships between them in RDFS and OWL, but none of the constructs we have seen so far can create descriptions of the sort we want in our Major League Baseball Player example. This is done in OWL using a language construct called a `Restriction`.

Consider the case of a `MajorLeaguePlayer`. We informally defined a `MajorLeaguePlayer` as someone who plays on a `MajorLeagueTeam`. The intuition behind the name `Restriction` is that membership in the class `MajorLeaguePlayer` is restricted to those things that play for a `MajorLeagueTeam`. Since a `Restriction` is a special case of a `Class`, we will sometimes refer to a `Restriction` as a *Restriction Class* just to make that point clear.

More generally, a `Restriction` in OWL is a `Class` defined by describing the individuals it contains. This simple idea forms the basis for extension of models in OWL: If you can describe a set of individuals in terms of known classes, then you can use that description to define a new class. Since this new class is now also an existing class, it can be used to describe individuals for inclusion in a new class, and so on. We will return to the baseball player example later in this chapter, but first we need to learn more about the use of restriction classes.

Example: Questions and Answers

To start with, we will use a running example of managing questions and answers, as if we were modeling a quiz, examination, or questionnaire. This is a fairly simple area that nevertheless illustrates a wide variety of uses of restriction classes in OWL.

Informally, a questionnaire consists of a number of questions, each of which has a number of possible answers. A question includes string data for the text of the question, whereas an answer includes string data for the text of the answer. In contrast to a quiz or examination, there are typically no "right" answers in a questionnaire. In questionnaires, quizzes, and examinations, the selection of certain answers may preclude the posing of other questions.

This basic structure for questionnaires can be represented by classes and properties in OWL. Any particular questionnaire is then represented by a set of individual questions, answers, and concepts, and particular relationships between them.

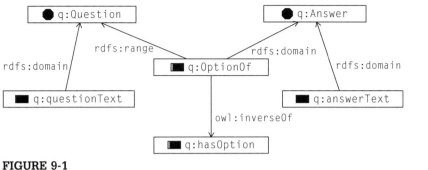

FIGURE 9-1

Question, answer, and the properties that describe them.

The basic schema for the questionnaire is as follows and is shown diagrammatically in Figure 9-1. Throughout the example, we will use the namespace *q:* to refer to elements that relate to questionnaires in general, and the namespace *d:* to refer to the elements of the particular example questionnaire.

```
q:Answer a owl:Class.
q:Question a owl:Class.
q:optionOf a owl:ObjectProperty;
   rdfs:domain q:Answer;
   rdfs:range q:Question;
   owl:inverseOf q:hasOption.
q:hasOption a owl:ObjectProperty .
q:answerText a owl:DatatypeProperty;
   rdfs:domain q:Answer;
   rdfs:range xsd:string.
q:questionText a owl:FunctionalProperty,
               owl:DatatypeProperty;
   rdfs:domain q:Question;
   rdfs:range xsd:string.
```

A particular questionnaire will have questions and answers. For now, we will start with a simple questionnaire that might be part of the screening for the helpdesk of a cable television and Internet provider:

What system are you having trouble with?

Possible answers (3): Cable TV, High-Speed Internet, Both

What television symptom(s) are you seeing?

Possible answers (4): No Picture, No Sound, Tiling, Bad Reception

This is shown as follows and graphically in Figure 9-2.

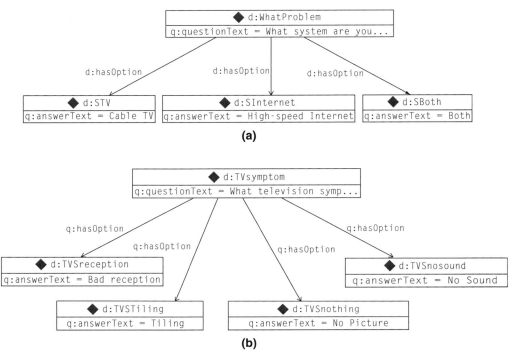

FIGURE 9-2

Some particular questions and their answers.

```
d:WhatProblem a q:Question;
    q:hasOption d:STV, d:SInternet, d:SBoth;
    q:questionText "What system are you having trouble with?" .

d:STV a q:Answer;
    q:answerText "Cable TV".

d:SInternet a q:Answer;
    q:answerText "High-speed Internet".

d:SBoth a q:Answer;
    q:answerText "Both".

d:TVsymptom a q:Question;
    q:questionText "What television symptoms are you having?";
    q:hasOption d:TVSnothing, d:TVSnosound, d:TVStiling,
    d:TVSreception .

d:TVSnothing a q:Answer;
    q:answerText "No Picture".

d:TVSnosound a q:Answer;
    q:answerText "No Sound".
```

```
d:TVStiling a q:Answer;
  q:answerText "Tiling".

d:TVSreception a q:Answer;
  q:answerText "Bad reception".
```

Consider an application for managing a questionnaire in a web portal. This application performs a query against this combined data to determine what question(s) to ask next. Then for each question, it presents the text of the question itself and the text of each answer, with a select widget (e.g., radio button) next to it. We haven't yet defined enough information for such an application to work, and we have made no provisions to determine which questions to ask before any others or how to record answers to the questions. We start with the latter.

We first define a new property `hasSelectedOption`, a subproperty of `hasOption`:

```
q:hasSelectedOption a owl:ObjectProperty;
  rdfs:subPropertyOf q:hasOption .
```

When the user who is taking a questionnaire answers a question, a new triple will be entered to indicate that a particular option for that question has been selected. That is, if the user selects "Cable TV" from the options of the first question `d:WhatProblem`, then the application will add the triple

```
d:WhatProblem q:hasSelectedOption d:STV .
```

to the triple store. Notice that there is no need to remove any triples from the triple store; the original `d:hasOption` relationship between `d:WhatProblem` and `d:STV` still holds. As we develop the example, the model will provide ever-increasing guidance for how the selection of questions will be done.

Adding "Restrictions"

The language construct in OWL for creating new class descriptions based on descriptions of the prospective members of a class is called the Restriction (`owl:Restriction`). An `owl:Restriction` is a special kind of class (i.e., `owl:Restriction` is a `rdfs:subClassOf owl:Class`). A Restriction is a class that is defined by a description of its members in terms of existing properties and classes.

In OWL, as in RDF, the AAA slogan holds: Anyone can say Anything about Any topic. Hence, the class of all things in owl (`owl:Thing`) is unrestricted. A `Restriction` is defined by providing some description that limits (or restricts) the kinds of things that can be said about a member of the class. So if we have a property `orbitsAround`, it is perfectly legitimate to say that anything `orbitsAround` anything else. If we restrict the value of `orbitsAround` by saying that its object must be `TheSun`, then we have defined the class of all things that orbit around the sun (*i.e.* our solar system).

Kinds of Restrictions

OWL provides a number of restrictions, three of which are `owl:allValuesFrom`, `owl:someValuesFrom`, and `owl:hasValue`. Each describes how the new class is constrained by the possible asserted values of properties.

Additionally, a restriction class in OWL is defined by the keyword `owl:onProperty`. This specifies what property is to be used in the definition of the restriction class. For example, the restriction defining the objects that orbit around the sun will use `owl:onProperty orbitsAround`, whereas the restriction defining major league players will use `owl:onProperty playsFor`.

A restriction is a special kind of a class, so it has individual members just like any class. Membership in a restriction class must satisfy the conditions specified by the kind of restriction (`owl:allValuesFrom`, `owl:someValuesFrom`, or `owl:hasValue`), as well as the `onProperty` specification.

owl:someValuesFrom

`owl:someValuesFrom` is used to produce a restriction of the form "All individuals for which at least one value of the property P comes from class C." In other words, one could define the class `AllStarPlayer` as "All individuals for which at least one value of the property `playsFor` comes from the class `AllStarTeam`." This is what the restriction looks like:

```
[ a owl:Restriction;
    owl:onProperty :playsFor;
    owl:someValuesFrom :AllStarTeam]
```

Notice the use of the [...] notation. As a reminder from Chapter 3, this refers to an anonymous node (a `bnode`) described by the properties listed here; that is, this refers to a single bnode, which is the subject of three triples, one per line (separated by semicolons).

The restriction class defined in this way refers to exactly the class of individuals that satisfy these conditions on `playsFor` and `AllStarTeam`. In particular, if an individual actually has some value from the class `AllStarTeam` for the property `playsFor`, then it is a member of this restriction class. Note that this restriction class, unlike those we've learned about in earlier chapters, has no specific name associated with it. It is defined by the properties of the restriction (i.e., restrictions on the members of the class) and thus it is sometimes referred to in the literature as an "unnamed class."

EXAMPLE **Answered Questions**

In the questionnaire example, we addressed the issue of recording answers to questions by defining a property `hasOption` that relates a question to answer options and a subproperty `hasSelectedOption` to indicate those answers that have been selected by the individual who is taking the questionnaire. Now we want to address the problem of selecting which question to ask.

There are a number of considerations that go into such a selection, but one of them is that (under most circumstances) we do not want to ask a question for which we already have an answer. This suggests a class of questions that have already been answered. We will define the set of `AnsweredQuestions` in terms of the properties we have already defined. Informally, an answered question is any question that has a selected option.

An answered question is one that has some value from the class *Answer* for the property `hasSelectedOption`. This can be defined as follows:

```
q:AnsweredQuestion owl:equivalentClass
[ a owl:Restriction;
            owl:onProperty q:hasSelectedOption;
            owl:someValuesFrom q:Answer ] .
```

Since

```
d:WhatProblem q:hasSelectedOption d:STV.
```

and

```
d:STV a Answer.
```

are asserted triples, the individual `d:WhatProblem` satisfies the conditions defined by the restriction class. That is, there is at least one value (someValue) for the property `hasSelectedOption` that is in the class *Answer*. Individuals that satisfy the conditions specified by a restriction class are inferred to be members of it. This inference can be represented as follows:

```
d:WhatProblem a [ a owl:Restriction;
                    owl:onProperty q:hasSelectedOption;
                    owl:someValuesFrom q:Answer ]
```

and thus, according to the semantics of `equivalentClass`,

```
d:WhatProblem a AnsweredQuestion.
```

These definitions and inferences are shown in Figure 9-3.

owl:allValuesFrom

`owl:allValuesFrom` is used to produce a restriction class of the form "the individuals for which all values of the property P come from class C." This restriction looks like the following:

```
[ a owl:Restriction;
    owl:onProperty P;
    owl:allValuesFrom C]
```

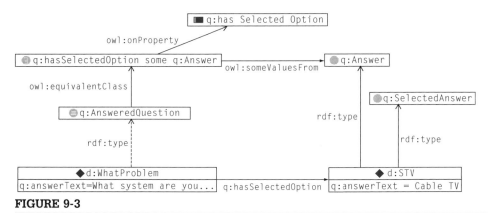

FIGURE 9-3

Definition of q:AnsweredQuestion and the resulting inferences for d:WhatProblem. Since d:WhatProblem has something (d:STV) of type q:Answer on property q:hasSelectedOption, it is inferred (*dotted line*) to be a member of AnsweredQuestion.

The restriction class defined in this way refers to exactly the class of individuals that satisfy these conditions on P and C. If an individual x is a member of this allValuesFrom restriction, a number of conclusions can follow, one for each triple describing x with property P. In particular, every value of property P for individual x is inferred to be in class C. So, if individual MyFavoriteAllStarTeam (a member of the class BaseballTeam) is a member of the restriction class defined by owl:onProperty hasPlayer and owl:allValuesFrom StarPlayer, then every player on MyFavoriteAllStarTeam is a StarPlayer. So, if MyFavorite AllStarTeam hasPlayer Kaneda and MyFavoriteAllStarTeam hasPlayer Gonzales, then both *Kaneda* and *Gonzales* must be of type StarPlayer.

There is a subtle difference between someValuesFrom and allValuesFrom. Since someValuesFrom is defined as a restriction class such that there is at least one member of a class with a particular property, then it implies that there must be such a member. On the other hand, allValuesFrom technically means "if there are any members, then they all must have this property." This latter does not imply that there are any members. This will be more important in later chapters.

EXAMPLE   Question Dependencies

In our questionnaire example, we might want to ask certain questions only after particular answers have been given. To accomplish this, we begin by defining the class of all selected answers, based on the property hasSelectedOption we have already defined. We can borrow a technique from Chapter 4 to do this. First, we define a class for the selected answers:

```
q:SelectedAnswer a owl:Class ;
   rdfs:subClassOf q:Answer .
```

We want to ensure that any option that has been selected will appear in this class. This can be done easily by asserting that

```
q:hasSelectedOption rdfs:range q:SelectedAnswer .
```

This ensures that any value V that appears as the object of a triple of the form

```
? q:hasSelectedOption V .
```

is a member of the class SelectedAnswer. In particular, since we have asserted that

```
d:WhatProblem q:hasSelectedOption d:STV .
```

we can infer that

```
d:STV a q:SelectedAnswer .
```

Now that we have defined the class of selected answers, we describe the questions that can be asked only after those answers have been given. We introduce a new class called EnabledQuestion; only questions that also have type EnabledQuestion are actually available to be asked:

```
q:EnabledQuestion a owl:Class.
```

When an answer is selected, we want to infer that certain dependent questions become members of EnabledQuestion. This can be done with a restriction, owl:allValuesFrom.

To begin, each answer potentially makes certain questions available for asking. We define a property called enablesCandidate for this relationship. In particular, we say that an answer enables a question if selecting that answer causes the system to consider that question as a candidate for the next question to ask:

```
q:enablesCandidate a owl:ObjectProperty;
            rdfs:domain q:Answer ;
               rdfs:range q:Question .
```

In our example, we only want to ask a question about television problems if the answer to the first question indicates that there is a television problem:

```
d:STV q:enablesCandidate d:TVsymptom.
d:SBoth q:enablesCandidate d:TVsymptom.
```

That is, if the answer to the first question, "What system are you having trouble with?," is either "Cable TV" or "Both," then we want to be able to ask the question "What television symptoms are you having?"

The following `owl:allValuesFrom` restriction does just that: It defines the class of things all of whose values for `d:enablesCandidate` come from the class `d:EnabledQuestion`:

```
[ a owl:Restriction;
    owl:onProperty q:enablesCandidate;
    owl:allValuesFrom q:EnabledQuestion]
```

Which answers should enforce this property? We only want this for the answers that have been selected. How do we determine which answers have been selected? So far, we only have the property `hasSelectedOption` to indicate them. That is, for any member of `SelectedAnswer`, we want it to also be a member of this restriction class. This is exactly what the relation `rdfs:subClassOf` does for us:

```
q:SelectedAnswer rdfs:subClassOf
   [ a owl:Restriction;
       owl:onProperty q:enablesCandidate;
       owl:allValuesFrom q:EnabledQuestion].
```

That is, a selected answer is a subclass of the unnamed restriction class.

Let's watch how this works, step by step. When the user selects the answer "Cable TV" for the first question, the type of `d:STV` is asserted to be `Selected-Answer`, like the preceding.

```
d:STV a q:SelectedAnswer.
```

However, because of the `rdfs:subClassOf` relation, `d:STV` is a member of the restriction class, that is, it has the restriction as its type:

```
d:STV a
   [ a owl:Restriction;
       owl:onProperty q:enablesCandidate;
       owl:allValuesFrom q:EnabledQuestion].
```

Any individual who is a member of this restriction necessarily satisfies the `allValuesFrom condition`; that is, any individual that it is related to by `d:enablesCandidate` must be a member of `d:EnabledQuestion`. Since

```
d:STV q:enablesCandidate d:TVsymptom.
```

we can infer that

```
d:TVsymptom a q:EnabledQuestion.
```

as desired. Finally, since we have also asserted the same information for the answer `d:SBoth`,

```
d:SBoth q:enablesCandidate d:TVsymptom.
```

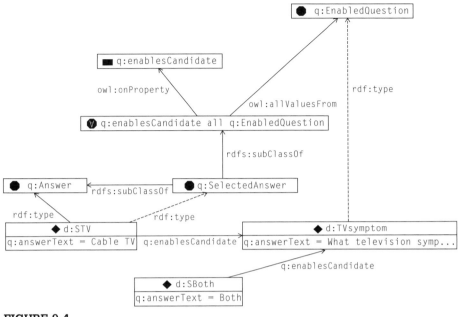

FIGURE 9-4

`d:STV enablesCandidate TVSymptom`, but it is also a member of a restriction on the property `enablesCandidate`, stipulating that all values must come from the class `q:EnabledQuestion`. We can therefore infer that `d:TVSymptom` has type `q:EnabledQuestion`.

We can see this inference and the triples that led to it in Figure 9-4. Restrictions are shown in the figures using a shorthand called the *Manchester Syntax* (named after its development at the University of Manchester). The shorthand summarizes a restriction using the keywords `all`, `some`, and `has` to indicate the restriction types `owl:allValuesFrom`, `owl:someValuesFrom`, and `owl:hasValue`, respectively. The restriction property (indicate in triples by `owl:onProperty`) is printed before the keyword, and the target class (or individual, in the case of `owl:hasValue`) is printed after the keyword. We see an example of an `owl:allValuesFrom` restriction in Figure 9-4. It is important to note that this is only a shorthand; all the information needed for inferences is expressed in RDF triples.

Since `SBoth` also enables the candidate `TVSymptom`, the same conclusion will be drawn if the user answers "Both" to the first question. If we were to extend the example with another question about Internet symptoms `d:InternetSymptom`, then we could express all the dependencies in this short questionnaire as follows:

```
d:STV q:enablesCandidate d:TVsymptom.
d:SBoth q:enablesCandidate d:TVsymptom.
```

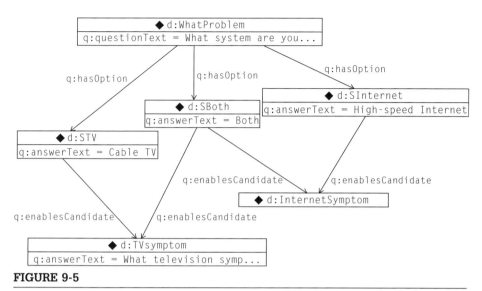

FIGURE 9-5

Questions and the answers that enable them.

```
d:SBoth q:enablesCandidate d:InternetSymptom.
d:SInternet q:enablesCandidate d:InternetSymptom.
```

The dependency tree is shown graphically in Figure 9-5.

EXAMPLE **Prerequisites**

In the previous example, we supposed that when we answered one question, it made all of its dependent questions eligible for asking. Another way questions are related to one another in a questionnaire is as prerequisites. If a question has a number of prerequisites, all of them must be answered appropriately for the question to be eligible.

Consider the following triples that define a section of a questionnaire:

```
d:NeighborsToo a q:Question;
    q:hasOption d:NTY, d:NTN, d:NTDK;
    q:questionText "Are other customers in your building also
    experiencing problems?" .

d:NTY a q:Answer;
    q:answerText "Yes, my neighbors are experiencing the same
    problem.".

d:NTN a q:Answer;
    q:answerText " No, my neighbors are not experiencing the
    same problem.".
```

```
d:NTDK a q:Answer;
    q:answerText "I don't know.".
```

This question makes sense only if the current customer lives in a building with other customers and is experiencing a technical problem. That is, this question depends on the answers to two more questions, shown following. The answer to the first question (d:othersinbuilding) should be d:OYes, and the answer to the second question (d:whatissue) should be d:PTech:

```
d:othersinbuilding
    a q:Question ;
    q:hasOption d:ONo , d:OYes ;
    q:questionText
            "Do you live in a multi-unit dwelling with other
    customers?" .

d:OYes a q:Answer;
    q:answerText "Yes." .

d:ONo a q:Answer;
    q:answerText " No.".

d:whatIssue
    a q:Question ;
    q:hasOption d:PBilling , d:PNew, d:PCancel, d:PTech ;
    q:questionText
            "What can customer service help you with today?".

d:PBilling a q:Answer;
    q:answerText "Billing question." .

d:PNew a q:Answer;
    q:answerText "New account".

d:PCancel a q:Answer;
    q:answerText "Cancel account".

d:PTech a q:Answer;
    q:answerText "Technical difficulty".
```

A graphic version of these questions can be seen in Figure 9-6.

Challenge 22 How can we model the relationship between d:NeighborsToo, d:whatIssue, and d:othersinbuilding so that we will only ask d:NeighborsToo when we have appropriate answers to both d:whatIssue and d:othersinbuilding?

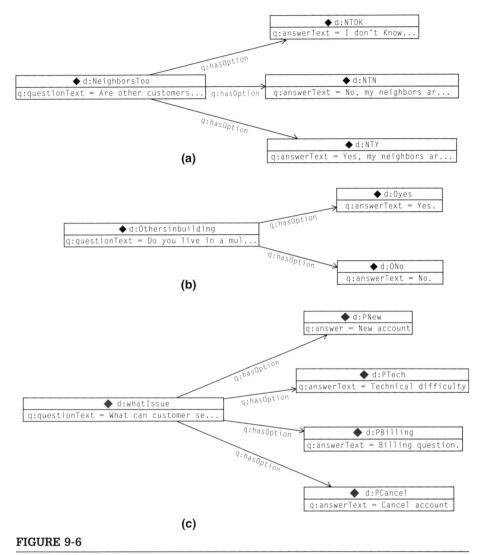

FIGURE 9-6

Questions about neighbors have two prerequisite questions.

We introduce a new property `q:hasPrerequisite` that will relate a question to its prerequisites:

```
q:hasPrerequisite
   rdfs:domain q:Question ;
   rdfs:range q:Answer .
```

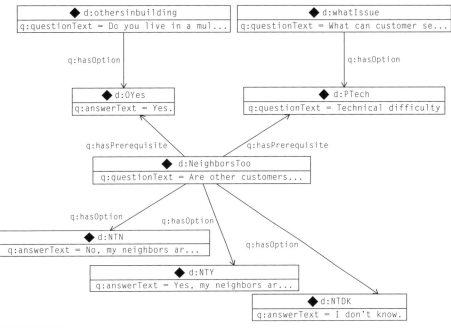

FIGURE 9-7

Some questions and their prerequisites.

We can indicate the relationship between the questions using this property:

```
d:NeighborsToo q:hasPrerequisite d:PTech, d:OYes .
```

This prerequisite structure is shown in graphical form in Figure 9-7.

Now we want to say that we will infer something is a `d:EnabledQuestion` if all of its prerequisite answers are selected. We begin by asserting that

```
[ a owl:Restriction ;
   owl:onProperty q:hasPrerequisite;
   owl:allValuesFrom q:SelectedAnswer ]
      rdfs:subClassOf q:EnabledQuestion .
```

Notice that we can use the restriction class just as we could any other class in OWL, so in this case we have said that the restriction is a subclass of another class. Any question that satisfies the restriction will be inferred to be a member of `d:EnabledQuestion` by this subclass relation. But how can we infer that something satisfies this restriction?

For an individual x to satisfy this restriction, we must know that every time there is a triple of the form

```
x hasPrerequisite y .
```

y must be a member of the class d:SelectedAnswer. But by the Open World assumption, we don't know if there might be another triple of this form for which y is not a member of d:SelectedAnswer. Given the Open World assumption, how can we ever know that all prerequisites have been met?

The rest of this challenge will have to wait until we discuss the various methods by which we can (partially) close the world in OWL. The basic idea is that if we can say how many prerequisites a question has, then we can know when all of them have been selected. If we know that a question has only one prerequisite, and we find one that is satisfied, then it must be the one. If we know that a question has no prerequisites at all, then we can determine that it is an Enabled-Question without having to check for any SelectedAnswers at all.

owl:hasValue

The third kind of restriction in OWL is called owl:hasValue. As in the other two restrictions, it acts on a particular property as specified by owl:onProperty. It is used to produce a restriction whose description is of the form "All individuals that have the value A for the property P" and looks as follows:

```
[ a owl:Restriction;
    owl:onProperty P;
    owl:hasValue A]
```

Formally, the hasValue restriction is just a special case of the someValuesFrom restriction, in which the class C happens to be a singleton set {A}.

Although it is "just" a special case, owl:hasValue has been identified in the OWL standard in its own right because it is a very common and useful modeling form. It effectively turns specific instance descriptions into class descriptions. For example, "The set of all planets orbiting the sun" and "The set of all baseball teams in Japan" are defined using hasValue restrictions.

EXAMPLE **Priority Questions**

Suppose that in our questionnaire, we assign priority levels to our questions. First we define a class of priority levels and particular individuals that define the priorities in the questionnaire:

```
q:PriorityLevel a owl:Class .
q:High a q:PriorityLevel .
q:Medium a q:PriorityLevel .
q:Low a q:PriorityLevel .
```

Then we define a property that we will use to specify the priority level of a question:

```
q:hasPriority
        rdfs:range q:PriorityLevel .
```

We have defined the range of `q:hasPriority` but not its domain. After all, we might want to set priorities for any number of different sorts of things, not just questions.

We can use `owl:hasValue` to define the class of high-priority items:

```
q:HighPriorityItem owl:equivalentClass
[ a owl:Restriction;
         owl:onProperty q:hasPriority;
         owl:hasValue q:High ] .
```

These triples are shown graphically in Figure 9-8. Note that where before we defined subclasses and superclasses of a restriction class, here we use `owl:equivalentClass` to specify that these classes are the same. So we have created a named class (`q:HighPriorityItem`) that is the same as the unnamed restriction class, and we can use this named class if we want to make other assertions or to further restrict the class.

We can describe `Medium` and `Low` priority questions in the same manner:

```
q:MediumPriorityItem owl:equivalentClass
[ a owl:Restriction;
         owl:onProperty q:hasPriority;
         owl:hasValue q:Medium ] .
q:LowPriorityItem owl:equivalentClass
[ a owl:Restriction;
         owl:onProperty q:hasPriority;
         owl:hasValue q:Low ] .
```

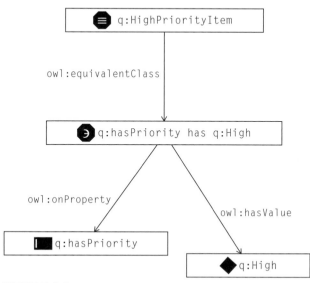

FIGURE 9-8

Definition of a `HighPriorityItem` as anything that has value High for the `hasPriority` property.

If we assert the priority level of a question, such as the following:

```
d:WhatProblem q:hasPriority q:High .
d:InternetSymptom q:hasPriority q:Low .
```

then we can infer the membership of these questions in their respective classes:

```
d:WhatProblem a q:HighPriorityItem .
d:InternetSymptom a q:LowPriorityItem .
```

We can also use `owl:hasValue` to work "the other way around." Suppose we assert that d:TVsymptom is in the class `HighPriorityItem`:

```
d:TVsymptom a q:HighPriorityItem .
```

Then by the semantics of `owl:equivalentClass`, we can infer that d:TVsymptom is a member of the restriction class and must be bound by its stipulations. Thus, we can infer that

```
d:TVsymptom q:hasPriority q:High .
```

Notice that there is no stipulation in this definition to say that a `HighPriorityItem` must be a question; after all, we might set priorities for things other than questions. The only way we know that d:TVsymptom is a q:Question is that we already asserted that fact. In the next chapter, we will see how to use set operations to make definitions that combine restrictions with other classes.

CHALLENGE PROBLEMS

As we saw in the previous examples, the class constructors in OWL can be combined in a wide variety of powerful ways. In this section, we present a series of challenges that can be addressed using these OWL constructs. Often the application of the construct is quite simple; however, we have chosen these challenge problems because of their relevance to modeling problems that we have seen in real modeling projects.

Challenge: Local Restriction of Ranges

We have already seen how `rdfs:domain` and `rdfs:range` can be used to classify data according to how it is used. But in more elaborate modeling situations, a finer granularity of domain and range inferences is needed. Consider the following example of describing a vegetarian diet:

```
:Person a owl:Class .
:Food a owl:Class .
```

```
:eats rdfs:domain :Person .
:eats rdfs:range :Food .
```

From these triples and the following instance data

```
:Maverick :eats :Steak .
```

we can conclude two things:

:Maverick a :Person .
:Steak a :Food .

The former is implied by the domain information, and the latter by the range information.

Suppose we want to define a variety of diets in more detail. What would this mean? First, let's suppose that we have a particular kind of person, called a Vegetarian, and the kind of food that a Vegetarian eats, which we will call simply VegetarianFood, as subclasses of Person and Food, respectively:

```
:Vegetarian a owl:Class ;
   rdfs:subClassOf :Person .
:VegetarianFood a owl:Class ;
   rdfs:subClassOf :Food .
```

Suppose further that we say

```
:Jen a :Vegetarian ;
   :eats :Marzipan .
```

We would like to be able to infer that

```
:Marzipan a :VegetarianFood .
```

but not make the corresponding inference for Maverick's steak until someone asserts that he, too, is a vegetarian.

Challenge 23   It is tempting to represent this with more domain and range statements—thus:

```
:eats rdfs:domain :Vegetarian .
:eats rdfs:range :VegetarianFood .
```

But given the meaning of rdfs:domain and rdfs:range, we can draw inferences from these triples that we do not intend. In particular, we can infer

:Maverick a :Vegetarian .
:Steak a :VegetarianFood .

which would come as a surprise both to Maverick and the vegetarians of the world.

How can the relationship between vegetarians and vegetarian food be correctly modeled with the use of the owl:Restriction?

SOLUTION

We can define the set of things that only eat `VegetarianFood` using a restriction, `owl:allValuesFrom`; we can then assert that any `Vegetarian` satisfies this condition using `rdfs:subClassOf`. Together, it looks like this:

```
:Vegetarian rdfs:subClassOf
    [ a owl:Restriction;
       owl:onProperty :eats ;
       owl:allValuesFrom :VegetarianFood] .
```

Let's see how it works. Since

```
:Jen a :Vegetarian .
```

we can conclude that

```
:Jen a [ a owl:Restriction;
    owl:onProperty :eats ;
       owl:allValuesFrom :VegetarianFood] .
```

Combined with the fact that

```
:Jen :eats :Marzipan .
```

we can conclude that

```
:Marzipan a :VegetarianFood .
```

as desired. How does `Maverick` fare now? We won't say that he is a `Vegetarian` but only, as we have stated already, that he is a `Person` . That's where the inference ends; there is no stated relationship between `Maverick` and `Vegetarian` , so there is nothing on which to base an inference. Maverick's steak remains simply a `Food` , not a `VegetarianFood`.

The entire model and inferences are shown in Figure 9-9.

Challenge: Filtering Data Based on Explicit Type

We have seen how tabular data can be used in RDF by considering each row to be an individual, the column names as properties, and the values in the table as values. We saw sample data in Table 3-10, which we repeat on page 200 as Table 9-1. Some sample triples from this data are shown in Table 9-2.

Each row from the original table appears in Table 9-2 as an individual in the RDF version. Each of these individuals has the same type—namely, `mfg:Product`—from the name of the table. This data includes only a limited number of possible values for the "Product_Line" field, and they are known in advance (e.g., "Paper machine," "Feedback line," "Safety Valve," etc.).

A more elaborate way to import this information would be to still have one individual per row in the original table but to have rows with different types

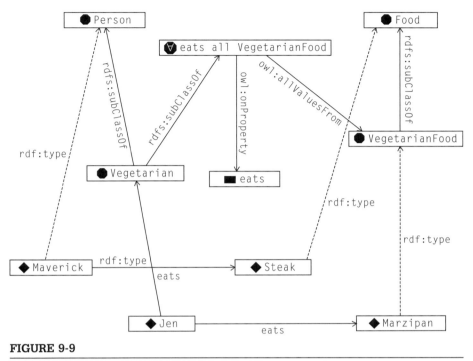

FIGURE 9-9

Definition of a Vegetarian as a restriction on what the person eats.

depending on the value of the Product Line column. For example, the following triples (among others) would be imported:

```
mfg:Product1 rdf:type ns:Paper_machine .
mfg:Product4 rdf:type ns:Feedback_line .
mfg:Product7 rdf:type ns:Monitor .
mfg:Product9 rdf:type ns:SafetyValve .
```

This is a common situation when actually importing information from a table. It is quite common for type information to appear as a particular column in the table. If we use a single method for importing tables, all the rows become individuals of the same type. A software-intensive solution would be to write a more elaborate import mechanism that allows a user to specify which column should specify the type. A model-based solution would use a model in OWL and an inference engine to solve the same problem.

Challenge 24   Build a model in OWL so we can infer the type information for each individual, based on the value in the "Product Line" field but using just the simple imported triples described in Chapter 3.

Table 9-1 Typical Tabular Data for RDF Import

			Product			
ID	Model Number	Division	Product Line	Manufacture Location	SKU	Available
1	ZX-3	Manufacturing support	Paper machine	Sacramento	FB3524	23
2	ZX-3P	Manufacturing support	Paper machine	Sacramento	KD5243	4
3	ZX-3S	Manufacturing support	Paper machine	Sacramento	IL4028	34
4	B-1430	Control Engineering	Feedback Line	Elizabeth	KS4520	23
5	B-1430X	Control Engineering	Feedback Line	Elizabeth	CL5934	14
6	B-1431	Control Engineering	Active Sensor	Seoul	KK3945	0
7	DBB-12	Accessories	Monitor	Hong Kong	ND5520	100
8	SP-1234	Safety	Safety Valve	Cleveland	HI4554	4
9	SPX-1234	Safety	Safety Valve	Cleveland	OP5333	14

SOLUTION

Since the classes of which the rows will be members (i.e., the product lines) are already known, we first define those classes:

```
ns:Paper_Machine rdf:type owl:Class .
ns:Feedback_Line rdf:type owl:Class .
ns:Active_Sensor rdf:type owl:Class .
ns:Monitor rdf:type owl:Class .
ns:Safety_Valve rdf:type owl:Class .
```

Each of these classes must include just those individuals with the appropriate value for the property mfg:Product_Product_Line. The class constructor that achieves this uses an owl:hasValue restriction, as follows:

```
ns:Paper_Machine owl:equivalentClass
    [ a owl:Restriction;
        owl:onProperty mfg:Product_Product_Line
        owl:hasValue "Paper machine"] .
```

Table 9-2 Sample Triples

Subject	Predicate	Object
mfg:Product1	rdf:type	mfg:Product
mfg:Product1	mfg:Product_ID	1
mfg:Product1	mfg:Product_ModelNo	ZX-3
mfg:Product1	mfg:Product_Division	Manufacturing support
mfg:Product1	mfg:Product_Product_Line	Paper machine
mfg:Product1	mfg:Product_Manufacture_Location	Sacramento
mfg:Product1	mfg:Product_SKU	FB3524
mfg:Product1	mfg:Proudct_Available	23
mfg:Product2	rdf:type	mfg:Product
mfg:Product2	mfg:Product_ID	2
mfg:Product2	mfg:Product_ModelNo	ZX-3P
mfg:Product2	mfg:Product_Division	Manufacturing support
mfg:Product2	mfg:Product_Product_Line	Paper machine
mfg:Product2	mfg:Product_Manufacture_Location	Sacramento
mfg:Product2	mfg:Product_SKU	KD5243
mfg:Product2	mfg:Proudct_Available	4
mfg:Product3	rdf:type	mfg:Product
mfg:Product4	rdf:type	mfg:Product
mfg:Product5	rdf:type	mfg:Product …

```
ns:Feedback_Line owl:equivalentClass
  [ a owl:Restriction;
    owl:onProperty mfg:Product_Product_Line
    owl:hasValue "Feedback line"] .

ns:Active_Sensor owl:equivalentClass
  [ a owl:Restriction;
    owl:onProperty mfg:Product_Product_Line
    owl:hasValue "Active sensor"] .

ns:Monitor owl:equivalentClass
  [ a owl:Restriction;
    owl:onProperty mfg:Product_Product_Line
    owl:hasValue "Monitor"] .
```

```
ns:Safety_Valve owl:equivalentClass
  [ a owl:Restriction;
     owl:onProperty mfg:Product_Product_Line
     owl:hasValue "Safety Valve"] .
```

Each of these definitions draws inferences as desired. Consider `mfg:Product1` ("ZX-3"), for which the triple

```
mfg:Product1 mfg:Product_Product_Line "Paper machine" .
```

has been imported from the table. The first triple ensures that `mfg:Product1` satisfies the conditions of the restriction for `Paper_Machine`. Hence,

```
mfg:Product1 rdf:type [ a owl:Restriction;
        owl:onProperty mfg:Product_Product_Line
        owl:hasValue "Paper machine" ] .
```

can be inferred. Since this restriction is equivalent to the definition for `mfg:Paper_Machine`, we have

```
mfg:Product1 rdf:type mfg:Paper_Machine .
```

as desired.

Furthermore, this definition maintains coherence of the data, even if it came from a source other than the imported table. Suppose that a new product is defined according to the following RDF:

```
os:ProductA rdf:type mfg:Paper_Machine .
```

The semantics of `owl:equivalentClass` means that all members of `mfg:Paper_Machine` are also members of the restriction. In particular,

```
os:ProductA rdf:type [ a owl:Restriction;
        owl:onProperty mfg:Product_Product_Line
        owl:hasValue "Paper Machine" ] .
```

Finally, because of the semantics of the restriction, we can infer

```
os:ProductA mfg:Product_Product_Line "Paper Machine" .
```

The end result of this construct is that regardless of how product information is brought into the system, it is represented both in terms of `rdf:type` and `mfg:Product_Product_Line` consistently.

Challenge: Relationship Transfer in SKOS

When mapping from one model to another, or even when specifying how one part of a model relates to another, it is not uncommon to make a statement of the form "Everything related to A by property p should also be related to B but by property q." Some examples are "Everyone who plays for the All Star team is governed by the league's contract" and "Every work in the *Collected Works of Shakespeare* was written by Shakespeare." We refer to this kind of mapping as `relationship transfer`, since it involves transferring individuals in a relationship with one entity to another relationship with another entity.

In Chapter 8, we saw how SKOS provides a framework for describing knowledge organization systems like thesauri, taxonomies, and controlled vocabularies. Not surprisingly, the issue of relationship transfer appears in this system, as well. We saw a special-purpose rule for managing collections—namely: If we have triples of the form

```
X skos:narrower C .
C skos:member Y .
```

then we can infer the triple

```
X skos:narrower Y .
```

In the case in which a collection `C` is narrower than a concept `X`, we can say, "Every member of `C` is also narrower than `X`." That is, the rule that governs the treatment of `skos:narrower` in the context of a `skos:Collection` is a relationship transfer.

Challenge 25   Represent the SKOS rule for propagating `skos:narrower` in the context of a `skos:Collection`, using constructs in OWL. For example, represent the constraint

```
IF agro:MilkBySourceAnimal skos:member Y .
THEN agro:Milk skos:narrower Y .
```

in OWL.

SOLUTION

First, let's define an inverse for `skos:member`:

```
skos:isMemberOf owl:inverseOf skos:member .
```

We already have an inverse for `skos:narrower`, which is `skos:broader`. With these inverses, we can restate the problem as

```
IF Y skos:isMemberOf agro:MilkBySourceAnimal .
THEN Y skos:broader agro:Milk .
```

How do we specify, in OWL, the set of all things `Y` that are members of `agro:MilkBySourceAnimal`? We can use an `owl:hasValue` restriction for that.

```
agro:MembersOfMilkSource owl:equivalentClass
    [ a owl:Restriction ;
        owl:onProperty skos:isMemberOf ;
        owl:hasValue agro:MilkBySourceAnimal ] .
```

We can also describe the set of all things that have `agro:Milk` as a broader category. We will call it `agro:NarrowerThanMilk`, since these things are narrower than `Milk` (i.e., `Milk` is broader than they are):

```
agro:NarrowerThanMilk owl:equivalentClass
    [ a owl:Restriction ;
        owl:onProperty skos:broader ;
        owl:hasValue agro:Milk ] .
```

Now, to say that all members of one of these classes is in the other, we simply use `rdfs:subClassOf`—thus:

```
ex:MembersOfMilkSource rdfs:subClassOf agro:NarrowerThanMilk .
```

You can think of this `rdfs:subClassOf` as something like an IF/THEN relationship: IF something is a member of the subclass, THEN it is a member of the superclass. In this case, both the subclass and the superclass are restrictions; when this happens, the IF/THEN takes on more meaning. In this case, it takes on the meaning IF an individual `skos:isMemberOf agro:MilkBySourceAnimal`, then that individual (has) `skos:broader` (concept) `agro:Milk`. With the inverses as just defined, this is equivalent to saying

```
IF
agro:MilkBySourceAnimal skos:member X
THEN
agro:Milk skos:narrower X
```

as desired.

RELATIONSHIP TRANSFER IN FOAF

A similar situation arises in FOAF with groups of people. Recall that FOAF provides two ways to describe members of a group: the `foaf:member` relation, which relates an individual member G of `foaf:Group` to the individuals who are in that group, and that same group G, which is related to an `owl:Class` by the `foaf:membershipClass` property. We take an example from the life of Shakespeare to illustrate this.

Suppose we define a `foaf:Group` for `Shakespeares_Children`, as follows:

```
b:Shakespeares_Children
a foaf:Group ;
    foaf:name "Shakespeare's Children" ;
    foaf:member b:Susanna , b:Judith , b:Hamnet ;
    foaf:membershipClass b:ChildOfShakespeare .
b:ChildOfShakespeare a owl:Class .
```

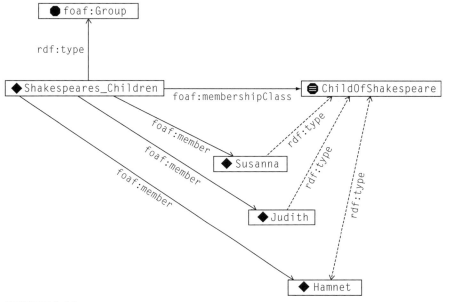

FIGURE 9-10

Inferences based on *membershipClass* in FOAF.

FOAF specifies that the following rule should hold:

```
IF
    b:Shakespeares_Children foaf:member ?x
THEN
?x rdfs:type b:ChildOfShakespeare .
```

Figure 9-10 shows graphically the result of this rule in the case of Shakespeare's family. The fine lines represent asserted triples, and the three bold lines represent the triples that are to be inferred.

Challenge 26 How can we get the inferences shown in Figure 9-10 by using only the constructs from OWL (i.e., without special-purpose rules)?

SOLUTION

The solution parallels the solution for relationship transfer in SKOS, but in this case, the relationship we are transferring to is rdf:type. We begin as we did in that example—by defining an inverse of foaf:member:

```
b:memberOf owl:inverseOf foaf:member .
```

Now we can define `ChildOfShakespeare` to be (equivalent to) the class of all individuals who are `b:memberOf b:Shakespeares_Children`, **using an** `owl:hasValue` **restriction:**

```
b:ChildOfShakespeare
   a owl:Class ;
   rdfs:label "Child of Shakespeare";
   owl:equivalentClass
      [ a owl:Restriction ;
      owl:hasValue b:Shakespeares_Children ;
      owl:onProperty b:memberOf
      ] .
```

Let's follow the progression of Shakespeare's children through this inference. From Figure 9-10, we begin with three triples:

```
b:Shakespeares_Children foaf:member b:Hamnet .
b:Shakespeares_Children foaf:member b:Judith .
b:Shakespeares_Children foaf:member b:Susanna .
```

By the semantics of `owl:inverseOf`, **we can infer**

```
b:Hamnet foaf:memberOf b:Shakespeares_Children .
b:Judith foaf:memberOf b:Shakespeares_Children .
b:Susanna foaf:memberOf b:Shakespeares_Children .
```

Therefore, all three are also members of the restriction defined previously, so we can conclude that

```
b:Hamnet rdf:type b:ChildOfShakespeare .
b:Judith rdf:type b:ChildOfShakespeare .
b:Susanna rdf:type b:ChildOfShakespeare .
```

Following similar reasoning, we can also turn this inference around backward; if we instead assert that

```
b:Hamnet rdf:type b:ChildOfShakespeare .
b:Judith rdf:type b:ChildOfShakespeare .
b:Susanna rdf:type b:ChildOfShakespeare .
```

we can infer that

```
b:Shakespeares_Children foaf:member b:Hamnet .
b:Shakespeares_Children foaf:member b:Judith .
b:Shakespeares_Children foaf:member b:Susanna .
```

Discussion

Just because we can represent something in OWL, it doesn't necessarily mean that we *have to* do so. How do the solutions we've proposed compare to those that were actually taken by the SKOS and FOAF developers?

As we have seen, SKOS uses a special-purpose rule to define the meaning of `skos:narrower` in the context of a `skos:Concept` and a `skos:Collection`. This means that a SKOS user can express the relationship between `Milk` and `MilkBySourceAnimal` simply by asserting the triple

```
agro:Milk skos:narrower agro:MilkBySourceAnimal .
```

Then the rule takes care of the rest. This is certainly much simpler for the SKOS user than having to construct the pair of restrictions.

This advantage for the rule-based approach goes even further: SKOS in fact defines the rule with a bit more generality, as follows:

```
X P C .
P rdf:type skos:CollectableProperty .
C skos:member Y .
```

Then we can infer the triple

```
X P Y .
```

That is, this rule works for any `skos:CollectableProperty`, which includes `skos:narrower`, `skos:broader`, and `skos:related`. A single rule can express the constraints for three different properties. To do the same using the OWL relationship transfer pattern, you would have to repeat the pattern once for each property and for each concept/collection pair for which you want to specify the relationship. Seen from this point of view, the rule seems like a far superior solution.

On the other hand, writing a special-purpose rule into the SKOS description has its own drawbacks. What language should the rules be written in? What processor will process the rules? The pragmatic answers are that the rules are written in the natural language that the specification is written in and the processing will be done by each application rather than by a general-purpose inference engine. This has the drawback that every application developer has to understand the rule from the imprecise natural language description and has to specially implement the rule. In contrast, the OWL solution (any OWL solution) can make use of generic software, and it takes advantage of standard semantics. For better or worse, the SKOS specification, at the time of this writing, has chosen to express this rule in prose, leaving its implementation to each application.

The situation for FOAF is a bit different. Unlike the situation for SKOS, there is only one property *(foaf:membershipClass)* that is affected by the transfer rule. Furthermore, a FOAF user has to assert the triple

```
b:Shakespeares_Children    foaf:membershipClass    b:ChildOf
    Shakespeare.
```

for the transfer rule to come in to play (in contrast to SKOS, this isn't built into some other construct like `skos:Collection`). That is, the FOAF user is already explicitly indicating at what point the rule is to be invoked.

Furthermore, the ground-up evolutionary strategy of FOAF argues against putting special-purpose meanings into the specification, since there is a good chance that these things could be changed or superseded by future versions. As it stands, any FOAF user can already express (in OWL) the relationship between a `foaf:Group` and its `foaf:members`, or indeed any other class and property as needed or desired. This is quite in accord with the AAA slogan and in particular with the ground-up empowerment of the FOAF user community that is manifest in the rest of the FOAF project.

Since the SKOS effort is focused and under the control of a single committee, it is possible to put a few rules into its specification and still keep some control over how the rules interact. Furthermore, SKOS is not domain-specific; it is intended to be usable across many domains. As such, SKOS must anticipate that any number of concept/collection pairs might require this rule.

When modeling in a more vertical domain, some of these conditions may not hold. Certainly it is not common for most modelers to be seeking W3C recommendation status or some other approval as a standard, which means that any rules that are put into the model can have possible adverse interactions with other rules. It is not uncommon when modeling a particular vertical domain to find that there are a few very distinguished instances in which some part of the model needs to be replicated at another place; *The Complete Works of Shakespeare* and the "All Star Team" are examples of this. In these cases, the relationship transfer is part of the description of these concepts, and is not something that needs to be repeated an indefinite number of times.

In such cases, it may be just as convenient to describe the relationships using constructs in OWL. This seems to be the case for group membership in OWL; the modeler is making a very special statement about a group when they relate it to its `membershipClass`. It is not out of the question to have a somewhat involved way to express this relationship, especially if it can be done without cluttering up the FOAF model itself.

A final comment about the comparative practice of expressing rules as part of a standards document versus an explicit representation in a semantic model has to do with the very nature of modeling as an intellectual pursuit. One reason to model knowledge about a domain in the first place is to understand the ramifications of that model, and to understand when there are conflicts between one viewpoint of the world and another. When rules are represented as part of a practice (e.g., encoded into a standard), the rules are not themselves available for automated analysis. That is, suppose that a rule in FOAF were to have some adverse interaction with a rule from SKOS. How would we know not to use these two models together? In the next chapter, we introduce notions of inconsistency and contradiction and examine how representations that remain within the OWL standard can detect such interactions in advance of their application to any actual web data.

ALTERNATIVE DESCRIPTIONS OF RESTRICTIONS

In this book, we describe OWL and its semantics with respect to the interpretation of OWL as RDF triples as defined in the W3C OWL documents. Other characterizations have been used during the history of OWL and even appear in user interfaces of some tools. Each characterization uses its own vocabulary to describe exactly the same things. In this section we review some of the most common language you will encounter when discussing OWL restrictions and classes, and we also provide a recommendation for best-practice terminology.

The semantics of `rdfs:subClassOf` and `owl:equivalentClass` are quite easy to characterize in terms of the inferences that hold

```
X rdfs:subClassOf Y .
```

can be understood as a simple IF/THEN relation; if something is a member of X, then it is also a member of Y.

```
X owl:equivalentClass Y .
```

can be understood as an IF and only IF relation, that is two IF/THEN relations, one going each way; if something is a member of X, then it is also a member of Y, and vice versa.

These relations remain unchanged in the case where X and/or Y are restrictions. We can see these relationships with examples taken from the solar system. Consider two classes: one is a named class `SolarBody`, which we'll call class A for purposes of this discussion. The other is the unnamed class defined by a restriction `onProperty` orbits that it `hasValue TheSun`, which we'll call class B. We can say that all solar bodies orbit the sun by asserting

```
A rdfs:subClassOf B .
```

In other words, if something is a solar body, then it orbits the sun.

Other terms are used in the literature for this situation. For example, it is sometimes described by saying that "orbiting the sun is a necessary condition for `SolarBody`." The intuition behind this description is that if you know that something is a `SolarBody`, then it is necessarily the case that it orbits the sun. Since such a description of the class `SolarBody` describes the class but does not provide a complete characterization of it (that is, you cannot determine from this description that something is a member of `SolarBody`), then this situation is also sometimes denoted by saying that "orbiting the sun is a `partial` definition for the class `SolarBody`."

If, on the other hand, we say that solar bodies are the same as the set of things that orbit the sun, we can express this in OWL compactly as

`A owl:equivalentClass B .`

Now we can make inferences in both directions: If something orbits the sun, then it is a `SolarBody`, and if it is a `SolarBody`, then it orbits the sun. This situation is sometimes characterized by saying that "orbiting the sun is a `necessary` and `sufficient` condition for `SolarBody`." The intuition behind this description is that if you know something is a `SolarBody`, then it is necessarily the case that it orbits the sun. But furthermore, if you want to determine that something is a `SolarBody`, it is sufficient to establish that it orbits the sun. Furthermore, since such a description does fully characterize the class `SolarBody`, this situation is also sometimes denoted by saying that "orbiting the sun is a `complete` definition for the class `SolarBody`."

Finally, if we say that all things that orbit the sun are solar bodies, we can express this compactly in OWL as

`B rdfs:subClassOf A .`

That is, if something orbits the sun, then it is a `SolarBody`. Given the usage of the words *necessary* and *sufficient*, one could be excused for believing that in this situation one would say that "orbiting the sun is a `sufficient condition` for `SolarBody`." However, it is not common practice to use the word `sufficient` in this way. Despite the obvious utility of such a statement from a modeling perspective and its simplicity in terms of OWL (it is no more complex than a `partial` or `complete` definition), there is no term corresponding to `partial` or `complete` for this situation.

Because of the incomplete and inconsistent way words, such as *partial*, *complete*, *sufficient*, and *necessary*, have been traditionally used to describe OWL, we strongly discourage their use and recommend instead the simpler and consistent use of the OWL terms `rdfs:subClassOf` and `owl:equivalentClass`.

SUMMARY

A key functionality of OWL is the ability to define restriction classes. The unnamed classes are defined based on restrictions on the values for particular properties of the class. Using this mechanism, OWL can be used to model situations in which the members of a particular class must have certain properties. In RDFS, the domain and range restrictions can allow us to make inferences about all the members of a class (such as `playsFor` relating a baseball player to a team). In OWL, one can use restriction statements to differentiate the case between something that applies to all members of a class versus some members, and even to insist on a particular value for a specific property of all members of a class.

When restrictions are used in combination with the constructs of RDFS (especially `rdfs:subPropertyOf` and `rdfs:subClassOf`), and when they are cascaded with one another (restrictions referring to other restrictions), they can be used to model complex relationships between properties, classes, and individuals. The advantage of modeling relationships in this way (over informal specification) is that interactions of multiple specifications can be understood and even processed automatically.

OWL also provides other kinds of restrictions that can be placed on the members of a class using other kinds of `onProperty` restrictions. We discuss these in the next chapter.

Fundamental Concepts

The following fundamental concepts were introduced in this chapter.

owl:Restriction—The building block in OWL that describes classes by restricting the values allowed for certain properties.

owl:hasValue—A type of restriction that refers to a single value for a property.

owl:someValuesFrom—A type of restriction that refers to a set from which some value for a property must come.

owl:allValuesFrom—A type of restriction that refers to a set from which all values for a property must come.

owl:onProperty—A link from a restriction to the property it restricts.

Counting and Sets in OWL

10

Restrictions provide a concise way to describe a class of individuals in terms of the properties we know that describe the individuals themselves. As we saw in the previous chapter, we can use this construct to define notions like *Vegetarian* (describing someone in terms of they type of food that they eat), to sift information from a table (describing something according to a value of one property), and to manage groups of people or terms (describe something based on its membership in a group). The restrictions defined in Chapter 9 are powerful methods for defining classes of individuals.

In this chapter, we see that OWL augments this capability with a full set theory language, including intersections, unions, and complements. These can be used to combine restrictions together (e.g., the set of planets that go around the sun *and* have at least one moon) or to combine the classes we use to define restrictions (a *Vegetarian* is someone who eats food that is *not Meat*). This combination provides a potent system for making very detailed descriptions of information.

OWL also includes restrictions that refer to *cardinalities*—that is, referring to the number of distinct values for a particular property some individual has. So we can describe "the set of planets that have at least three moons" or "the teams that contain more than one all-star player." Reasoning with cardinalities in OWL is surprisingly subtle. Perhaps not surprising, when one considers that reasoning is taking place under the Open World assumption and the Non-Unique Naming assumption.

Perhaps we shouldn't be surprised that it is difficult to count how many distinct things there are when one thing might have more than one name (i.e., more than one URI), and we never know when someone might tell us about a new thing we didn't know about before. These are the main reasons why cardinality inferencing in OWL is quite conservative in the conclusions it can draw.

UNIONS AND INTERSECTIONS

We begin with the basic logical combinations, which are familiar from set theory. OWL provides a facility for defining new classes as unions and intersections of previously defined classes. All set operations can be used on any class definition at all in OWL, including named classes and restrictions. This allows OWL to express a wide variety of combinations of classes and conditions. The semantics for the constructors is as one would expect, matching the set operations of the same name.

Syntactically, they use the list constructs of RDF, as follows:

```
U1 a owl:Class;
    owl:unionOf ( ns:A ns:B ...) .
I1 a owl:Class;
    owl:intersectionOf ( ns:A ns:B ...) .
```

The union of two or more classes includes the members of all those classes combined; the intersection includes the members that belong to every one of the classes.

The intersection of two (or more) classes is a new class; this can be represented in OWL/RDF by either naming that class (as just shown) or by defining an anonymous class (an individual of type `owl:Class`), which is defined to be the intersection of other classes using the property `owl:intersectionOf` (likewise `owl:unionOf`). An anonymous class of this sort can be used again in a model by naming using `owl:equivalentClass`, as follows:

```
bb:MajorLeagueBaseballPlayer owl:equivalentClass
    [ a owl:Class;
        owl:intersectionOf
    ( bb:MajorLeagueMember bb:Player bb:BaseballEmployee ) ] .
```

Although the semantics of `intersectionOf` and `unionOf` are straightforward, they have a particular application to Semantic Web modeling when used in conjunction with restrictions.

Natural language descriptions of restrictions often have a notion of intersection built-in. "All planets orbiting the sun" is actually the intersection of all things that orbit the sun (`hasValue` restriction) and all planets. The set of major league baseball players is the intersection of the things that play on a major league team (`someValuesFrom` restriction) and baseball players. Intersections work just as well on restrictions as they do on named classes; we can define these things directly using intersections:

```
:SolarPlanet a owl:Class;
    owl:intersectionOf (
        :Planet
        [ a owl:Restriction;
```

```
        owl:onProperty :orbits;
        owl:hasValue :TheSun
      ] ) .
   :MajorLeagueBaseballPlayer a owl:Class;
      owl:intersectionOf (
        :BaseballPlayer
        [ a owl:Restriction;
        owl:onProperty :playsFor;
        owl:someValuesFrom :MajorLeagueTeam
      ] ) .
```

EXAMPLE **High-Priority Candidate Questions**

In the previous chapter, we defined a class of candidate questions based on dependencies of selected answers, and we defined priorities for the questions themselves. We will use the set constructors to combine these two to form a class of candidate questions of a particular priority. An application that asks questions and records answers using this construct would only ask high-priority questions that have been enabled by answers given so far.

First, let's revisit the description of `SelectedAnswer` that classifies dependent questions as `EnabledQuestion`:

```
q:SelectedAnswer rdfs:subClassOf
   [ a owl:Restriction;
      owl:onProperty q:enablesCandidate;
      owl:allValuesFrom q:EnabledQuestion].
```

We now want to define a class of questions that we are ready to ask, based on two criteria: First, if they have been enabled by the description above and, second, if they are high priority. This is done with an `intersectionOf` contstructor:

```
q:CandidateQuestion owl:equivalentClass
   [ a owl:Class;
      owl:intersectionOf
         ( q:EnabledQuestion q:HighPriorityQuestion ) ] .
```

With this description of `q:CandidateQuestion`, only questions with value `q:High` for the property `q:hasPriority` can become candidates.

Alternately, we could make a more relaxed description for candidate questions that include medium-priority questions:

```
q:CandidateQuestion owl:equivalentClass
   [ a owl:intersectionOf
      ( q:EnabledQuestion
         [ a owl:unionOf
```

```
( q:HighPriorityQuestion
  q:MediumPriorityQuestion ) ] ) ] .
```

Closing the World

A key to understanding how set operations and counting works in OWL is the impact of the *Open World Assumption*. Not only does it make counting difficult, but even the notion of set complement is subtle when you assume that a new fact can be discovered at any time. Who's to say that something isn't a member of a class when the very next statement might assert that it actually is? Fortunately, there are ways in OWL to assert that certain parts of the world are closed; in such situations, inferences having to do with complements or counting become much clearer.

Consider, for example, the following bit of dialogue:

> RIMBAUD: *I saw a James Dean movie last night.*
> ROCKY: *Was it* Giant?
> RIMBAUD: *No.*
> ROCKY: *Was it* East of Eden?
> RIMBAUD: *No.*
> ROCKY: *James Dean only made three movies; it must have been* Rebel Without a Cause.
> RIMBAUD: *Yes, it was.*

This sort of inference relies on the fact that James Dean made only three movies. In light of the open world assumption, how can we make such a claim? After all, in an open world, someone could come along at any time and tell us about a fourth James Dean movie. We will use the example of James Dean's movies to illustrate how OWL provides a controlled means for modeling closed aspects of the world.

Enumerating Sets with *owl:oneOf*

In the James Dean example, it wasn't necessary that we reject the open world assumption completely. We simply needed to know that for a particular class (James Dean movies), all of its members are known. When one is in a position to enumerate the members of a class, a number of inferences can follow.

OWL allows us to enumerate the members of a class using a construct called `owl:oneOf`, as shown here:

```
ss:SolarPlanet rdf:type owl:Class;
    owl:oneOf ( ss:Mercury ss:Venus ss:Earth
        ss:Mars ss:Jupiter ss:Saturn
            ss:Uranus ss:Neptune).
```

The class `SolarPlanet` is related via the property `owl:oneOf` to a list of the members of the class. Informally, the meaning of this is that the class `SolarPlanet` contains these eight individuals and no others. `owl:oneOf` places a limit on the AAA slogan. When we say that a class is made up of exactly these items, nobody else can say that there is another distinct item that is a member of that class. Thus, `owl:oneOf` should be used with care and only in situations in which the definition of the class is not likely to change—or at least not change very often. In the case of the solar planets, this didn't change for 50 years. We can probably expect that it won't change again for quite a while.

Although `owl:oneOf` places a limitation on the AAA slogan and Open World assumption, it places no limitation on the Nonunique Naming assumption. That is, `owl:oneOf` makes no claim about whether, say, Mercury might be the same as Venus.

When combined with `owl:someValuesFrom`, `owl:oneOf` provides a generalization of `owl:hasValue`. Whereas `owl:hasValue` specifies a single value that a property can take, `owl:someValuesFrom` combined with `owl:oneOf` specifies a distinct set of values that a property can take.

Challenge 27   In the dialogue with Rimbaud, Rocky used the fact that James Dean made only three movies to help determine what movie Rimbaud had seen. How do we represent this in OWL?

SOLUTION

Since James Dean has been dead for more than 50 years, it seems a sad but safe bet that he won't be making any more movies. We can therefore express the class of James Dean movies using `owl:oneOf` as follows:

```
:JamesDeanMovie a owl:Class;
    owl:oneOf ( :Giant :EastOfEden :Rebel ).
```

Informally, this states that the class `JamesDeanMovie` is made up of only `Giant`, `EastOfEden`, and `Rebel`. What is the formal meaning of `owl:oneOf`? As usual, we define the meaning of a construct in terms of the inferences that can be drawn from it. In the case of `owl:oneOf`, there are a number of inferences that we can draw.

First, we can infer that each instance listed in `owl:oneOf` is indeed a member of the class. From our assertion about `:JamesDeanMovie`, we can infer that each of these things is a James Dean movie:

```
:Giant rdf:type :JamesDeanMovie .
:EastOfEden rdf:type :JamesDeanMovie .
:Rebel rdf:type :JamesDeanMovie .
```

The meaning of `owl:oneOf` goes further than simply asserting the members of a class; it also asserts that these are the *only* members of this class. In terms of inferences, this means that if we assert that some new thing is a member of the class, then it must be `owl:sameAs` one of the members listed in the `owl:oneOf` list. In our James Dean example, if someone were to introduce a new member of the class—say:

```
:RimbaudsMovie rdf:type :JamesDeanMovie .
```

then we can infer that Rebel must be `owl:sameAs` one of the other movies already mentioned.

This inference differs from the inferences that we have seen so far. Up to this point, we were able to express inferences in terms of new triples that can be inferred. In this case, the inference tells us that *some* triple from a small set holds, but we don't know which one. We can't assert any new triples, and we can't respond to a query any differently.

How do we turn this kind of inference into something from which we assert a triple? If we compare where we are now with the conversation between Rocky and Rimbaud, we are right at the point where Rocky has heard from Rimbaud that he saw a James Dean Movie. Rocky doesn't know which movie he has seen, but because of his background knowledge, he knows that it was one of three movies. How does Rocky proceed? He eliminates candidates until he can conclude which one it is. To do this in OWL, we must be able to say that some individual is *not* the same as another.

Differentiating Individuals with owl:differentFrom

There's an old joke about the three major influences on the price of a piece of real estate: location, location, and location. The joke is, of course, that when you promised to name three influences, any reasonable listener expects you to give three *different* influences. Because of the *nonunique naming assumption* in the Semantic Web, we have to be explicit about these things and name things that are, in fact, different from one another. OWL provides `owl:differentFrom` for this. Its use is quite simple: To assert that one resource is different from another requires a single triple:

```
ss:Earth owl:differentFrom ss:Mars .
```

Informally, this triple means that we can rely on the fact that `ss:Earth` and `ss:Mars` refer to different resources when making arguments by counting or by elimination. Formally, `owl:differentFrom` supports a number of inferences when used in conjunction with other constructs like `owl:cardinality` and `owl:oneOf`, as we shall see.

Challenge 28   Use OWL to model the dialogue between Rocky and Rimbaud so that OWL can draw the same inference that Rocky did—namely, that Rimbaud saw *Rebel Without a Cause*.

SOLUTION

At the beginning of the dialogue, Rocky knows that the movie Rimbaud saw was one of the three movies: `EastOfEden`, `Giant`, or `Rebel`. We have already shown how to represent this using `owl:oneOf`. But he doesn't know which one. He can make a guess: Perhaps it was `Giant`. If he is right, we can simply assert that

> `:RimbaudsMovie owl:sameAs :Giant .`

But what if (as was the case in the dialogue) he was wrong, and Rimbaud didn't see `Giant`? We express this in OWL, using `owl:differentFrom`, as follows:

> `:RimbaudsMovie owl:differentFrom :Giant .`

This narrows things down a bit, but we still don't know whether Rimbaud saw *East of Eden* or *Rebel Without a Cause*. So Rocky tries again: Was the movie *East of Eden*? When the answer is negative, we have another `owl:different From` triple:

> `:RimbaudsMovie owl:differentFrom :EastOfEden .`

Now we are in the position that Rocky was in at the end of the dialogue; we know that there are just three James Dean movies, and we know that Rimbaud did not see *Giant* or *East of Eden*. Just as Rocky was able to conclude that Rimbaud saw *Rebel Without a Cause*, the semantics of `owl:oneOf` and `owl:differentFrom` allow us to infer that

> `:RimbaudsMovie owl:sameAs :Rebel .`

We can see these assertions and the inference in Figure 10-1.

DIFFERENTIATING MULTIPLE INDIVIDUALS

The nonunique naming assumption allowed us to use a new resource—`RimbaudsMovie`—to stand in for an indeterminate movie. With appropriate use of modeling constructs, we were able to get inferences about which movie it actually was, using `owl:sameAs` to indicate the answer. The nonunique naming assumption applies to all resources. For instance, even though we intuitively

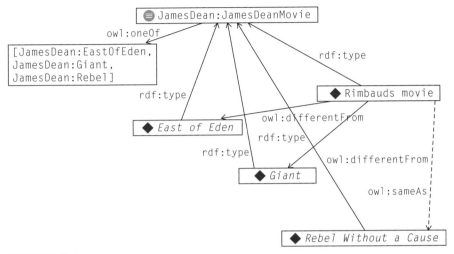

FIGURE 10-1

Rimbauld's movie is neither *Giant* nor *East of Eden,* so we infer that it is *Rebel Without a Cause.*

know that `ss:Earth` and `ss:Mars` do not refer to the same thing, we need to state that in our model. We did this before using `owl:differentFrom`. We also want to say that `ss:Earth` is different from `ss:Jupiter` and `ss:Venus`, `ss:Venus` is different from `ss:Mars`, and so on.

To simplify the specification of lists of items, all of which are different from one another, OWL provides `owl:AllDifferent` and `owl:distinctMembers`—two constructs. Using these, we will specify that a list of individuals is distinct from one another. The list of items is specified as an RDF list. We specify that this list should be treated as a set of mutually different individuals by referring to it in a triple using `owl:distinctMembers` as a predicate. The domain of `owl:distinctMembers` is `owl:AllDifferent`.

It is customary for the subject of an `owl:distinctMembers` triple to be a bnode, so the statement that all eight planets are mutually distinct would be expressed in N3 as

```
[ a owl:AllDifferent;
   owl:distinctMembers (ss:Mercury
                        ss:Venus
                        ss:Earth
                        ss:Mars
                        ss:Jupiter
                        ss:Saturn
                        ss:Uranus
                        ss:Neptune) ] .
```

Formally, this is the same as asserting the 28 `owl:differentFrom` triples, one for each pair of individuals in the list. In the case of James Dean's movies, we can assert that the three movies are distinct in the same way:

```
[ a owl:AllDifferent;
  owl:distinctMembers (:EastOfEden
                       :Giant
                       :Rebel) ] .
```

The view of this bit of N3 in terms of triples is shown in Figure 10-2. The movies are referenced in an RDF list (using `rdf:first` and `rdf:next` to chain the entities together). For longer lists (like the planets), the chain continues for each entity in the list.

Earlier we saw that the class `JamesDeanMovie` was defined using `owl:oneOf` to indicate that these are the only James Dean movies in existence. Now we have gone on to say that additionally these three movies are distinct. It is quite

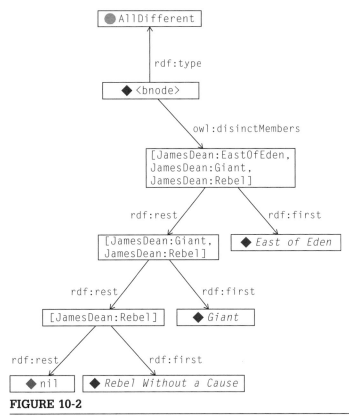

FIGURE 10-2

Using `owl:AllDifferent` and `owl:distinctMembers` to indicate that the three James Dean movies are distinct. The movies are referred to in an RDF list.

common to use `owl:oneOf` and `owl:allDifferent` together in this way to say that a class is made up of an enumerated list of distinct elements.

CARDINALITY

So far, we have seen restrictions that define classes based on the presence of certain values for given properties. OWL allows a much finer-grained way to define classes, based on the number of distinct values a property takes. Such a restriction is called a *cardinality restriction*. This seemingly simple idea turns out to have surprising subtlety when modeling in OWL. Cardinality restrictions allow us to express constraints on the number of individuals that can be related to a member of the restriction class. For example, a baseball team has exactly nine (distinct) players. A person has two (biological) parents. Cardinality restrictions can be used to define sets of particular interest, like the set of one-act plays or the set of books that are printed in more than one volume.

The syntax for a cardinality restriction is similar to that for the other restrictions we have already seen. Here is the restriction that defines the class of things that have exactly nine players:

```
[ a owl:Restriction;
  owl:onProperty :hasPlayer;
  owl:cardinality 9]
```

Of course, instead of 9, we could have any nonnegative integer. We can also use cardinality restrictions to specify upper and lower bounds:

```
[ a owl:Restriction;
  owl:onProperty :hasPlayer;
  owl:minCardinality 10]
```

and

```
[ a owl:Restriction;
  owl:onProperty :hasPlayer;
  owl:maxCardinality 2]
```

These specify the set of things that have at least 10 players and at most 2 players, respectively. Specifying that the `owl:cardinality` is restricted to n is the same saying that both the `owl:minCardinality` and `owl:maxCardinality` are restricted to the same value n. Cardinality refers to the number of *distinct* values a property has; it therefore interacts closely with the nonunique naming assumption and `owl:differentFrom`.

The semantics of cardinality restrictions are similar to those of other restrictions. If we can prove that a individual has exactly (respectively at least, at most) n distinct values for the property P, then it is a member of the corresponding owl:cardinality (respectively owl:minCardinality, owl:maxCardinality) restriction. So a rugby union team (with 17 players) and a soccer team (with 11) are both members of the restriction class with minimum cardinality 10; a bridge team (with two players) is not, though it is a member of the restriction class with max cardinality 2.

Similarly, if we assert that something is a member of an owl:cardinality restriction, then it must have exactly n distinct values for the property P. So if we define a baseball team to be a subclass of the restriction class with exact cardinality 9, we can conclude that a baseball team has exactly nine (distinct) players. Similar conclusions follow from restrictions on minimum and maximum cardinality. We will demonstrate the use of cardinality restrictions through a series of challenge problems based on the James Dean example.

Challenge 29   Rocky and Rimbaud continue their conversation.

> RIMBAUD: *Do you own any James Dean movies?*
> ROCKY: *They are the only ones I own.*
> RIMBAUD: *Then I guess you don't own very many movies! No more than three.*

Model these facts in OWL so that Rimbaud's conclusion follows from the OWL semantics.

SOLUTION

First we model Rocky's statement that he owns only James Dean movies. We will need a property called ownsMovie to indicate that someone owns a movie:

```
:ownsMovie a owl:ObjectProperty .
```

In OWL, we make general statements about an individual by asserting that the individual is a member of a restriction class. So we can say that Rocky owns only James Dean movies by using the owl:allValuesFrom restriction from Chapter 9:

```
:JamesDeanExclusive owl:equivalentClass
   [ a owl:Restriction ;
      owl:onProperty :ownsMovie ;
      owl:allValuesFrom :JamesDeanMovie] .
:Rocky a :JamesDeanExclusive .
```

Rocky is a member of the class JamesDeanExclusive, which is the class of things for which all the values of ownsMovie come from the class JamesDeanMovie.

How can we model Rimbaud's conclusion? We define the class of things that don't own many movies (where by "not many," we mean at most three) as follows:

```
:FewMovieOwner owl:equivalentClass
   [ a owl:Restriction ;
```

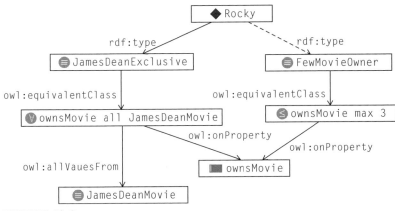

FIGURE 10-3

We asserted that Rocky is a `JamesDeanExclusive`; we infer that he owns only a few movies.

```
    onProperty :ownsMovie ;
    maxCardinality 3] .
```

Now Rimbaud's conclusion can be formulated as a triple:

```
:Rocky a :FewMovieOwner .
```

This triple can be inferred from the model because all the values of the property `ownsMovie` for Rocky come from the class `JamesDeanMovie`, and there are only three of them, and they are all distinct, so Rocky can own at most three movies. This inference is shown in Figure 10-3.

Challenge 30   Model this situation and conclusion in OWL.

> *RIMBAUD: How many movies do you own, then?*
> *ROCKY: Three.*
> *RIMBAUD: That's all of them; so you must own the one I saw last night,*
>   Rebel Without a Cause.

SOLUTION

We assert that Rocky owns exactly three movies by asserting that he is a member of an `owl:cardinality` restriction class for "the set of things that own exactly three movies":

```
:ThreeMovieOwner owl:equivalentClass
   [ a owl:Restriction ;
       owl:onProperty :ownsMovie ;
       owl:cardinality 3 ] .
:Rocky a :ThreeMovieOwner .
```

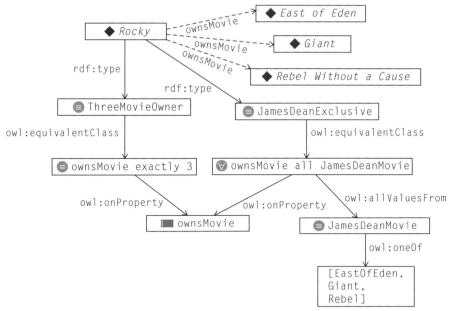

FIGURE 10-4

Rimbauld owns three movies, and he owns only James Dean movies, so he must own each of them.

Since Rocky owns exactly three distinct movies, and all of his movies are members of `JamesDeanMovie`, and there are just three different `JamesDeanMovies`, he must own each of them. In particular, we can infer

    :Rocky :ownsMovie :Rebel .

These assertions and inferences can be seen in Figure 10-4.

Small Cardinality Limits

OWL provides the facility to use any natural number as a cardinality. We have seen how this provides an inference engine with the information needed to determine membership in a class based on counting the number of distinct individuals that satisfy some condition. The particular restrictions of cardinalities to the small numbers 0 and 1 have special modeling utility.

minCardinality 1:   The restriction of the `minCardinality` to 1 indicates the set of individuals for which some for the specified property is required. The **Restriction** `onProperty ownsMovie minCardinality 1` explicitly specifies the set of individuals that own at least one movie.

maxCardinality 1: The restriction of `maxCardinalilty` to 1 specifies that a value is unique (but need not exist). The Restriction `onProperty ownsMovie maxCardinality 1` explicitly specifies the set of individuals who own at most one movie—in other words, they have limited themselves to a single movie.

minCardinality 0: The restriction of the `minCardinality` to 0 describes a set of individuals for which the presence of a value for the `onProperty` is optional. In the semantics of OWL, this is superfluous (since properties are always optional anyway), but the explicit assertion that something is optional can be useful for model readability. The Restriction `onProperty ownsMovie minCardinality 0` explicitly specifies the set of individuals for which owning a movie is optional.

maxCardinality 0: The restriction of the `maxCardinality` to 0 indicates the set of individuals for which no value for the specified property is allowed. The Restriction `onProperty ownsMovie maxCardinality 0` explicitly specifies the set of individuals that own no movies.

These four special cases of cardinality are closely related. `minCardinality 1` and `maxCardinality 0` form a partition of `minCardinality 0`; that is, `minCardinality 1` and `maxCardinality 0` are disjoint from one another, they are both subclasses of `minCardinality 0`, and together (`minCardinality 1` union `maxCardinality 0`) they make up all of `minCardinality 0` (which is equivalent to `owl:Thing`, the class of all individuals).

SET COMPLEMENT

The complement of a set is the set of all things not in that set. The same definition applies to Classes in OWL. The complement of a class is another class whose members are all the things not in the complemented class. Since a complement applies to a single class, we can define it using a single triple:

```
ex:ClassA owl:complementOf ex:ClassB .
```

Although set complements seem quite straightforward, they can be easily misused, and OWL (like any formal system) can be quite unforgiving in such situations.

For example, we might be tempted to say that minor league players are the complement of major league players (asserting that there are just these two types of players and that nobody can be both).

```
bb:MinorLeaguePlayer owl:complementOf bb:MajorLeaguePlayer .
```

From this description, all of the players who are not `bb:MajorLeaguePlayers` will be included in `bb:MinorLeaguePlayer`. However, the complement class includes everything that is not in the referred class, so in addition to hopeful rookies, the class `bb:MinorLeaguePlayer` includes managers, fans, and indeed anything else in the universe, like movies or planets.

To avoid such a situation, common practice is not to refer to complementary classes directly. Instead, it is common practice to combine complement with intersection.

```
bb:MinorLeaguePlayer owl:intersectionOf
    ([ a owl:Class ;
        owl:complementOf bb:MajorLeaguePlayer ]
    bb:Player ).
```

That is, a `MinorLeaguePlayer` is a **Player** who is not a `MajorLeaguePlayer`.

Thus, members of `bb:MinorLeaguePlayer` include only members of the class `bb:Player` but does not include players that are included in `bb:MajorLeague-Player`. This is much closer to the natural meaning suggested by the name. This definition makes use of a bnode to specify an anonymous class. There is no need to name the class that is the complement of `bb:MajorLeaguePlayer`, so it is specified anonymously using the bnode notation *"[a owl:Class ...]."*

Challenge 31   Rocky's friend Paul joins in the discussion.

> PAUL: *Are you talking about James Dean? I love him! I have all his movies.*
> RIMBAUD: *But you aren't obsessive, are you? I mean, you have other movies,*
>   *too, don't you?*
> ROCKY: *I'm not obsessive!*
> PAUL: *Of course, I have some movies that aren't James Dean movies.*
> ROCKY: *You must have at least four movies then!*

Model this situation and conclusion in OWL.

SOLUTION

For this challenge, we need to have an inverse for `ownsMovie`:

```
:ownedBy owl:inverseOf :ownsMovie .
```

We can define the class of all the movies that Paul owns as follows:

```
:PaulsMovie a owl:Class;
    owl:intersectionOf
        ([ a owl:Restriction;
            owl:onProperty :ownedBy;
            owl:hasValue :Paul]
            :Movie ) .
```

Paul says that he owns every James Dean movie—that is, every `JamesDeanMovie` is a `PaulsMovie` (but possibly not vice versa), so we assert

```
:JamesDeanMovie rdfs:subClassOf :PaulsMovie .
```

Paul claims to own other movies, too. We can express that by saying

```
:Paul a [ a owl:Restriction ;
          owl:onProperty :ownsMovie ;
          owl:someValuesFrom
            [ owl:complementOf :JamesDeanMovie]].
```

Let's look at this one in some detail.

```
[ owl:complementOf :JamesDeanMovie]
```

is an anonymous class (bnode) that includes everything that is not a James Dean movie.

```
[ a owl:Restriction ;
  owl:onProperty :ownsMovie ;
  owl:someValuesFrom [ owl:complementOf :JamesDeanMovie]]
```

is an anonymous class (bnode) of all the things that have some value for `ownsMovie` that isn't a James Dean movie. We claim that Paul is such a thing.

Finally, we define the class of people who own four or more movies, using `owl:minCardinality`.

```
:ManyMovieOwner
   owl:equivalentClass
     [ a owl:Restriction;
         owl:onProperty :ownsMovie;
         owl:minCardinality 4] .
```

Now, Paul owns all of James Dean's movies (all three of them) and at least one that isn't a James Dean movie. That makes (at least) four in all; so we can infer that *Paul* qualifies as a member of `ManyMovieOwner`.

```
:Paul rdf:type :ManyMovieOwner .
```

These assertions and conclusion can be seen in Figure 10-5.

DISJOINT SETS

We have seen how we can use `owl:complementOf` to describe the class that includes all the individuals that are not in some class. A related idea is that two sets have no individual in common. When this happens, we say that the sets are *disjoint*, and we represent this situation in OWL using `owl:disjointWith`, as follows:

```
:Man owl:disjointWith :Woman .
:Meat owl:disjointWith :Fruit .
:Fish owl:disjointWith :Fowl .
```

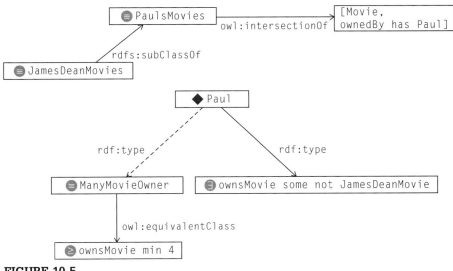

FIGURE 10-5

Paul owns every James Dean movie, and he owns some others, so he owns at least four movies.

For any members of disjoint classes, we can infer that they are `owl:different-From` one another—for instance, we might assert that

```
:Irene a :Woman .
:Ralph a :Man .
```

we can infer that

```
:Irene owl:differentFrom :Ralph .
```

This simple idea can have powerful ramifications when combined with other constructs in OWL, as we can see in the following challenge problems.

Challenge 32   Our moviegoers continue their conversation:

> PAUL: *I am a big movie fan. Not only do I own all the James Dean movies, but I also have movies with Judy Garland, Tom Cruise, Dame Judi Dench, and Antonio Banderas!*
>
> ROCKY: *You must own at least seven movies!*
>
> PAUL: *How do you know that?*
>
> ROCKY: *Because none of those people played in movies together!*

Model this situation and conclusion in OWL.

SOLUTION

How do we express, in OWL, that Paul owns a Judy Garland movie? We assert that Paul is a member of the class of things that own Judy Garland movies. Thus, the statements that Paul has made about the movies he owns can be modeled in OWL using an `owl:someValuesFrom` restriction for each one:

```
:Paul a [ a owl:Restriction ;
        owl:onProperty :ownsMovie ;
        owl:someValuesFrom :JudyGarlandMovie ] .
:Paul a [ a owl:Restriction ;
        owl:onProperty :ownsMovie ;
        owl:someValuesFrom :JudiDenchMovie ] .
:Paul a [ a owl:Restriction ;
        owl:onProperty :ownsMovie ;
        owl:someValuesFrom :TomCruiseMovie ] .
:Paul a [ a owl:Restriction ;
        owl:onProperty :ownsMovie ;
        owl:someValuesFrom :AntonioBanderasMovie ] .
```

We can define the set of people who own seven or more movies using `owl:minCardinality`:

```
:SevenMovieOwner a owl:Restriction ;
                 owl:onProperty ownsMovie ;
                 owl:minCardinality 7 .
```

How do we know that Paul is a member of this class? As Rocky points out in the dialogue, we don't know until we know that all the sets of movies he mentioned are disjoint. That is, we need to know

```
JamesDeanMovie owl:disjointWith JudyGarlandMovie .
JamesDeanMovie owl:disjointWith TomCruiseMovie .
JamesDeanMovie owl:disjointWith JudiDenchMovie .
JamesDeanMovie owl:disjointWith AntonioBanderasMovie .
JudyGarlandMovie owl:disjointWith TomCruiseMovie .
JudyGarlandMovie owl:disjointWith JudiDenchMovie .
JudyGarlandMovie owl:disjointWith AntonioBanderasMovie .
TomCruiseMovie owl:disjointWith JudiDenchMovie .
TomCruiseMovie owl:disjointWith AntonioBanderasMovie .
JudiDenchMovie owl:disjointWith AntonioBanderasMovie .
```

Now we know that Paul has three James Dean movies and at least one movie from each of the other actors named here. Furthermore, none of these movies appears twice, since all of the sets are disjoint. An inference engine can confirm that Rocky is justified in counting to seven movies, and

```
:Paul a :SevenMovieOwner .
```

FIGURE 10-6

Paul owns three James Dean movies (Figure 10-5), plus one each from other actors, making seven (or more) in total.

These assertions and inferences can be seen in Figure 10-6.

Notice how `owl:someValuesFrom` interacts with cardinality; each restriction of `someValuesFrom` guarantees the existence of one value for the specified property. When these values are known to be distinct, we can count (at least) one per `someValuesFrom` restriction.

Just as we had `owl:AllDifferent` as a way to specify that several individuals are mutually distinct, we could have something like `owl:AllDisjoint` to indicate that a set of classes are mutually disjoint. As it happens, the OWL standard did not include such a construct, though some proposals for extensions to OWL include such a facility.

PREREQUISITES REVISITED

We have already explored how prerequisites can be modeled in OWL using `owl:allValuesFrom`. At that point, we had a problem with the Open World Assumption—namely, how can we tell that all prerequisites have been satisfied if we have to assume that someone can come along and set new prerequisites at any time? We'll use prerequisites to demonstrate a number of ways we can close the world.

As a reminder from Chapter 9, we modeled the fact that something that has all its prerequisites satisfied (i.e., selected) is an `EnabledQuestion` as follows:

```
q:hasPrerequisite a owl:ObjectProperty .

[ a owl:Restriction ;
  owl:onProperty hasPrerequisite;
  owl:allValuesFrom q:SelectedAnswer ]
    rdfs:subClassOf q:EnabledQuestion .
```

If something satisfies the restriction (all its values are members of Selected-Answer), then it is also a member of EnabledQuestion.

No Prerequisites

Let's start with the simple situation in which we know that there are no prerequisites at all. If something has no prerequisites, then there are no conditions to be checked, so it should be an EnabledQuestion. How can we know that something has no prerequisites?

We can assert the number of distinct values that an individual has for some property by using the cardinality restrictions. In particular, if we say that

```
c:WhatProblem a [ a owl:Restriction ;
                  owl:onProperty q:hasPrerequisite ;
                  owl:cardinality 0 ] .
```

Then we know that there are no triples of the form

```
c:WhatProblem q:hasPrerequisite ? .
```

That is, WhatProblem has no prerequisites. Therefore it satisfies the restriction

```
c:WhatProblem a [ a owl:Restriction ;
                  owl:onProperty hasPrerequisite;
                  owl:allValuesFrom q:SelectedAnswer ].
```

hence

```
c:WhatProblem a q:EnabledQuestion .
```

The interpretation of owl:allValuesFrom in such a situation—that is, when we know that there are no values from the indicated class (or even no values at all!) can be a bit confusing. If there are no values at all, how can all of them be members of some class? The correct way to think about owl:allValuesFrom is as something that sets prerequisites, regardless of the name of the restricted property. Let's take a simple example: If a person has no children, then all of their children are boys.

First we define the set of people all of whose children are boys, with an allValuesFrom restriction:

```
:ParentOfBoysOnly owl:equivalentClass
  [ a owl:Restriction ;
      owl:onProperty :hasChild ;
      owl:allValuesFrom :Boy ] .
```

How do we decide about membership in this class? Each triple with predicate hasChild places a prerequisite for its subject to be a member of the class. So the triple

```
:ElizabethII :hasChild :Charles .
```

places a prerequisite for `ElizabethII` to be a member of `ParentOfBoysOnly`—namely, that `Charles` must be a `Boy`. In this case, the prerequisite is satisfied.

But in order for `ElizabethII` to be a member of `ParentOfBoysOnly`, all prerequisites must be satisfied. In particular, if we assert that

```
:ElizabethII :hasChild :Anne .
```

we have a prerequisite that isn't satisfied, so we won't be able to infer that `ElizabethII` is a member of `ParentOfBoysOnly`.

How can we ever know in the face of the Open World Assumption that all prerequisites will be satisfied? One way is if we assert that there are none. For instance, Elizabeth's famous ancestor, `ElizabethI`, was famous for having died childless. We can assert this in OWL by asserting her membership in a restriction class of `cardinality 0`, thus:

```
:ElizabethI a [ a owl:Restriction ;
               owl:onProperty :hasChild ;
               owl:cardinality 0].
```

Now we know that there are no prerequisites on `ElizabethI`, so we can infer

```
:ElizabethI a :ParentOfBoysOnly .
```

Many people find this result counterintuitive—that someone with no children would have all of their children be boys. This conclusion is much more intuitive if you think of `owl:allValuesFrom` as working with prerequisites; it is intuitive to say that something that has no prerequisites is satisfied. In the semantics of OWL, this is the appropriate interpretation of `owl:allValuesFrom`.

Counting Prerequisites

Another way to determine that something has satisfied all of its prerequisites is to count how many of them there are. Just as we have done with counting James Dean movies, we can count prerequisites. Suppose we know that something has exactly one prerequisite:

```
TvSymptom a [ a owl:Restriction ;
              owl:onProperty hasPrerequisite ;
              owl:cardinality 1 ] .
```

and that, furthermore, we actually know one prerequisite, and its type:

```
TvSymptom q: hasPrerequisite d:STV .

d:STV a q:SelectedAnswer .
```

We know that one of the prerequisites is a member of the class `q:Selected-Answer`. We also know that there aren't any others (since the cardinality says there is just one of them). So we know that all of the prerequisites are members of the class `q:SelectedAnswer`:

```
c:TVSymptom a [ a owl:Restriction ;
                owl:onProperty hasPrerequisite ;
                owl:allValuesFrom q:SelectedAnswer ] .
```

Just as in the James Dean examples, we can make inferences from larger counts if we know that all the entities are different. If we know, for example, that

```
c:TVTurnedOn a [ a owl:Restriction ;
                 owl:onProperty hasPrerequisite ;
                 owl:cardinality 2 ] .

c:TVTurnedOn q:hasPrerequisite c:TVSnothing .
c:TVTurnedOn q:hasPrerequisite c:STVSnosound .
c:TVSnothing owl:differentFrom c:STVSnosound .

c:TVSnothing a q:SelectedAnswer .
c:STVSnosound a q:SelectedAnswer .
```

we can infer that

```
c:TVTurnedOn a [ a owl:Restriction ;
                 owl:onProperty hasPrerequisite ;
                 owl:allValuesFrom q:SelectedAnswer ] .
```

since there are only two prerequisites, and we know which two they are.

Guarantees of Existence

The issue of prerequisites revealed a subtlety in the interpretation of `owl:allValuesFrom`—namely, that the membership of an individual `A` in an `allValuesFrom` restriction on property P does not guarantee that any triple of the form

```
A P ? .
```

exists at all. What should be the corresponding situation in the case of `someValuesFrom`? That is, if we say that an individual `A` is a member of a restriction `onProperty` P `someValuesFrom` another class `C`, should we insist that there is some triple of this form?

```
A P ? .
```

The interpretation of `someValuesFrom` is that we do know that there is a pair of triples of the form

```
A P X .
X rdf:type C .
```

Evidently, if we have both of these triples, then we certainly have a triple of the desired form. That is, in contrast to `allValuesFrom`, `someValuesFrom` does guarantee that some value is given for the specified property.

The case for `hasValue` is even more evident than that for `someValuesFrom` Not only does `hasValue` guarantee that there is such a triple, but it even specifies exactly what it is. That is, if A is a member of the restriction `onProperty P hasValue X`, we can infer the triple

    A P X .

CONTRADICTIONS

Challenge 33   Model this situation and conclusion in OWL.

> ROCKY: *You're a Judy Garland fan? I have a couple of her movies, too!*
> RIMBAUD: *Wait a minute! That can't be right! You said that you own only James Dean movies, and now you say you have a Judy Garland movie. They weren't in any movie together!*

SOLUTION

This solution requires us to introduce a new aspect of inferencing in OWL. The simplest form of inferencing we have seen was where we inferred new triples based on asserted ones. With the more advanced notions beyond RDFS-Plus, we saw how some inferences could not themselves be represented as triples but could result in new triples when combined with other assertions. But in this example, there are no new triples to be inferred at all.

Rimbaud does not make any new assertions about Rocky. Instead, he brings into question the validity of something that Rocky has asserted. In OWL terms, we say that Rimbaud has found a *contradiction* in what Rocky has said.

In this case, the contradiction arose because Rocky has made the following statements:

```
:JamesDeanExclusive owl:equivalentClass
        [ a owl:Restriction ;
            owl:onProperty :ownsMovie ;
            owl:allValuesFrom :JamesDeanMovie] .

:Rocky a :JamesDeanExclusive .

:Rocky a [ a owl:Restriction ;
            owl:onProperty :ownsMovie ;
            owl:someValuesFrom :JudyGarlandMovie] .

:JudyGarlandMovie owl:disjointWith :JamesDeanMovie .
```

The `owl:someValuesFrom` restriction guarantees that Rocky owns some Judy Garland movie (though we don't know which one), and the `owl:allValuesFrom` restriction tells us that this movie must also be a James Dean movie. Although such a movie would have undoubtedly been very popular, unfortunately we also know from the `owl:disjointWith` triple that there is no such movie; somewhere in this model there is a contradiction.

These assertions are shown in Figure 10-7; no inferences are shown, since the model contains a contradiction.

The OWL semantics can tell us that there is a contradiction in this example, but it cannot tell us which assertion is wrong. The validity of an assertion has nothing to do with the OWL standard or its semantics; it has to do with the domain that is being modeled. Did Rocky lie about owning only James Dean movies? Or is he lying now about owning Judy Garland movies? Or, perhaps we are mistaken, and there is a Judy Garland/James Dean collaboration out there that nobody knows about (that is, we were mistaken when we said that these two classes were disjoint). There is no way to know which of these statements is incorrect. But OWL can tell us that their combination results in a contradiction.

The notion of contradiction gets to the heart of what we mean by modeling. A model is a description of the world and can be mistaken; that is, the model may not actually correspond to the actual state of affairs. The tools that surround OWL models help us to determine the nature of our models. If they are logically inconsistent, then we know that either our model is defective or our understanding of how it relates to the world is mistaken.

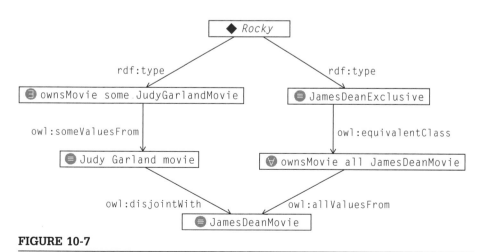

FIGURE 10-7

All of Rocky's films are James Dean films, but some of them are Judy Garland films.

UNSATISFIABLE CLASSES

A contradiction arises when the assertions that have been made simply cannot all be true. There is a fundamental disagreement in the asserted statements. A similar situation can arise when we define a class in an inconsistent way. A slight variation on the previous example shows how this can happen. First, suppose we define the class of people who own Judy Garland movies that Rocky claims to be a member of:

```
:JudyGarlandMovieOwner owl:equivalentClass
    [ a owl:Restriction ;
        owl:onProperty :ownsMovie ;
        owl:someValuesFrom :JudyGarlandMovie] .
```

Now, instead of claiming that Rocky is a member of both this class and `James-DeanExclusive`, let's define the class of such people:

```
:JDJG owl:intersectionOf
    ( :JudyGarlandMovieOwner :JamesDeanExclusive ) .
```

Rocky has claimed to be a member of this class; this claim led to a contradiction.

We can define this class without asserting that Rocky is a member of it. Although this does not lead to a contradiction, the same argument that showed that Rocky cannot (consistently) be a member of this class can be used to show that *nothing* can be a member of this class, or that this class is empty. When we can prove that a class is empty, we say that the class itself is *unsatisfiable*. Although a contradiction indicates that some statement in the model is in conflict with others, an unsatisfiable class simply means that there can be no individuals who are members of that class. Of course, if we go on to assert that some individual is a member of an unsatisfiable class (as Rocky did, when he claimed to be a member of *JDJG*), and then the model contains a contradiction.

Figure 10-8 shows these assertions and the conclusions that follow. *JDJG* is a subclass of both `JudyGarlandMovieOwner` and `JamesDeanExclusive`, since it is defined as the intersection of these two classes. But it is also inferred to be subclass of `owl:Nothing`. This indicates in OWL that it can have no members, since `owl:Nothing` is the class that corresponds to the empty set.

Propagation of Unsatisfiable Classes

Once a model contains an unsatisfiable class, it is easy for other class definitions to be unsatisfiable as well. Here are a few of the simpler ways in which this can happen:

subclass: A subclass of an unsatisfiable class is itself unsatisfiable. If the subclass could (without contradiction) have an individual member, then so could the superclass.

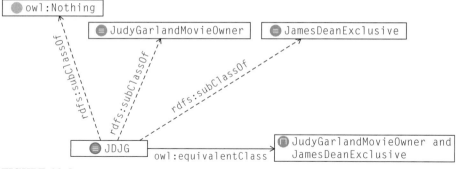

FIGURE 10-8

JDJG is the intersection of people who only own James Dean movies and people who own Judy Garland movies.

someValuesFrom: A restriction (on any property) with `owl:someValuesFrom` an unsatisfiable class is itself unsatisfiable, since `owl:someValuesFrom` requires that there be some value that the property can indicate.

domain and range: If a property has an unsatisfiable `domain` or `range`, then the property becomes basically unusable. Any `someValuesFrom` restriction on that property is unsatisfiable. If any triple is asserted using that property as predicate, then the model results in a contradiction.

intersection of disjoints: The `owl:intersectionOf` two disjoint classes is unsatisfiable. The intersection of any class with an unsatisfiable class is unsatisfiable.

Some operations do not propagate unsatisfiable classes; the union of an unsatisfiable class and another class can be satisfiable. A restriction `owl:allValuesFrom` an unsatisfiable class can still be satisfiable (but none of its members can have any value for the property specified by `owl:onProperty` in the restriction).

These rules seem intuitive enough in isolation; their usefulness in modeling comes in during analysis of the results of an inference engine. Many inference engines will report on unsatisfiable classes, but in the face of several such classes, it can be difficult to tell just what is going on. Although some engines have tools to assist the modeler in tracking this, the use of these tools requires some understanding of how unsatisfiable classes can arise. This short list is not exhaustive, but it covers most of the common cases.

INFERRING CLASS RELATIONSHIPS

In the previous discussion, most of the inferences we drew were about individuals: Wenger is an Analyst, Jupiter is a Solar Planet, Kaneda is a Star Player, or Shakespeare married Anne Hathaway. In this chapter, we have begun to draw conclusions about classes—for example, *JDJG* is unsatisfiable. OWL allows us to draw a wide range of conclusions about classes. We can, in some circumstances, infer that one class is a subclass of another or that a class is the domain (or range) of a property. There are countless possibilities for how this can happen, but there are a few common patterns that are worth calling out. We'll return to our descriptions of baseball teams for examples:

Intersection and subclass: The intersection of two (or more) classes is a subclass of each intersected class. If `AllStarBaseballTeam` is the intersection of `AllStarTeam` and `BaseballTeam`, then it is also `rdfs:subClassOf` each of those classes.

Union and subclass: The union of two (or more) classes is a superclass of each united class. If `JBallTeam` is the union of `PacificLeagueTeam` and `CentralLeagueTeam`, then `PacificLeagueTeam` and `CentralLeagueTeam` are both `rdfs:subClassOf JBallTeam`.

Complement and subclass: Complement reverses the order of subclass. For example, if `AllStarBaseballTeam` is a subclass of `BaseballTeam`, then the complement of `BaseballTeam` is a subclass of the complement of `AllStarBaseballTeam`.

Subclass propagation through restriction: The subclass relationships propagate through restrictions. If `AllStarBaseballTeam` is a subclass of `BaseballTeam`, then the restriction (on any property—say, `playsFor`) `owl:allValuesFrom AllStarBaseballTeam` is a subclass of the restriction (on the same property `playsFor`) `owl:allValuesFrom BaseballTeam`. If we call the first restriction `AllStarBaseballPlayer` and the second restriction `BaseballPlayer` (both are reasonable names for these restrictions), then this pattern says that `AllStarBaseballPlayer` is a subclass of `BaseballPlayer`. The same propagation principle holds for any property and also for `owl:someValuesFrom`; If `AllStarBaseballTeam` is a subclass of `BaseballTeam`, then the restriction on property `playsFor` some values from `AllStarBaseballTeam` is a subclass of the restriction on property `playsFor` some values from `BaseballTeam`.

hasValue, someValuesFrom, and subClassOf: Propagation for `owl:hasValue` works a bit differently from the way it works for `owl:allValuesFrom` or `owl:someValuesFrom`, since `owl:hasValue` refers to an individual, not a class. Suppose that the individual `TokyoGiants` is a member of class `BaseballTeam`; the restriction on property `playsFor owl:hasValue TokyoGiants` is a subclass of the restriction on property `playsFor owl:someValuesFrom BaseballTeam`.

Relative cardinalities: Subclass relations between cardinality restrictions arise from the usual rules of arithmetic on whole numbers. For example, if a `ViableBaseballTeam` must have at least nine players on its roster (`owl:minCardinality 9`), and a `FullBaseballTeam` has exactly 10 players on the roster (`owl:cardinality 10`), then `FullBaseballTeam` is a subclass of `ViableBaseballTeam`.

owl:someValuesFrom **and** *owl:minCardinality:* If we say that something has some value from a particular class, then we can infer that it has at least one such value. So if `BaseballTeam` has some pitcher (i.e., `BaseballTeam` is a subclass of the restriction `owl:onProperty hasPlayer owl:someValuesFrom Pitcher`), we can infer that it has at least one pitcher (i.e., `BaseballTeam` is a subclass of the restriction `owl:onProperty hasPlayer owl:minCardinality 1`). Note that the same conclusion does not hold for `owl:allValuesFrom`; in short, `someValuesFrom` guarantees that there is some value; `allValuesFrom` makes no such guarantee.

> The ability in OWL to infer class relationships is a severe departure from Object Oriented modeling. In OO modeling, the class structure forms the backbone of the model's organization. All instances are created as members of some class, and their behavior is specified by the class structure. Changes to the class structure have far-reaching impact on the behavior of the system. In OWL, it is possible for the class structure to change as more information is learned about classes or individuals.
>
> These aspects of OWL are not the result of whimsical decisions on the part of the OWL designers; they are a direct consequences of the basic assumptions about the web—that is, the AAA slogan, the Open World nature of the web, and the fact that names on the web are not unique. A strict data model (like an object model) is useful when there is top-down governance of the system (as is the case when building a software system), but it doesn't work in an open, free system like the Web. Our understanding of the structure of knowledge will change as we discover more things—we cannot escape that! OWL at least provides a consistent and systematic way to understand those changes.

The logic underlying OWL goes beyond these propagation rules and encompasses inferences about subclasses regarding cardinalities. The technical details of the logic are beyond the scope of this book. In short, any class relationship that can be proven to hold, based on the semantics of restrictions, unions, intersections, and so on, will be inferred. The propagation patterns presented here don't cover all the possible class relationship inferences, but they are the most common patterns that appear in semantic models.

The ability in OWL to infer class relationships enables a style of modeling in which subclass relationships are rarely asserted directly. Instead, relationships between classes are described in terms of unions, intersections, complements and restrictions, and the inference engine determines the class structure. If more information is learned about a particular class or individual, then more class structure can be inferred. Subclass relationships are asserted only in that the members of one class are included in another.

Table 10-1 Overview of Entities in the Baseball Model

AllStarBaseballPlayer	≡ playsFor some AllStarBaseballTeam
AllStarBaseballTeam	≡ BaseballTeam ∩ AllStarTeam
AllStarPlayer	≡ playsFor some AllStarTeam
AllStarTeam	⊆ Employs some AllStarPlayer
BaseballPlayer	≡ playsFor some BaseballTeam
BaseballTeam	⊆ employs some BaseballPlayer
JballTeam	≡ PacificLeagueTeam ∪ CentralLeagueTeam ⊆ BaseballTeam
CarpPlayer	≡ playsFor hasValue Carp (the Carp is the name of the baseball team from Hiroshima)
CentralLeagueTeam	≡ oneOf Carp, Giants, BayStars, Tigers, Dragons, Swallows
PacificLeagueTeam	≡ oneOf Lions, Hawks, Fighters, BlueWave, Buffaloes, Marines
Player	domain of playsFor
Team	range of playsFor
playsFor	Inverse of employs

The baseball model demonstrates this principle at work-we summarize the statements about baseball players and their teams in Table 10-1.

In Table 10-1, we write ≡ if the class in the left column is defined as equivalent to the expression in the right column, and ⊆ if the class is a subclass of the expression in the right column. Notice that the only direct subclass assertion (i.e., one class is a subclass of another) is for JBallTeam, which is asserted to be a subclass of BaseballTeam. All other assertions in the model either refer to logical combinations (intersections or unions) or to restrictions. Thus, the class tree as asserted is shown in Figure 10-9.

We can infer a number of subclass relationships from the definitions of the model in Table 10-1 and the subclass inferencing patterns we have seen.

- Since AllStarBaseballTeam is the intersection of BaseballTeam and AllStarTeam, then AllStarBaseballTeam is a subclass of BaseballTeam and AllStarTeam.

- Both AllStarBaseballPlayer and AllStarPlayer are someValuesFrom restrictions on the same property, playsFor, referencing AllStarBaseballTeam and AllStarTeam, respectively. The fact that AllStarBaseballTeam is a subclass of AllStarPlayer can be propagated, so we can infer that

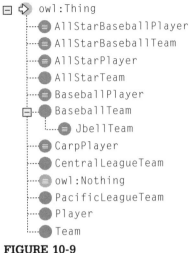

FIGURE 10-9

Class tree for the baseball ontology, as asserted.

AllStarBaseballPlayer is a subclass of AllStarPlayer. **Similar reasoning allows us to infer that** AllStarBaseballPlayer **is a subclass of** BaseballPlayer.

- Since JBallTeam **is the union of** PacificLeagueTeam **and** CentralLeague-Team, **we can conclude that** PacificLeagueTeam **and** CentralLeagueTeam **are subclasses of** JBallTeam.

- Since the Hiroshima Carp is a CentralLeague **team, it is also a** JBallTeam **and thus a** BaseballTeam. **A** CarpPlayer **is a** hasValue **restriction on the Carp; thus, we can infer that** CarpPlayer **is a subclass of** BaseballPlayer.

- The domain of playsFor **is also used to make class inferences. Since** All-StarPlayer **is equivalent to the** someValuesFrom **restriction** onProperty playsFor, **any individual member of** AllStarPlayer playsFor **some team. But the domain of** playsFor **is Player, so that individual must also be a Player. We have just shown that any** AllStarPlayer **must be a Player; thus,** AllStarPlayer **is a subclass of Player.**

- Even the range information gets into the act; since an AllStarTeam *employs* some AllStarPlayer, **and since employs is the inverse of** playsFor, **that means that some person** playsFor **any** AllStarTeam. **But the range of** playsFor **is Team, so** AllStarTeam **must be a team, as well.**

We can see the inferred class structure in Figure 10-10. Notice that every class is involved in some class inferencing pattern so that in contrast to the asserted model, the inferred model has considerable depth to its class tree.

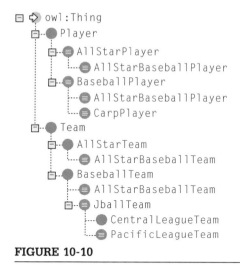

FIGURE 10-10

Inferred structure of the Baseball model.

REASONING WITH INDIVIDUALS AND WITH CLASSES

From an RDF perspective, inferencing about individuals and inferencing about classes is very similar. In both cases, new triples are added to the model based on the triples that were asserted. From a modeling perspective, the two kinds of reasoning are very different. One of them draws specific conclusions about individuals in a data stream, while the other draws general conclusions about classes of individuals. These two kinds of reasoning are sometimes called A-box reasoning (for individuals) and T-box reasoning (for classes). The curious names A-box and T-box are historical and no longer have any relevance.

The utility of reasoning about individuals in a Semantic Web context is clear, and we have seen a number of examples of it throughout this book. We inferred things about the wife of Shakespeare, which movies belong to which people, and what terms are broader than others. All of these things are examples of reasoning about an individual. Information specified in one information source is transformed according to a model for use in another context. Mappings from one context to the next are specified using constructs like `rdfs:subClassOf`, `rdfs:subPropertyOf`, and various `owl:Restrictions`. Data can then be transformed and processed according to these models and the inferences specified in the RDFS and OWL standards for each of them.

The utility of reasoning about classes is more subtle. It can take place in the absence of any data at all! Class reasoning determines the relationships between classes of individuals. It determines how data are related in general. In advance of seeing any data about the Pacific League, we can determine that any team in that league is a baseball team. There is no need to process all the particular teams, or indeed any of them. We can guarantee that this is the case. Even if new teams join the league, we know that this will still be true. In this sense, class reasoning is similar to a compilation of the model. Whereas individual reasoning processes particular data items as input, Class reasoning determines general relationships among data and records those relationships with `rdfs:subClassOf`, `rdfs:subPropertyOf`, `rdfs:domain`, or `rdfs:range`. Once these general relationships have been inferred, processing of individual data can be done much more easily.

When we use individual and class reasoning together in a single system, we have a powerful system that smoothly integrates general reasoning with specific data transformations. This allows us to smoothly manage information based on whatever information we come across, generic or specific.

SUMMARY

At each level of our exposition of the Semantic Web languages from RDF to RDFS to the various levels of OWL, we have introduced new notions of how to understand a model. For RDF, the fundamental aspect of the model had to do with data sharing and federation. RDF answers the question "How do I get all the information I know about a single thing in one place?" For RDFS, we introduced the notion of inference, answering the question "Given that I know certain things about my data, what else can I figure out?" RDFS-Plus and the basic use of OWL gave us more comprehensive capabilities to infer new information from old. As we move on to the advanced features OWL, we are still working within the paradigm of inferencing as the source of meaning of our models, but we expand the sort of inferencing we can make to include inferences not just about our data but also about the model itself.

Up to this point, we could, for the most part, ignore the ramifications of the Open World Assumption of the Semantic Web. With the advanced constructs of OWL, where we can draw conclusions based on arguments of enumeration and elimination (as well as arguments based on properties and types, as we did with RDFS and RDFS-Plus), the impact of the open world becomes more apparent.

Armed with the concepts and constructs OWL from this chapter, we are now in a position to examine some more comprehensive OWL models. We can see how a modeler can use the constructs of OWL to describe how data from different sources will be federated on the Semantic Web. Just as we saw for RDFS-Plus, a model can mediate information from sources that have not yet been examined. Advanced OWL provides more powerful and complete ways to make this happen.

Fundamental Concepts

The following fundamental concepts were introduced in this chapter:

owl:unionOf, *owl:intersectionOf*, *owl:complementOf*—Basic set operations applied to classes. Each of these is used to create a new class, based on the specified set operation applied to one or more defined classes.

Open World Assumption—This idea was introduced in Chapter 1, but strategies for closing the world for certain purposes were introduced here.

owl:oneOf—Specifies that a class consists just of the listed members

owl:differentFrom—Specifies that one individual is not owl:sameAs another. This is particularly useful when making counting arguments.

owl:disjointWith—Specifies that two classes cannot share a member. This is often used as a sort of wholesale version of owl:differentFrom.

owl:cardinality, *owl:minCardinality*, *owl:maxCardinality*—Cardinality specifies information about the number of distinct values for some property. Combined with owl:oneOf, owl:differentFrom, owl:disjointWith, and so on, it can be the basis of inferences based on counting the number of values for a property.

Contradiction—With the advanced constructs of OWL, it is possible for a model to express a contradiction—that is, for a model to be logically inconsistent.

Satisfiability (unsatisfiability)—With the advanced constructs of OWL, it is possible to infer that a class can have no members, so such a class is *unsatisfiable*.

Using OWL in the Wild

11

OWL provides a wide variety of modeling capabilities for relating information in flexible and powerful ways. We have seen a number of examples of how these constructs can be combined to represent complex relationships among various data sources. In this chapter, we delve into two detailed examples of how OWL can be used in real-world modeling situations.

Our examples feature applications from two government ontologies: one for modeling enterprise architectures and one in the life sciences. In both cases, the semantic model provides a set of reference concepts to be used as a basis for other work. In the first case, the model provides guidance for a description of the enterprise architecture of a government agency. The model has to mediate the simultaneous challenges of providing centralized advice for the development and maintenance of an enterprise architecture (after all, this is the government), while allowing a degree of autonomy for the agencies. We will see how a combination of RDF and OWL can be used to satisfy these requirements. In the life sciences case, the model provides a central repository for a controlled vocabulary. In this case, the challenge is to build and maintain a model that can serve the needs of a widely differentiated community, while still providing some degree of unity in their operation. When you read this chapter, you will not learn a lot about enterprise architecture or cancer research.

This chapter is not about solving the problems essential to these fields but rather about how they can use Semantic Web modeling to bring the advantages of a Web solution to their practice. For example, the value of explicit, executable enterprise architecture is controversial in many circles; we will not resolve this issue here. Once you accept (as the U.S. government has) that executable enterprise architecture is valuable, there still remains the problem of how hundreds of semiautonomous agencies working in a federated way can achieve the value of a distributed representation of their architecture. Allowing each agency the autonomy it needs, while respecting the central commonality required by participation in a single government, is a key challenge to instituting an executable federal enterprise architecture.

In contrast to an executable enterprise architecture, the value of cancer research is not usually contested. But this field also has requirements having to do with distribution of information and work. Each research team around the world has its own approach and methodology for pursuing its research. How can each team have the autonomy it needs to make its advances yet still participate in a worldwide community so that efforts from various teams can be used synergistically? The Semantic Web is about enabling the network effect in these efforts. The purpose of the models described here is to achieve an effective balance between federation (commonality) and autonomy (variability).

In both of these cases, we find once again that a little bit of OWL goes a long way. Most of the value in the federal enterprise architecture case comes from the use of RDF to describe how a centralized model can be extended by multiple agencies. But in addition to the use of RDF to extend the model, there are some constraints on the enterprise architecture that can be described using a little bit of OWL. There is no need for elaborate recombining models, only a handful of modeling patterns are used again and again. In the case of the cancer research ontology, a centralized model has been created in which OWL is used to describe how the various concepts related to research in the genetic basis of cancer are related to one another. These definitions, maintained in an ongoing effort by the U.S. National Cancer Institute, provide a common reference point for research teams from around the world to coordinate their results.

THE FEDERAL ENTERPRISE ARCHITECTURE REFERENCE MODEL ONTOLOGY

The federal government in the United States determined that some coherence was necessary among numerous government agencies in terms of information systems, their form, and their content. Toward this end, the government instituted an ongoing effort called the Federal Enterprise Architecture. The idea of an Enterprise Architecture is that it should be possible to describe, in a coherent, formal and machine-readable way, the information systems, components, and information content of a government agency. Even once the agencies represent their enterprise architecture in such a way, there is no guarantee that the decisions made by various agencies will be consistent. For this reason, the government defined the Federal Enterprise Architecture Reference Model (FEA-RM). The idea behind a reference model is that it is not an enterprise architecture itself but is a starting point for someone who plans to design an enterprise architecture. If every agency uses the same reference model as a starting point for its own enterprise architecture, then the hope is that we can guarantee, or at least encourage, some degree of consistency among the architectures of the various agencies.

The first edition of the Federal Enterprise Architecture was delivered as a series of documents written in natural language with an assortment of diagrams. Although the documents were very well organized, it was still possible for an enterprise architect in any particular agency to simply pay lip service to the federal reference model by "spinning" a story about why a nonconformant model is conformant to the reference model. It was felt that a more effective way to deliver the model would be in a formal, machine-readable (and, as far as possible, automatically verifiable) form.

REFERENCE MODELS AND COMPOSABILITY

Toward this end, the U.S. government sponsored a project to cast the FEA-RM into OWL (FEARMO). The FEARMO project chose RDF as the data modeling language to support the composability that is required by a reference model. The reference model itself is represented as an RDF graph; each agency customization is represented as a set of triples, which is merged with this graph. This ensures that each agency has a core structure (based on the FEA-RM) on which they all agree, but at the same time, each agency can add its own extra structure as it sees fit. For example, consider the fragment of the FEARMO shown in Figure 11-1.

The FEA-RM defines a business area called Management of Government Resources. In the original FEA document, components in the model are said

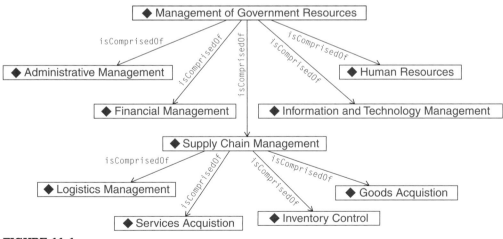

FIGURE 11-1

Sample business areas from the FEARMO.

to "comprise" one another or to be "comprised of" one another. Figure 11-1 shows that this business area is comprised of five components. Components at this level are called *Lines of Business*. The line called `SupplyChainManagement` consists of four other components, called subfunctions.

The RDF representation of the FEARMO followed the modularity of the textual FEA-RM by defining a number of distinct namespaces for the various parts of the FEA-RM. Although these namespaces are used consistently in the published models, we will take some liberties for the sake of simplicity of diagrams and triples in this description by leaving out the particulars of the namespaces.

An agency can extend the FEA-RM by adding new lines of business in a business area, or new subfunctions to a line of business. Figure 11-2 shows such an extension, in which an agency has added an extra subfunction called `Fleet-Management` to the `SupplyChainManagement` line of business. This extension is expressed with the single triple:

```
:SupplyChainManagement :isComprisedOf :FleetManagement.
```

So far, the FEARMO has not used any feature of OWL at all, only basic RDF. Even at this level, the model provides a valuable service in that it expresses how an agency can extend the model, and it provides a compact way for the agency to express just its extensions.

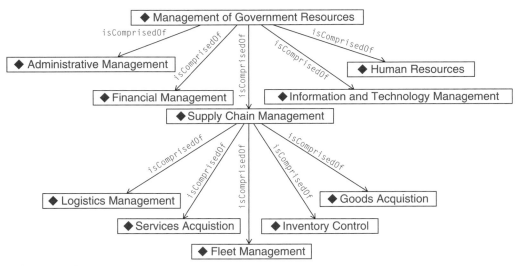

FIGURE 11-2

An agency extension to Figure 11-1. This agency has an additional subfunction of `SupplyChainManagement` for `FleetManagement`.

RESOLVING AMBIGUITY IN THE MODEL: SETS VERSUS INDIVIDUALS

The bulk of the FEA-RM is made up of tree structures of this sort, in which a number of components are described as consisting of other components. There are four sections to the FEA-RM: the Performance Reference Model, the Business Reference Model (of which a small excerpt was shown in Figure 11-1), the Service Component Reference Model, and the Technology Reference Model.

The original FEA-RM was expressed in English. One of the challenges of recasting an informal model (expressed in natural language) into a formal model (e.g., expressed in OWL) is sorting out the ambiguities in the informal model. One recurring source of ambiguity in the FEA-RM is the distinction between sets of components and components. For example, in Figure 11-1, should we view `SupplyChainManagement` as a set of four subfunctions, or should we see it as a component in its own right, with properties of its own (e.g., a responsible party or a budget line item)? Both of these viewpoints are viable and useful in the model. How do we deal with this?

In the FEARMO, this ambiguity is dealt with by noticing that in a graph like the one in Figure 11-1, we can view every node as a component but still acknowledge that there is utility in explicitly naming "the set of all things that `ManagementOfGovernmentResources` *is comprised of.*" Fortunately, it is a simple matter to express such a class using a `hasValue` restriction, as shown in Figure 11-3. We need to define an inverse for `isComprisedOf` to make the restriction; `comprises` is an obvious name for this property.

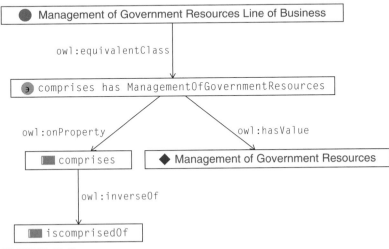

FIGURE 11-3

OWL definition of "the set of all things that `ManagementOfGovernmentResources` is comprised of."

This pattern should be familiar by now; we saw similar uses of `hasValue` in Chapter 9 (pages 202, 204), where we defined "The children of `Shakespeare`" and "the terms narrower than `Milk`." The `hasValue` restriction gives us a simple way to move from an individual (like `ManagementOfGovernmentResources`, `Milk`, or `Shakespeare`) to the set of individuals related to it by some given property.

When we combine Figures 11-2 and 11-3 and show the inferences entailed by OWL, we get the set of triple shown in Figure 11-4. The `owl:hasValue` restriction ensures that the members of the class `LOB_ManagementOfGovernment-Resources` are exactly the individuals that comprise the line of business `ManagementOfGovernmentResources`. Since these relationships are inferred, they will be maintained even when new members of the class `ManagementOfGovern-mentResources` are asserted, or if we learn of a new subfunction that comprises `ManagementOfGovernmentResources`.

There are ample opportunities in the FEARMO to use this pattern; in fact, at each point in any of the FEA-RM trees, we can refer to the set of components of which some other component is comprised. Since the FEARMO is intended to be a reference model, any of these sets are likely to be used in some agency extension. The FEARMO therefore includes definitions like the one shown in Figure 11-3 for every intermediate node in any tree. (This design

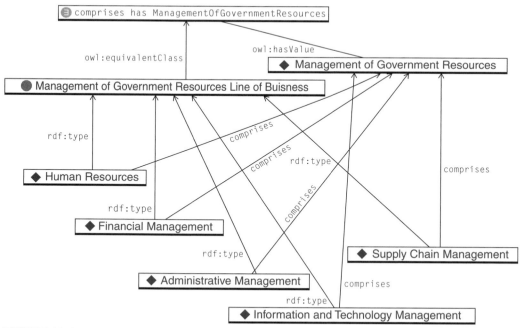

FIGURE 11-4

After inferencing. The members of the class `LOB_ManagementOfGovernmentResources` are exactly the individuals that comprise `ManagementOfGovernmentResources`.

pattern is a special case of the relationship transfer pattern we saw previously.) In this case, the pattern transfers a relationship to some individual (in this example, the relationship `comprises` for `ManagementOfGovernmentResources`) to the `rdf:type` relation for a specified class (in this example, `LOB_ManagementOf-GovernmentResources`). This particular use of the relationship transfer pattern is so specific and pervasive that we give it its own name. Since it defines a class whose membership tracks a property of an individual, we call it the *Class-Individual Mirror* pattern.

CONSTRAINTS BETWEEN MODELS

The FEA-RM describes several layers of components in the four reference models: for Business, Performance, Service Components, and Technology. This is in itself a remarkable undertaking, since these models identify hundreds of specific entities that can play a role in the enterprise architecture of an agency. But the FEA-RM goes even further to describe constraints between these models.

For example, one level of the Performance Reference Model describes a number of Measurement Categories. Instead of specifying all the things that each measurement category is comprised of (as we saw for the Business Reference Model in Figure 11-1), for certain measurement categories, the Performance Reference Model stipulates that they are comprised of things that come from the Business Reference Model.

Let's look at a specific example. The Performance Reference Model defines a Measurement Area called the Mission and Business Results Measurement Area (this is called `MA_MissionAndBusinessResults` in the FEARMO). Rather than listing the components that comprised it, the PRM stipulates that the things that comprise it are exactly the lines of business that comprise three specific business areas, including the Management of Government Resources business area outlined in Figures 11-1 through 11-4. To state this as a constraint in natural language, we have

> *Anything that comprises* `ManagementOfGovernmentResources` *should also comprise* `MA_MissionAndBusinessResults`.

How can this be modeled in OWL?

Fortunately, since the FEARMO already uses the Class-Individual Mirror pattern throughout the model, there is a simple way to express this relationship directly in OWL. That is, it already has a definition (through Class-Individual Mirror) of "the set of all individuals that comprise `ManagementOfGovernment-Resources`" (in FEARMO, that class is called `LOB_ManagementOfGovernment-Resources`). It also already has a definition of "the set of all individuals that comprise `MA_MissionAndBusinessResults`" (in FEARMO, this class is called `prm:LineOfBusinessMeasurementCategory`). Given that these two classes have already been defined, and recalling that the type propagation rule of `rdfs:sub-ClassOf` means that members of one class will be inferred to also be members of the other, FEARMO can model the constraint that all individuals that comprise `ManagementOfGovernmentResources` should also comprise `MA_MissionAnd-BusinessResults` with the single triple

```
LOB_ManagementOfGovernmentResources rdfs:subClassOf
    prm:LineOfBusinessMeasurementCategory.
```

Let's have a closer look at how this works.

First, we look at the definition of `prm:LineOfBusinessMeasurementCategory` in Figure 11-5. This is defined with the same pattern as the one in Figure 11-3. Any individual that comprises `prm:MA_MissionAndBusinessResults` is a member of this class, and vice versa.

Now suppose we have a new individual that comprises `ManagementOf-GovernmentResources`. The chain of inferences is shown in Figure 11-6. Reading counterclockwise from the bottom of the figure, we have the new line of business that comprises `ManagementOfGovernmentResources`. Because of the Class-Individual Mirror pattern for `LOB_ManagementOfGovernmentResources` (detailed in Figure 11-3 and summarized here in Figure 11-6), we can infer that the new line of business is a member of (i.e., has `rdf:type`) `LOB_ManagementOfGovern-mentResources`. Since we just asserted that `LOB_ManagementOfGovernment-Resources` is `rdfs:subClassOf prm:LineOfBusinessMeasurementCategory`, we can infer that the new line of business is also a member of `prm:LineOfBusiness-MeasurementCategory`. Now we can use the Class-Individual Mirror pattern again but this time to infer that the new line of business comprises `MA_MissionAnd-BusinessResults`, as desired.

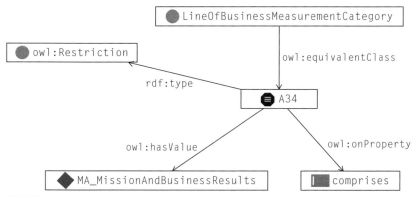

FIGURE 11-5

`LineOfBusinessMeasurementCategory` is defined using the Class-Individual Mirror pattern. The *Class* is called `LineOfBusinessMeasurementCategory`; the individual is `MA_MissionAndBusinessResults`. The Restriction is an anonymous class, shown here as a formulaic node A34.

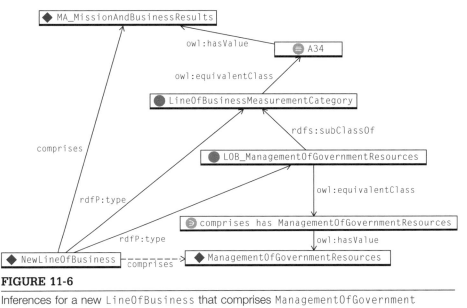

FIGURE 11-6

Inferences for a new LineOfBusiness that comprises ManagementOfGovernment
Resources.

OWL AND COMPOSITION

As a reference model, one of the main values of the FEARMO is the capability to combine it with agency models in a modular way. As a complex document, the original FEA-RM was already divided into four sections, each of which has its own value but also have a value as an integrated whole. This is not an unusual situation in software deployment. Most software languages have features for managing modularity of this sort. OWL is no different in this regard, and it has language features for modularizing semantic models. These language features have no semantics for the model (they allow no new triples to be inferred), but they help us, as humans, to organize a model in a modular way.

owl:Ontology

OWL provides a built-in class whose members correspond to modular parts of a semantic model. It is customary for the URI of an *Ontology* to correspond to the URL of the file on the web where the ontology is stored. This makes use of a slightly different syntax in N3 than we have used so far. It is possible to spell out a URI by enclosing it in angle brackets:

```
<http://www.workingontologist.com/Examples/ch14/shakespeare.
  owl> a owl:Ontology.
```

Unlike the other constructs in OWL, the meaning of membership in `owl:Ontology` is not given by inference. In fact, one could say that it has no formal meaning at all. Informally, an instance of `owl:Ontology` corresponds to a set of RDF triples. In particular, it corresponds to exactly the triples that are stored in the file that is found at the URL specified by the URI of the Ontology instance. There is no connection in the model between an instance of `owl:Ontology` and the triples to which it corresponds.

Although such an individual has no significance from the point of view of model semantics, it can be quite useful when specifying modularity of semantic models. The primary way to specify modularity is with the property `owl:imports`.

owl:imports

This is a property that connects two instances of the class `owl:Ontology`. Just as is the case with `owl:Ontology` itself, no inferences are drawn based on `owl:imports`. But the meaning in terms of modularity of models is clear: When any system loads triples from the file corresponding to an instance of `owl:Ontology`, it can also find any file corresponding to an imported ontology and load that as well. This load can, in turn, trigger further imports, which trigger further loads, and so on. There is no need to worry about the situation in which there is a circuit of imports (e.g., prm imports brm imports fea imports prm). A simple policy of taking no action when a file is imported for a second time will guarantee that no vicious loops will occur. The resulting set of triples is the union of all triples in all imported files.

In the case of FEARMO, there is a somewhat elaborate import structure, as shown in Figure 11-7. The four main divisions of FEARMO are called *srm*, *prm*, *brm*, and *trm*. The `rdfs:subClassOf` triples that connect the PRM to the

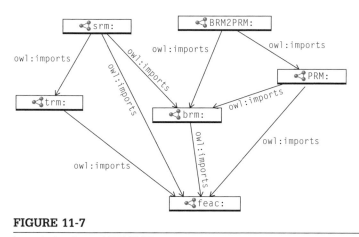

FIGURE 11-7

Import structure of FEARMO.

BRM, as illustrated in Figure 11-6, are included in a model called *BRM2PRM*, which, naturally enough, imports *brm* and *prm*. The *srm* imports *brm* and *prm*, and everything imports some common triples from a module called *feac*. Any part of this structure can be referenced independently; all the necessary modules can then be found by tracing the `owl:imports` links from one ontology to the next.

Although `owl:imports` is the workhorse of model modularity, OWL includes a handful of properties for version control. They also have no meaning for the inference semantics of OWL and so have no significance in terms of modeling, but they are useful to OWL as a computer language. (Note that only minimal support for these constructs is provided in most OWL tools, and they are not widely used.)

These are, for the most part, self-explanatory:

versionInfo: An annotation property for specifying version information, either human readable or for use by other version control systems.

priorVersion: Refers one ontology to another ontology that is a prior version.

backwardCompatibleWith: Like `priorVersion` but further states the new ontology is backward compatible with the previous one.

incompatibleWith: Like `priorVersion` but further states that the new ontology is incompatible with the previous one.

DeprecatedClass and *DeprecatedProperty:* Used to specify that a class or property, respectively, is deprecated in a particular version (and should no longer be used).

ADVANTAGES OF THE MODELING APPROACH

The inferences in Figure 11-6 follow from the OWL standard and can be done automatically by any OWL inference engine. What is the advantage of modeling the enterprise architecture like this?

To see the advantages of modeling in this way, we need to examine the alternatives. How else might the constraints between the performance and business reference models be maintained? One way to maintain this relationship is through work practice. Whenever a new line of business is established that comprises `ManagementOfGovernmentResources`, a person could be given the task to make a corresponding update to the `MA_MissionAndBusinessResults` measurement area. This solution requires documentation of that work practice and a reliance that it will continue to be done in the same way, even if personnel in the organization change. This is difficult to achieve in practice.

Another way to maintain the relationship would be to write a special-purpose program that watches for additions to the business model and makes corresponding changes to the performance model. It is easier to keep such a system working in the face of new personnel, but it has the disadvantage that because the solution is written in general-purpose program code, it is difficult to maintain and evolve the software or to make certain that the process is done the same way throughout the work flow. The relationship between the business and performance models is not explicitly stated anywhere, and it is difficult for future personnel to maintain software they don't understand.

In the presence of an inference engine, the modeling solution given by the FEARMO is very similar to the programmatic solution. The inference engine plus the model together constitute a program that takes the appropriate action. Whenever a new line of business is established, a corresponding measurement area is also updated. The difference is that the FEARMO makes explicit the relationship between the business and reference models in a way that is separate from any other processing around the enterprise architecture.

The code that supports this constraint is not embedded in a general-purpose language with the rest of the processing of data or user interfaces, or any other aspect of an agency's information system. The constraint is maintained by a standard inference engine. The relationship is expressed, in this case, in a single statement whose meaning is given by standard semantics.

This advantage is especially meaningful in the context of a reference model like FEA-RM. The utility of a reference model lies in its extensibility. When an agency makes an addition to the model (e.g., by adding a new line of business, which might just comprise `ManagementOfGovernmentResources`), it should make a corresponding addition to the performance measurement areas. How can this stipulation be unambiguously communicated and enforced? Custom code is not a solution to this problem at all—no single piece of code specified centrally (i.e., by the federal government) can be expected to run in the context of every agency's systems. A semantic model can make such a specification and can do it unambiguously because of the standard meaning of the constructs in OWL. An agency can choose to enforce it in any way that it likes, as long as it respects the formal meaning of the model. Thus, one agency might choose to use, say, an Oracle implementation of OWL, while another might use some other OWL reasoner built by a custom contractor, but the semantic model of OWL guarantees interoperability between them. A special-purpose program does not provide this capability.

THE NATIONAL CANCER INSTITUTE ONTOLOGY

The NCI Thesaurus is a public domain terminology produced by the U.S. National Cancer Institute (one of the National Institutes of Health). It is currently released in a number of forms, including OWL encoding. OWL is a natural model for this vocabulary, as we shall see, because it provides a means for specifying in a formal and unambiguous way the relationships between terms.

The need for a comprehensive NCI-wide terminology arose because NCI staff require access to timely and accurate information about activities related to the scientific mission of the Institute. The collection, storage, and retrieval of data related to NCI research programs are necessary to analyze, manage, and report about these activities. Although centralized coding of NCI-supported research-related activities met some of these needs, supplementary data coding had become common. This coding was assigned independently within various components of the Institute and was frequently based on locally developed term lists or other informal vocabulary, making it difficult to find and combine information across programs.

The NCI source vocabulary within the NCI ontology encompasses the terminology used by the various offices and divisions within the Institute, with the goal of providing a common vocabulary to increase the interoperability of information systems. The NCI vocabulary provides not only an initial Institute-wide integrated vocabulary but also rich mappings of NCI terminology to numerous other biomedical vocabularies.

The NCI ontology itself does not take advantage of the distributed nature of the Semantic Web in that it is stored and published in the form of one very large file, with all the class and property definitions within it. This has the advantage that it makes it easier to keep the ontology consistent and to do version control (a new version is released monthly), but it comes with some cost. At present, the NCI employs several full-time workers to maintain the ontology and uses a complex work flow control system to manage the builds.

The NCI ontology primarily provides class definitions (and relationships between classes) that can be used by others to link their data. By the middle of 2007, the ontology had over 50,000 class definitions, and it has been growing by several thousands of classes a year over the past few years.

REQUIREMENTS OF THE NCI ONTOLOGY

Cancer research draws on a number of disciplines in the life sciences, including genetics, chemistry, and biology (among many others). Research in each of these fields includes a wide variety of specialized terminology. For this research to yield actionable results, some connection among the various fields must be made in a systematic way. But because of the complexity of each field, it is difficult to track what information in one field is relevant in another.

A small example of the situation is shown in Figure 11-8. The figure shows fragments of the terminology hierarchies for *Genes, Species,* and *Biological Processes*. In addition to listing terms in each of these areas, the NCI ontology also specifies that the special case of *Gene* called *Oncogene* occurs only in the species *Human*, as opposed to a number of other possible species in which other

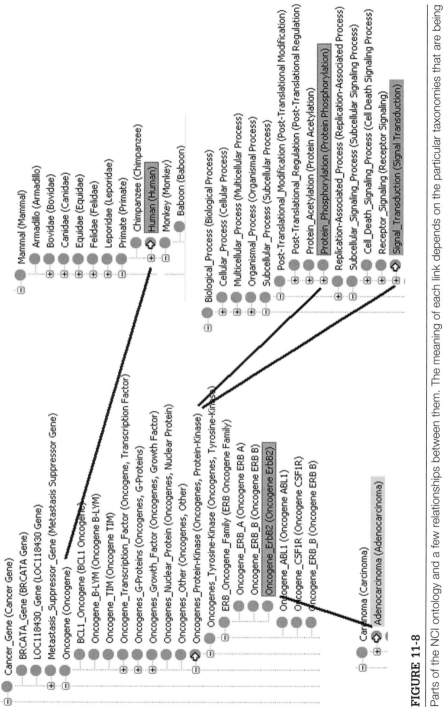

FIGURE 11-8

Parts of the NCI ontology and a few relationships between them. The meaning of each link depends on the particular taxonomies that are being linked—for example, an *Oncogene* occurs in species *Human*.

genes may occur. Furthermore, the genes in the more specific class called `Oncogenes_Protein_Kinase` have functions `Protein_Phosphorylation` and `Signal_Transduction`. Finally, the even more specific `Oncogene_ErbB2` is associated with the disease `Adenocarcinoma`. In managing this ontology, it is important to note that there are tens of thousands of terms from several different disciplines and it is quite a daunting task to track all of these associations.

Simple lists of corresponding terms cannot effectively address this problem. In the example in Figure 11-8, it isn't only the term *Oncogene* that is associated with the species *Human* but indeed every term below it in the terminology tree. The tree structure of each terminology space, as well as the ability to link the spaces together, is essential for the effective management of terminology for cancer research.

UPPER-LEVEL CLASSES

The NCI ontology is organized into several high-level classes that correspond to the various kinds of things that it describes. Each of these high-level classes is called a *Kind*. Each kind is defined as an OWL class that can be used to organize many subclasses. Some of the kinds are related to the biological aspects of oncology—for example:

```
NCI:Organism_Kind a owl:Class.
NCI:Gene_Kind a owl:Class.
```

and others. In addition, there are more general properties that are used for classifying treatments and processes in cancer care—for example:

```
NCI:Chemicals_and_Drugs_Kind a owl:Class.
NCI:Clinical_or_Research_Activity_Kind a owl:Class.
NCI:Chemotherapy_Regimen_Kind a owl:Class.
```

and finally, some that are used for classifying things used in cancer research or treatment, such as:

```
NCI:Equipment_Kind a owl:Class.
NCI:Technique_Kind a owl:Class.
```

There's also a kind for those things that don't really fit into other kinds or which are specific to NCI research:

```
NCI:NCI_Kind a owl:Class.
```

The kinds are linked to each other by a set of properties and their domains and ranges—for example:

```
NCI:Gene_In_Chromosomal_Location a rdf:Property,
    rdfs:domain NCI:Gene_Kind,
    rdfs:range NCI:Anatomy_Kind.
```

to assert that chromosomal locations link genes to parts of the anatomy.

As we saw in Figure 11-8, the primary use of ontology is to define more specific classes and to put constraints on how each property can relate classes in one tree to classes in another. How are the relationships shown in Figure 11-8 expressed in OWL? Let's take a closer look at the example of `Oncogene_ErbB2`:

```
NCI:Oncogene_ErbB2 a owl:Class;
   rdfs:subClassOf NCI:Gene_Kind;
   rdfs:subClassOf
      [a owl:Restriction;
         owl:onProperty NCI:Gene_Found_In_Organism;
         owl:someValuesFrom NCI:Human];
   rdfs:subClassOf
      [a owl:Restriction;
         owl:onProperty NCI:Gene_In_Chromosomal_Location;
         owl:someValuesFrom NCI:_17q21_1];
   rdfs:subClassOf
      [a owl:Restriction;
         owl:onProperty NCI:Gene_Has_Function;
         owl:someValuesFrom NCI:Protein_Phosorylation];
   rdfs:subClassOf
      [a owl:Restriction;
         owl:onProperty NCI:Has_Function;
         owl:someValuesFrom NCI:Signal_Transduction];
   rdfs:subClassOf
      [a owl:Restriction;
         owl:onProperty NCI:Gene_is_Biomarker_Type;
         owl:someValuesFrom NCI:Tumor_Marker];
   rdfs:subClassOf
      [a owl:Restriction;
         owl:onProperty NCI:Gene_Associated_With_Disease;
         owl:someValuesFrom NCI:Adenocarcinoma].
```

The triples in this example are shown graphically in Figure 11-9. In this way, the primary classification hierarchy is used to specify classes and the restrictions on the properties between them.

The pattern we see six times in Figure 11-9 (using `rdfs:subClassOf` and `owl:someValuesFrom`) occurs roughly 50,000 times in the NCI thesaurus; that's roughly once per class. This is the predominant modeling pattern in this ontology. So what does it mean in this context, and how is it used?

To see how this pattern is used in the NCI ontology, let's have a close look at a small part of the ontology: a pair of mappings from the `Gene_Kind` to the `Biological_Process_Kind` (see Figure 11-10). In this case, we are looking at two applications of the design pattern that maps one tree to another. In Figure 11-10, we see something of an odd situation: a `Cancer_Gene` has function `Tumorigenesis`, while an `Oncogene` has function `Oncogenesis`. This seems odd because although `Cancer_Gene` is more general than `Oncogene`,

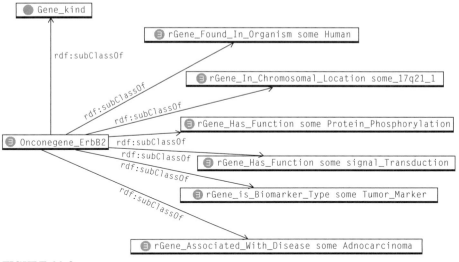

FIGURE 11-9

Definition of `Oncogene_ErbB2`. Each `owl:Restriction` class is shown here as a single node with a label in the Manchester syntax. Each one is a `someValuesFrom` restriction class, restricting a property to values from a particular class.

FIGURE 11-10

Mapping from the `Gene_Kind` to the `Biological_Process_Kind`. The links correspond to the `Has_Function` property in the ontology. Notice that the mapping "crosses levels," a higher-level Gene class is mapped to a lower-level process class.

`Tumorigenesis`, it is less general than `Oncogenesis`. When we draw it in a diagram, the mappings cross one another.

Just how odd is this? Is it something to worry about? What should be done about it? One value that OWL brings to a modeling effort like the NCI is clarity of the logical meaning of mappings of this sort. When we model this situation in OWL, we give it a formal meaning. More important, we can use that formal meaning to understand just what, if anything, is odd about the situation in which the mappings cross as they do in this case. More precisely, the formalism allows us to determine a formal description of the situation so that we have a clear understanding of what informally could only be understood as vaguely "odd."

In the NCI ontology, each of these mappings was represented with `owl:some-ValuesFrom` in a manner similar to what we see in Figure 11-9. Figure 11-11 shows a closer look at the `Oncogene/Cancer_Gene` situation and how it was modeled in OWL.

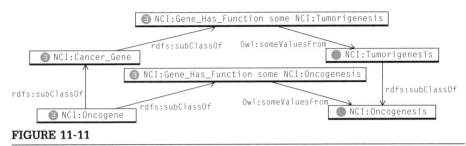

FIGURE 11-11

Representation of Figure 11-10 in OWL, NCI Ontology v. 3.09d.

Each of the gene classes is defined to be a subclass of a restriction class on the property `Gene_Has_Function`. Notice that the subclass relationship between the biological processes points in the opposite direction from the one between the genes; the more general gene is mapped to the more specific process.

What conclusions can we draw from this diagram? If we think this looks odd, perhaps it is because the model is inconsistent and there is an unsatisfiable class. As it happens, this model has none of these problems. Every class in Figure 11-11 is satisfiable, and the model is consistent. To see this, consider a single Oncogene that has a single Tumorigenesis function; both gene classes are nonempty (they contain the gene), the two genesis classes are nonempty (they contain the function), and every member of each restriction class is known to satisfy the restriction. The model is in fine shape.

Let's investigate a bit more closely. What else can we see from this model? We know that the `subClassOf` relationship can propagate through a `someValuesFrom` restriction. In this case, since `Tumorigenesis` is a subclass of `Oncogenesis`, we can conclude that one of the restriction classes is actually a subclass of the other, as shown in Figure 11-12.

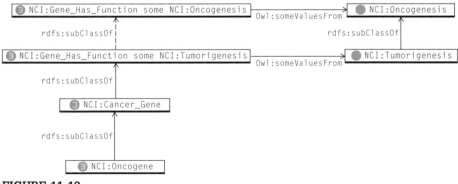

FIGURE 11-12

The subclass relation between Tumorigenesis and Oncogenesis propagates to the corresponding restrictions (*dashed line*).

What can we infer from this situation? It has already been asserted that Oncogene is a subclass of Cancer_Gene, which is a subclass of the Tumorigenesis restriction class, which is a subclass of the Oncogenesis restriction class. According to the type propagation rule for subclass (see Chapter 5), we already know that Oncogene is a subclass of the Oncogenesis restriction class. That is, the assertion in Figure 11-11 that Oncogene is a subclass of the Oncogenesis restriction class is redundant.

Redundancy in a model is not problematic; after all, any query or inference engine will treat an inferred triple the same as an asserted triple. Since the NCI ontology acts as a record of terminology decisions made by the NCI ontology committee, a situation like this does make you wonder if there might be a mistake somewhere. Why did someone feel the need to assert a (redundant) connection between Oncogene and Oncogensis? Were they unaware that it was redundant? Is it a mistake that this was a redundant assertion? Did they intend something more specific but were unable to express it in the current model?

We now have a better handle on our vague notion of "odd"—someone asserted something that could have been easily inferred. This could indicate an error in thinking or communication that could have an impact on the model. Now we have some idea what to investigate.

The resolution of questions of this sort, like the resolution of questions of consistency or satisfiabilty, cannot be done with OWL itself but must be considered by the authors and intended users of the model. In this case, a more recent version of the NCI ontology shows that indeed this situation has been rectified, as shown in Figure 11-13.

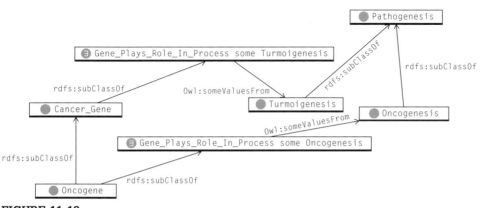

FIGURE 11-13

Newer version of Oncogene fragment of the NCI ontology, v. 7.05e, ca. 2007.

The relationship between Oncogene and Cancer_Gene is unchanged from the previous version, as are the subclass relationships with the restriction classes. But the relationships of the target classes Tumorigenesis and Oncogenesis have changed. Neither is now a subclass of the other, but they are both subclasses of the common superclass Pathogenesis. This resolves the redundancy from the earlier version while making a more specific statement about the relationships between the terms.

A further relationship between Tumorigenesis and Oncogenesis appears in the new version (but is not shown in Figure 11-13), in which the process Tumorigenesis is described as part of the process Oncogenesis, preserving the intended relationship between these two processes. The new model still uses two occurrences of the mapping pattern from a class in the Gene tree to a class in the Process tree, but in the new version, the anomaly of the crossing mappings has been resolved. Because of the semantics of OWL, we know exactly what aspects of the model were changed between the earlier and later versions.

DESCRIBING CLASSES IN THE NCI ONTOLOGY

Many of the classes in the NCI ontology correspond to genes (in particular, certain subclasses of the Gene_Kind class). Because of their importance in the life sciences, genes have been identified by a number of classification systems like Swiss_Prot and the GeneBank. It is essential for the interoperability of the NCI ontology that these identifiers be associated with the genes in the ontology whenever they are known. The obvious solution to this is to assert triples of the form such as

```
:FABP3_Gene a :Gene_Kind ;
        :Swiss_Prot "P05413" .
```

What inferences should we expect from such a statement? Since FABP3_Gene is a class, it could have subclasses. Would they or should they share the Swiss_Prot number of FABP3_Gene? The answer is certainly not! The Swiss_Prot number is supposed to be an identifier of a particular gene.

In Chapter 13 we will discuss the logical details of making assertions of this sort about classes, but at this point all we need to observe is that it is intentionally not desired that the property Swiss_Prot take part in any inferencing. In OWL, we can indicate that a property is not to be used for inferencing by asserting that it is an AnnotationProperty, thus:

```
:Swiss_Prot a owl:AnnotationProperty .
```

By making this declaration, we inform readers of the model as well as inference engines that this property is intended to add extra information to a class without having any impact on inferencing.

INSTANCE-LEVEL INFERENCING IN THE NCI ONTOLOGY

The combination of `rdfs:subClassOf` and `owl:someValuesFrom` is pervasive in the NCI ontology, but it does not entail any inferences about individual members of classes. Figure 11-14 shows an example of why this is the case.

Suppose we were to assert membership of two instances: `Gene_001` in `Gene_Kind` and `Patient001` in `Human`, as shown. Since there is some value in the class `Human` on the property `Gene_Found_In_Organism` for `Gene_001`, an OWL inference engine would infer that it is indeed a member of the restriction class as shown with the dashed line in Figure 11-14. But that is as far as the inferencing can go; no inference rules apply at this point. In particular, the type propagation rule for subclass does not apply. So far, we have inferred that `Gene_001` is a member of the superclass; the type propagation rule only applies if we know that it is a member of the subclass.

Perhaps it is not surprising that no useful instance-level inferences follow from the structure of the NCI ontology, since the NCI ontology was built as a way of managing terminology in cancer research and not the progress of individual patients. Nevertheless, more recent work on the NCI ontology has refined certain definitions to allow for more specific, instance-level inferencing.

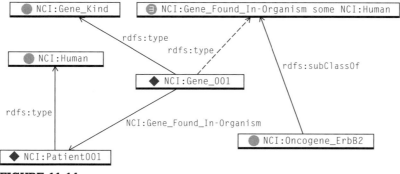

FIGURE 11-14

Potential instance level assertions in the NCI Ontology. Solid lines are asserted triples; dotted lines are inferred triples.

For instance, the definition of the Oncogene `ErbB2` in the newer version of NCI is given by

```
:Oncogene_ErbB2 owl:equivalentClass
  [a owl:Class;
   owl:intersectionOf
     (:ERB_Oncogene_Family
      [a owl:Restriction;
         owl:onProperty:Allele_In_Chromosomal_Location;
         owl:someValuesFrom :_17q21_1 ]
      [a owl:Restriction ;
         owl:onProperty :Gene_Found_In_Organism ;
         owl:someValuesFrom :Human ]
      [a owl:Restriction ;
         owl:onProperty :Gene_Plays_Role_In_Process ;
         owl:someValuesFrom :Cell_Proliferation ]
      [a owl:Restriction ;
         owl:onProperty :Gene_Plays_Role_In_Process ;
         owl:someValuesFrom :Tyrosine_Phosphorylation ]
      [a owl:Restriction ;
         owl:onProperty :Gene_Plays_Role_In_Process ;
         owl:someValuesFrom :Receptor_Signaling ]
      [a owl:Restriction ;
         owl:onProperty :Gene_Is_Biomarker_Type ;
         owl:someValuesFrom :Tumor_Marker ]
      [a owl:Restriction ;
         owl:onProperty :Gene_Associated_With_Disease ;
         owl:someValuesFrom :Adenocarcinoma ]
     )
  ].
```

If we contrast this with the definition of `ErbB2` in the earlier version of the NCI ontology, we see that `ErbB2` is still a subclass of seven restriction classes (since the intersection of all the restriction classes is a subclass of each of them). Now `ErbB2` is defined as being equivalent to the intersection of all those restriction classes. This means that should there be an instance that satisfies all of them (that is, a member of `ERB_Oncogene_Family` with an allele in chromosome location `_17q21_1` found in organism `Human`, etc.), then an inference engine would conclude that it is a member of `Oncogene_ErbB2`. In this version of NCI, such capabilities are only beginning to be explored.

There are a number of aspects of the NCI ontology that could be criticized as being misleading or even, in some cases, incorrect. For instance, what is the significance of naming something `Gene_Kind` instead of just *Gene*? Why does the model provide class-level inferences but no instance-level inferences? Is this really a problem or not? We have seen an example of how a particular issue with the NCI ontology (crossing mappings) has been resolved in later versions and how certain instance-level inferencing is being treated in current research.

In Chapter 12, we will explore some basics of ontology engineering and design, which suggest that some requirements be spelled out in advance of beginning the construction of a model. In the case of an ongoing project like the NCI ontology, the requirements are likely to shift as the project matures and is used by more and more people. We see evidence of that shift in the current move to include the definitions needed for inferencing about individuals as well as classes.

SUMMARY

On the face of it, the Federal Enterprise Architecture Reference Model Ontology and the NCI Ontology serve very different functions. The FEARMO is intended to be a starting point for several agencies, each of which will extend it. As such, it is specifically designed for distributed maintenance. The NCI ontology, on the other hand, is managed by a single body as a centralized controlled vocabulary.

If we look a bit more deeply, we see that these differences are superficial. In both cases, the important aspect of the model is that it can be used by many different people who have two conflicting needs: On the one hand, they need to have some commonality among their work. In the case of the agencies and their enterprise architecture, the federal government wants some unity among the agencies. In the case of the NCI, researchers around the world want to be able to correlate their results. On the other hand, each user of the models has some independent needs; the agencies have their own lines of business to pursue, and the researchers have their own methodologies and agendas.

Each ontology mediates these conflicting needs by providing a formal, unambiguous, and reusable model of the constraints between the concepts in the respective domains. Core concepts that are shared among the stakeholders are represented in a core model. Constraints that hold between these core concepts are also represented. In the case of FEARMO, these constraints govern what happens when the model is extended. In the NCI case, these constraints help to disambiguate terms and to keep track of which term is used in what way. Both Ontologies take advantage of the formal semantics of OWL to balance their conflicting requirements.

Another similarity between these two ontologies is found in their design. Each of these ontologies repeats a particular ontology design pattern over and over again. In the case of the NCI ontology, it is the `owl:someValuesFrom` pattern that links classes in one tree to classes in another. In the case of FEARMO, it is an `owl:hasValue` pattern that gathers up all the entities that comprise another into a class. In FEARMO, the pattern is repeated over 200 times. In the NCI Ontology, its pattern is repeated over 50,000 times! What role does such repetition play in ontology design?

In both cases, the respective pattern reveals an underlying pattern of how information is organized in the domain that the ontology describes. FEARMO is concerned with managing the composition of systems: What components are combined to form a system? What higher-level system do these systems participate in? The repetition of this pattern in the domain (systems composition) is reflected as repetition of a pattern in the model. Similarly, the terminology space that the NCI Ontology describes has many facets. Certain terms in each facet have known relationships to terms of another facet. The relationship between each pair of classes is the same—that is, how we can find our way through the terminology space.

From the point of view of model maintenance, these repeated patterns give future modelers a chance of understanding how the models work and what could be done to modify them. No single person can understand a model of 50,000 classes all at once. If there were 50,000 distinct logical relationships, understanding what inferences result from the model would be a similarly daunting task. Inference engines can, of course, compute the inferences, but understanding at a high level exactly what is going on is still a challenge for someone who wants to maintain or modify a model. Repetition of modeling patterns simplifies this task, making model maintenance possible.

Fundamental Concepts

The following fundamental concepts were introduced in this chapter:

owl:imports—Allows one ontology to refer explicitly to another. Triples from the imported ontology are available for inferencing in the importing ontology.

Versioning—OWL provides a number of resources for tracking changes in model versions and the dependencies between them.

Annotation—Properties in OWL that do not participate in inferencing. The versioning properties are examples of annotations.

Ontology Design Patterns—Repeated modeling idioms that provide coherence and unity to a large model.

Good and Bad Modeling Practices

12

In preceding chapters, we reviewed the constructs from RDF, RDFS, and OWL that go into a good model. We provided examples of successful models from a number of different backgrounds. Even after reaching this point, the prospect of creating a new model from scratch can seem daunting. Where should you begin? How do you tell a good model from a bad one?

Unlike the examples in the previous chapters, many of the examples in this chapter should not be used as templates or examples of good practice in building your own models. We indicate these examples with the label "antipattern" to indicate patterns that should *not* be emulated in your models.

GETTING STARTED

Often the first step of a journey is the most difficult one. How can you start the construction of a useful semantic model? Broadly speaking, there are three ways to get started, and the first comes directly from the nature of a web. Why build something if it is already available on the Web? One of the easiest ways to begin a modeling project is to find models on the Web that suit your needs. The second way is to leverage information assets that already have value for your organization.

It is not uncommon for an organization to have schemas, controlled vocabularies, thesauri, or other information organization artifacts that can provide an excellent source of vetted information for a semantic model. The third way is to engineer a model from scratch. In this case, certain standard engineering practices apply, including the development of requirements definitions and test cases.

Regardless of the manner in which a model was acquired, you must answer this question: Is this model, or some part of it, useful for my purposes? This poses two issues for the modeler: How do I express my intended purpose for a model? How do I determine whether a model satisfies some purpose?

Know What You Want

How can we express our intentions for the purpose of a model? In the case where we are engineering a model from scratch, we can express requirements for the model we are creating. One common practice for semantic models usually starts with the notion of "competency questions." Begin the modeling process by determining what questions the model will need to answer. Then construct the model so that these questions can be answered, and, to the extent possible, model no further than necessary to answer them.

Although competency questions provide a reasonable start for specifying the purpose of a model, they have some limitations in the context of modeling in the Semantic Web. The first drawback is that for models that have been found on the Web, or for other information artifacts that we have used as a basis for a new model, competency questions typically will not have been provided. It is not uncommon for a modeler to find themselves in a position of determining what a model can do, based simply on an examination of the model.

A more serious limitation stems from the observation that a model in the Semantic Web goes beyond the usual role of an engineered artifact with system requirements. On the Semantic Web, it is expected that a model will be merged with other information, often from unanticipated sources. This means that the design of a semantic model must not only respond to known requirements (represented with competency questions) but also express a range of variation that anticipates to some extent the organization of the information with which it might be merged.

Although this seems like an impossible task (and in its full generality, of course, it is impossible to anticipate all the uses to which a model might be applied), there are some simple applications of it, in light of the other guidelines. You model ShakespeareanWork as a class not only when you have a corresponding competency question (e.g., "What are the works of Shakespeare?") but also whenever you anticipate that someone else might be interested in that competency question. You model ShakespeareanWork as a subclass of ElizabethanWork not just in the case when you have a competency question of that form, (e.g., "What are all the kinds of Elizabethan works?") but also if you anticipate that someone might be interested in Shakespearean works and someone else might be interested in Elizabethan works, and you want the answers to both questions to be consistent (i.e., each ShakespeareanWork is also an ElizabethanWork).

This idea gets to the crux of how modeling in the Semantic Web differs from many other engineering modeling practices. Not only do you have to model for a particular engineering setting but for a variety of anticipated settings, as well. We have already seen examples of how this acts as a driving force behind our models in the wild. The NCI model is structured as it is, not primarily because a single stakeholder needs to understand the organization of the terminology of the life sciences but because members of a community of stakeholders with different goals need answers to a variety of questions, which must all be answered consistently. Similarly, the design decisions in FEARMO are not motivated by the needs of any single stakeholder but by the anticipated needs of a variety of agencies, each of which can or does organize information differently but all of which require a consistent source of information.

Inference Is Key

It is fine to talk about stakeholders, variation, and competency questions, but even when we do have a specific understanding of the intent of a model, how can we even determine whether the model, as constructed, meets that intention? We can appeal to the intuition behind the names of classes and properties, but this is problematic for a number of reasons. First is the issue known as "wishful naming." Just because someone has named a class `ElizabethanWork` doesn't mean that it will contain all or even any works that might deserve that name. Second is the issue of precision. Just what did the modeler mean by `ElizabethanWork`? Is it a work created *by* Queen Elizabeth or one that was created during her reign? Or perhaps it is a work created by one of a number of prominent literary figures (the `ElizabethanAuthors`), whose names we can list once and for all. To determine whether a model satisfies some intent, we need an objective way to know what a model means and, in the case of competency questions, how a model can answer questions.

There are two ways a Semantic Web model answers questions. The first is comparable to the way a database answers question: by having the appropriate data indexed in a way that can be directly accessed to answer the question. If we answer the question "What are the Elizabethan literary works?" this way, we would do so by having a class called, say, `ElizabethanWork` and maintain a list of works as members of that class.

This method for answering questions is fundamental to data management; at some point, we have to trust that we have some data that are correct or that are at least correct enough for our purposes. The special challenge of semantic modeling comes when we need to model for variability. How do we make sure that our answer to the question "What are the Shakespearean works?" is consistent with the answer to "What are the Elizabethan works?" (and how does this relate to the answer to the question "Who are the Elizabethan authors?"). This brings us to the second way a semantic model can answer questions: through the use of inferencing.

We can determine a model's answer to a particular question (or query) through an analysis of inferencing. What triples can we infer based on the triples that have already been asserted? If we require every `ShakespeareanWork` to be an `ElizabethanWork`, we can either build or find a model that asserts that `ShakespeareanWork` is a subclass of `ElizabethanWork`. If instead we want an `ElizabethanWork` to be one that was created or performed by an `Elizabethan-Author` and that `Shakespeare` is one of these authors, we build or find a model that will support the corresponding inferences (e.g., using `owl:someValuesFrom`). In all these cases, the consistency of the answers to the various questions is expressed and maintained through inferencing.

MODELING FOR REUSE

One of the principle drivers in the creation of a semantic model is that it will be used by someone other than its designer in a new context that was not fully anticipated. If you are designing a model, you must consider the challenges the people using your model might face. How can you make this job easier for them?

Insightful Names Versus Wishful Names

When you are reusing a model that you found on the Web, you'd like to know the intent of the various components of the model (classes, properties, individuals). The support that a model provides for question answering is given formally by the inferences that the model entails. As far as an inference engine is concerned, entities in the model could have any name at all, like *G0001* or *Node97*. But names of this sort are of little help when perusing a model to determine whether it can satisfy your own goals. Putting the shoe on the other foot, when you build a model, you are also selecting names for those who will want to link to your model and need to know what is in it, as well as for those, including yourself at a later date, who may have to maintain or extend the model. There's a fine line between good naming and wishful thinking, but keeping in mind that your model will be "read" by others is always good practice.

A closely related issue to naming is the use of annotations like `rdfs:label`, `rdfs:comment`, and `rdfs:seeAlso`. Even if you choose a name for a resource that you understand, and even one that is understood by the community you participate in, there could well be another community who will find that usage meaningless or even misleading. We have seen an example of this before with `skos:broader`. For someone with a background in thesaurus management, it is understood that skos:broader is used to connect a narrow term to a broader term, such as:

    :cheese skos:broader :dairy.

That is, `skos:broader` should be read as "has broader term." Other readers might expect this to be read "cheese is broader than dairy," and they would either be confused by the use of `skos:broader` or, worse, would misuse it in their own models. Judicious use of `rdfs:label` can alleviate this issue, as follows:

    skos:broader rdfs:label "has broader term" .

In addition to the selection of meaningful names and quality naming, some simple conventions can contribute to the understandability of a model. The conventions listed next have grown up as de facto standard ways to name entities on the Semantic Web, and are followed by the W3C itself as well as throughout this book.

Name resources in `CamelCase`: CamelCase is the name given to the style of naming in which multiword names are written without any spaces but with each word written in uppercase. We see this convention in action in W3C names like `rdfs:subClassOf` and `owl:InverseFunctionalProperty`.

Start class names with capital letters: We see this convention in the W3C class names `owl:Restriction` and `owl:Class`.

Start property names with lowercase letters: We see this convention in the W3C property names `rdfs:subClassOf` and `owl:inverseOf`. Notice that except for the first letter, these names are written in `CamelCase`.

Start individual names with capital letters: We see this convention at work in the `lit:Shakespeare` and `ship:Berengaria` examples in this book.

Name classes with singular nouns: We see this convention in the W3C class names `owl:DatatypeProperty` and `owl:SymmetricProperty` and in the examples in this book: `lit:Playwright`.

Keeping Track of Classes and Individuals

One of the greatest challenges when designing a semantic model is determining when something should be modeled as a class and when it should be modeled as an individual. This issue arises especially when considering a model for reuse because of the distributed nature of a semantic model. Since a semantic model must respond to competency questions coming from different stakeholders, it is quite possible that one work practice has a tradition of considering something to be a class, whereas another is accustomed to thinking of it as an instance.

As a simple example, consider the idea of an endangered species. For the field zoologists who are tracking the number of breeding pairs in the world (and in cases where the numbers are very small, give them all names), the species is a class whose members are the individual animals they are tracking. For the administrator in the federal agency that lists endangered species, the species is an instance to be put in a list (i.e., asserted as a member of the class of endangered species) or removed from that list. The designer of a single model who wants to answer competency questions from both of these stakeholder communities is faced with something of a challenge.

We have seen exactly this situation in FEARMO, where some stakeholders are interested in viewing a `LineOfBusiness` as an instance (to make assertions of the form "The General Services Agency is in the line of business of Management of Government Resources"). Other stakeholders view a particular line of business as a set of operations (called *subfunctions* in FEARMO) and so want to make assertions of the form "Supply chain management is an instance of Management of Government Resources." As was the case in FEARMO, this situation can often be modeled effectively using the Class-Individual Mirror pattern from Chapter 11.

Another source of difficulty arises from the flexibility of human language when talking about classes and instances. We can say that Shakespeare is an Elizabethan author or that a poem is a literary work. In the first sentence, we are probably talking about the individual called Shakespeare and his membership in a particular class of authors. In the second, we are probably talking about how one class of things (poems) relates to another (literary works). Both of these sentences us the words *is a(n)* to describe these very different sorts of relationships. In natural languages, we don't have to be specific about which relationships we mean. This is a drawback of using competency questions in natural language: The question "What are the types of literary works?" could be interpreted as a request for the individuals that are members of the class `LiteraryWork`, or it could be asking for the subclasses (types) of the class `LiteraryWork`. Either way of modeling this could be considered a response to the question.

Although there is no hard and fast rule for determining whether something should be modeled as an instance or a class, some general guidelines can help organize the process. The first is based on the simple observation that classes can be seen as sets of instances. If something is modeled as a class, then there should at least be a possibility that the class might have instances. If you cannot imagine what instances would be members of a proposed class, then it is a strong indication that it should not be modeled as a class at all. For example, it is unlikely, according to this guideline, that we should use a class to refer to the literary figure known as Shakespeare. After all, given that we usually understand that we are talking about a unique literary figure, what could possibly be the instances of the class `Shakespeare`? If there are none, then `Shakespeare` should properly be modeled as an instance.

If you can imagine instances for the class, it is a good idea to name the class in such a way that the nature of those instances is clear. There are some classes having to do with Shakespeare that one might want to define. For example, the works of the Bard, including 38 plays, 254 sonnets, 5 long poems, and so on could be a class of interest to some stakeholder. In such a case, the name of the class should not simply be `Shakespeare` but instead something like `ShakespeareanWork`. Considerable confusion can be avoided in the design phase by first determining what it is that is to be modeled (the Bard himself, his works, his family, etc.), then deciding if this should be a class or an instance, and then finally selecting a name that reflects this decision.

The second guideline has to do with the properties that describe the thing to be modeled. Do you know (or could you know) specific values for those properties or just in general that there is some value? For instance, we know in general that a play has an author, a first performance date, and one or more protagonists, but we know specifically about *The Tempest* that it was written by William Shakespeare, was performed in 1611, and has the protagonist Prospero. In this case, *The Tempest* should be modeled as an instance, and *Play* should be modeled as a class. Furthermore, *The Tempest* is a member of that class.

Model Testing

Once we have assembled a model—either from designed components, reused components, or components translated from some other source—how can we test it? In the case where we have competency questions, we can start by making sure it answers those. More important, in the distributed setting of the Semantic Web, we can determine (by analyzing the inferences that the model entails) whether it maintains consistent answers to possible competency questions from multiple sources. We can also determine test cases for the model. This is particularly important when reusing a model. How does the model perform (i.e., what inferences can we draw from it?) when it is faced with information that is not explicitly in the scope of its design? In the analysis to follow, we will refer generally to *model tests*—ways you can determine if the model satisfies its intent.

COMMON MODELING ERRORS

In light of the AAA slogan (Anybody can say Anything about Any topic), we can't say that anything is really a modeling error. In our experience teaching modeling to scientists, engineers, content managers, and project managers, we have come across a handful of modeling practices that may be counterproductive for the reuse goals of a semantic model. We can't say that the models are strictly erroneous, but we can say that they do not accomplish the desired goals of sharing information about a structured domain with other stakeholders.

We have seen each of the antipatterns described following in a number of models. Here, we describe each one in turn and outline its drawbacks in terms of the modeling guidelines just given. We have given each of them a pejorative (and a rather fanciful) name as a reminder that these are antipatterns—common pitfalls of beginning modelers. Whenever possible, we will also indicate good practices that can replace the antipattern, depending on a variety of possible desired intents for the model.

Rampant Classism (Antipattern)

A common reaction to the difficult distinction between classes and instances is simply to define everything as a class. This solution is encouraged by most modeling tools, since the creation of classes is usually the first primitive operation that a user learns. The temptation is to begin by creating a class with the name of an important, central concept and then extend it by creating more classes whose names indicate concepts that are related to the original. This practice is also common when a model has been created by automatic means from some other knowledge organization source, like a thesaurus. A thesaurus makes much less commitment about the relationship between terms than does a semantic model between classes or between classes and individuals.

As an example, someone modeling Shakespeare and his works might begin by defining a class called Shakespeare and classes called `Plays`, `Poems`, `Poets`, `Playwrights`, and `TheTempest`. Then, define a property (an `owl:ObjectProperty`) called `wrote` and assert that Shakespeare wrote all of these things by asserting triples like the following:

```
:Playwrights :wrote :Plays .
:Poets :wrote :Poems .
:Shakespeare :wrote :Plays .
:ModernPlays rdfs:subClassOf :Plays .
:ElizabethanPlays rdfs:subClassOf :Plays .
:Shakespeare :wrote :TheTempest .
:Shakespeare :wrote :Poems .
```

and perhaps even

```
:TheTempest rdfs:subClassOf :Plays .
```

This seems to makes sense because, after all, `TheTempest` will show up next to *Plays* in just about any ontology display tool. The resulting model is shown in Figure 12-1.

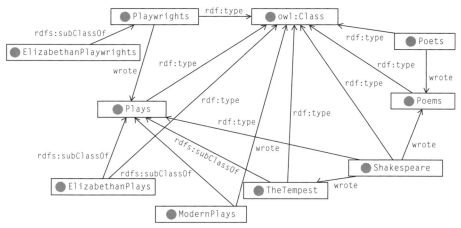

FIGURE 12-1

Sample model displaying rampant classism. Every node in this model has `rdf:type owl:Class`.

Given the AAA slogan, we really can't say that anything in this set of triples is "wrong." After all, anyone can assert these triples. But we can start by noting that it does not follow the simple syntactic conventions in that the class names are plurals.

This model reflects a style typical of beginning modelers. The triples seem to translate into a sensible sentence in English: "Shakespeare wrote poems"; "Shakespeare wrote *The Tempest*." If you render `rdfs:subClassOf` in English as *is a,* then you have "*The Tempest* is a plays," which aside from the plural at the end, is a reasonable sentence in English. How can we evaluate whether this model satisfies the intent of the modeler or of someone who might want to reuse this model? We'll consider some tests that can tell us what this model might be useful for.

Let's start with some simple competency questions. This model can certainly answer questions of the form "Who wrote *The Tempest*?" The answer is available directly in the model. It can also answer questions like "What type of thing writes plays? What type of thing writes poems?" Again, these answers are represented directly in the model.

Suppose we want to go beyond mere questions and evaluate how the model organizes different points of view. It seems on the face of it that a model like this should be able to make sure that the answer to a question like "What type of thing wrote Elizabethan plays?" would at the very least include the class of playwrights, since playwrights are things that wrote plays and Elizabethan plays are plays. Can this model support this condition? Let's look at the relevant triples and see what inferences can be drawn:

```
:Playwrights a owl:Class ;
    :wrote :Plays .
:ElizabethanPlays rdfs:subClassOf :Plays.
```

None of the inference patterns we have learned for OWL or RDFS apply here. In particular, there is *no* inference of the form

```
:Playwrights :wrote :ElizabethanPlays .
```

Another test criterion that this model might be expected to pass is whether it can distinguish between plays and types of plays. We do have some plays and types of plays in this model: *The Tempest* is a play, and Elizabethan play and modern play are types of plays. The model cannot distinguish between these two cases. Any query that returns *The Tempest* (as a play) will also return modern plays. Any query that returns Elizabethan play (as a type of play) will also return *The Tempest*. The model has not made enough distinctions to be responsive to this criterion.

If we think about these statements in terms of the interpretation of classes as sets, none of these results should come as a surprise. In this model, playwrights and plays are sets. The statement "Playwrights wrote plays" makes no statements about individual playwrights or plays; it makes a statement about the sets.

But sets don't write anything, whereas playwrights and poets do. This statement, when made about sets, is nonsense. The OWL inference semantics bear this out: The statement has no meaning, so no inferences can be drawn. `TheTempest` is modeled here as a class, even though there is no way to imagine what its instances might be; it is a play, not a set. Plays are written by people (and have opening dates, etc.), not sets.

Similar comments can be made about a statement like "Poets wrote poems." If triples like:

```
:Poets :wrote :Poems .
```

aren't meaningful, how should we render the intuition reflected by the sentence "Poets wrote poems"? This consideration goes beyond the simple sort of specification that we can get from competency questions. We could respond to questions like "Which people are poets?" or "Which things are poems?" with any model that includes these two classes. If we want the answers to these two questions to have some sort of consistency between them, then we have to decide just what relationship between *poems* and *poets* we want to represent.

We might want to enforce the condition "If someone is a poet, and he wrote something, then it is a poem." When we consider the statement in this form, it makes more sense (and a more readable model) if we follow the convention that names classes with singular nouns ("a poet," "a poem") rather than plurals (poets, poems).

We have already seen an example of how to represent a statement of this form. If something is an `AllStarTeam`, then all of its players are members of `StarPlayer`. Following that example, we can represent this same thing about poets and poems as follows:

```
:Poet rdfs:subClassOf [ a owl:Restriction ;
                        owl:onProperty :wrote ;
                        owl:allValuesFrom :Poem ] .
```

If we specify an instance of *poet*—say, *Homer*—and something he wrote—say, *The Iliad*—then we can infer that *The Iliad* is a *poem*, thus:

```
:Homer :wrote :TheIliad .
:Homer a :Poet .
:TheIliad a :Poem .
```

This definition may work fine for Homer, but what happens if we press the boundaries of the model a bit and see what inferences it can made about someone like Shakespeare

```
:Shakespeare :wrote :TheTempest .
:Shakespeare a :Poet .
:TheTempest a :Poem .
```

The conclusion that *The Tempest* is a poem is unexpected. Since it is common for poets to write things that don't happen to be poems, probably this isn't what we really mean by *"Poets wrote poems."* This is an example of a powerful method for determining the scope of applicability of a model. If you can devise a test that might challenge some of the assumptions in the model (in this case, the assumption that nobody can be both a poet and a playwright), then you can determine something about its boundaries.

What other results might we expect from the statement "Poets wrote poems"? We might expect that if someone is a *poet*, then they must have written at least one *poem*. (We have already seen a number of examples of this using `owl:someValuesFrom`.) In this case, this definition looks like this:

```
:Poet rdfs:subClassOf [ a owl:Restriction ;
                        owl:onProperty :wrote ;
                        owl:someValuesFrom :Poem ] .
```

The inferences we can draw from this statement are subtle. For instance, from the following fact about *Homer*

```
:Homer a :Poet .
```

we can infer that he wrote something that is a *poem*, though we can't necessarily identify what it is.

When we say, "Poets wrote poems," we might expect something even stronger: that having written a *poem* is exactly what it means to be a *poet*. Not only does being a poet mean that you have written a *poem*, but also, if you have written a *poem*, then you are a poet. We can make inferences of this sort by using `owl:equivalentClass` as follows:

```
:Poet owl:equivalentClass [a owl:Restriction ;
                           owl:onProperty :wrote ;
                           owl:someValuesFrom :Poem ] .
```

Now we can infer that Homer is a poet from the poem that he wrote

```
:Homer :wrote :TheIliad .
:TheIliad a :Poem .
:Homer a :Poet .
```

In general, linking one class to another with an object property (as in *Poets wrote poems* in this example) does not support any inferences at all. There is no inference that propagates properties associated with a class to its instances, or to its subclasses, or to its superclasses. The only inferences that apply to object properties are those (like the inferences having to do with `rdfs:domain` and `rdfs:range`, or inferences from an `owl:Restriction`) that assume that the subject and object (*Shakespeare* and *poems* in this case) are instances, not classes.

This illustrates a powerful feature of OWL as a modeling language. The constructs of OWL make very specific statements about what the model means, based on the inference standard. A sentence like "Poets wrote poems" may have some ambiguity in natural language, but the representation in OWL is much more specific. The modeler has to decide just what they mean by a statement like "Poets wrote poems," but OWL allows these distinctions to be represented in a clear way.

Exclusivity (Antipattern)

The rules of RDFS inferencing say that the members of a subclass are necessarily members of a superclass. The fallacy of exclusivity is to assume that the only candidates for membership in a subclass are those things that are already known to be members of the superclass.

Let's take a simple example. Suppose we have a class called *City* and a subclass called `OceanPort`, to indicate a particular kind of city

```
:OceanPort rdfs:subClassOf :City .
```

We might have a number of members of the class *City*, for example:

```
:Paris a :City .
:Zurich a :City .
:SanDiego a :City .
```

According to the AAA assumption, any of these entities could be an `OceanPort`, as could any other entity we know about—even things we don't yet know are cities, like New York or Rio de Janeiro. In fact, since Anyone can say Anything about Any topic, someone might assert that France or The Moon is an `OceanPort`. From the semantics of RDFS, we would then infer that France or The Moon are cities.

In a model that commits the error of exclusivity, we assume that because `OceanPort` is a subclass of `City`, the only candidates for `OceanPort` are those things we know to be cities, which so far are just *Paris, Zurich,* and *San Diego*. To see how the exclusivity fallacy causes modeling problems, let's suppose we are interested in answering the question "What are the cities that connect to an ocean?" We could propose a model to respond to this competency question as follows:

```
:OceanPort rdfs:subClassOf :City .

:OceanPort owl:equivalentClass
              [ a owl:Restriction ;
                  owl:onProperty :connectsTo ;
                  owl:someValuesFrom :Ocean ] .
```

These triples are shown graphically in Figure 12-2.

This model commits the fallacy of exclusivity; if we assume that only cities can be ocean ports, then we can answer the question by querying the members of the class `OceanPort`. But let's push the boundaries of this model. What inferences does it draw from some boundary instances that might violate some assumptions in the model? In particular, what if we consider something that is

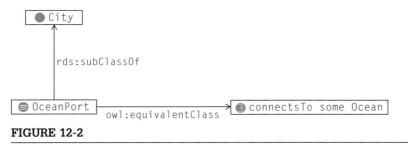

FIGURE 12-2

Eronneous definition of `OceanPort` as a city that connects to an Ocean.

not a city but still connects to an ocean? Suppose we have the following facts in our data set:

```
:Zurich :connectsTo :RiverLimmat .
:Zurich :locatedIn :Switzerland .
:Switzerland :borders :France .
:Paris :connectsTo :LaSeine .
:Paris :locatedIn :France .
:France :connectsTo :Mediterranean .
:France :connectsTo :AtlanticOcean .
:SanDiego :connectsTo :PacificOcean .
:AtlanticOcean a :Ocean .
:PacificOcean a :Ocean .
```

and so on.

From what we know about `SanDiego` and the `PacificOcean`, we can conclude that `SanDiego` is an `OceanPort`, as expected

```
:SanDiego :connectsTo :PacificOcean .
:PacificOcean a :Ocean .
:SanDiego a :OceanPort .
```

Furthermore, since

```
:OceanPort rdfs:subClassOf :City .
```

we can conclude that

```
:SanDiego a :City .
```

So far, so good, but let's see what happens when we look at *France*.

```
:France :connectsTo :AtlanticOcean .
:AtlanticOcean a :Ocean
```

Therefore, we can conclude that

```
:France a :OceanPort .
```

and furthermore,

> :France a :City .

This is not what we intended by this model, and it does not respond correctly to the question. The flaw in this inference came because of the assumption that only things known to be cities can be ocean ports, but according to the AAA assumption, anything can be an ocean port unless we say otherwise.

This fallacy is more a violation of the AAA slogan than any consideration of subclassing itself. The fallacy stems from assumptions that are valid in other modeling paradigms. For many modeling systems (like object-oriented programming systems, library catalogs, product taxonomies, etc.) a large part of the modeling process is the way items are placed into classes. This process is usually done by hand and is called *categorization* or *cataloguing*. The usual way to think about such a system is that something is placed intentionally into a class because someone made a decision that it belongs there. The interpretation of a subclass in this situation is that it is a refinement of the class. If someone wants to make a more specific characterization of some item, then they can catalogue it into a subclass instead of a class.

If this construct does not correctly answer this competency question, what model will? We want something to become a member of OceanPort just if it is both a City and it connects to an Ocean. We do this with an *intersection* as shown in Figure 12-3.

Now that we have defined an OceanPort as the intersection of City and a restriction, we can infer that OceanPort is a subclass of City. Furthermore, only individuals that are known to be cities are candidates for membership in OceanPort, so anomalies like the previous one for *France* cannot happen.

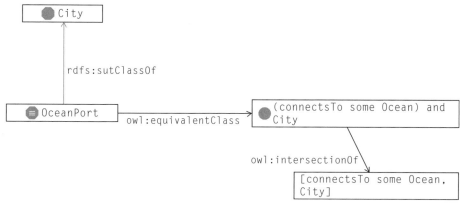

FIGURE 12-3

Correct model for an OceanPort as a *City* that also connects to an *Ocean*.

The Class Exclusivity fallacy is a common error for anyone who has experience with any of a number of different modeling paradigms. Semantic Web modeling takes the AAA assumption more seriously than any other common modeling system. Fortunately, the error is easily remedied by using the intersection pattern shown in Figure 12-3.

Objectification (Antipattern)

One common source of modeling errors is attempting to build a Semantic Web model that has the same meaning and behavior as an object system. Object systems, however, are not intended to work in the context of the three Semantic Web assumptions: AAA, Open World, and Nonunique Naming. In many cases, these differences in assumptions about the modeling context result in basic clashes of modeling interpretation.

A fundamental example of this kind of clash can be found in examining the role of a class in a model. In object modeling, a class is basically a template from which an instance is stamped. It makes little or no sense to speak of multiple classes (stamped out of two templates?) or of having a property that isn't in the class (where do you put it if there wasn't a slot in the template for it?).

In Semantic Web models, the AAA and the Open World assumptions are incompatible with this notion of a class. Properties in Semantic Web models exist independently of any class, and because of the AAA slogan, they can be used to describe any individual at all, regardless of which classes it belongs to. Classes are seen as sets, so membership in multiple classes is commonplace.

Let's consider a simple but illustrative example of how the intent of an object model is incompatible with modeling in the Semantic Web. Suppose an object model is intended to reflect the notion that a person has exactly two parents who are also people. These are the requirements an object model must satisfy:

1. A value for the property `hasParent` can be specified only for members of the `Person` class.

2. We will recognize as a mistake the situation in which only one value for `hasParent` is specified for a single person.

3. We recognize as a mistake the situation in which more than two values for `hasParent` are specified for a single person.

Before we even look at an OWL model that attempts to satisfy these conditions, we can make some observations about the requirements themselves. In particular, many of these requirements are at odds with the fundamental assumptions of Semantic Web modeling, as described by the AAA, Open World, and Nonunique Naming assumptions. Let's look at the requirements in turn.

Requirement 1 is at odds with the AAA slogan. The AAA slogan tells us that we cannot keep anyone from asserting a property of anything, so we can't enforce the condition that `hasParent` can only be specified for particular individuals. The Open World assumption complicates the situation even further: Since the next thing we learn about a resource could be that its type is *Person*, we can't even tell for sure whether something actually is a person.

Requirement 2 is at odds with the Semantic Web assumptions. In this case, the Open World assumption again causes problems. Just because we have not asserted a second parent for any individual does not mean that one doesn't exist. The very next Semantic Web page we see might give us this information. Thus, regardless of how we model this in OWL, there cannot be a contradiction in the case where too few parents have been specified.

Requirement 3 is not directly at odds with the Semantic Web assumptions, but the Nonunique Naming assumption makes this requirement problematic. We can indeed say that there should be just two parents, so if more than two parents are specified, a contradiction can be detected. This will only happen in the case where we know that all the (three or more) parents are distinct, using a construct like `owl:differentFrom`, `owl:allDifferent`, or `owl:disjointWith`.

The discrepancy between these requirements and an OWL model doesn't depend on the details of any particular model but on the assumptions behind the OWL language itself. An object model is designed for a very different purpose from an OWL model, and the difference is manifest in many ways in these requirements.

Despite this mismatch, it is fairly common practice to attempt to model these requirements in OWL. Here, we outline one such attempt and evaluate the inference results that the model entails. Consider the following model, which is a fairly common translation of an OO model that satisfies these requirements into OWL:

```
:Person a owl:Class .
:hasParent rdfs:domain :Person .
:hasParent rdfs:range :Person .

[ a owl:Restriction ;
    owl:onProperty :hasParent ;
    owl:Cardinality 2 ]
```

This model was created by translating parts of an object model directly into OWL, as follows:

1. When a property is defined for a class in an OO model, that class is listed as the domain of the property in OWL. The type of the property in the OO model is specified as the range in OWL.

2. Cardinality limitations in the object model are represented by defining a restriction class in OWL.

We have already seen that this model cannot satisfy the requirements as stated. How far off are we? What inference does this model support? What inferences does it not support?

According to the stated intent of this model, if we assert just the following fact:

```
:Willem :hasParent :Beatrix .
```

The model should signal an error, since only a `Person` can have a parent, and we have not asserted that `Willem` is a `Person`. If we fix this by asserting that

```
:Willem a :Person .
```

then the model should still indicate an error; after all, `Willem` must have two parents, not just one. If we also assert more parents for `Willem`:

```
:Willem :hasParent :Claus .
:Willem :hasParent :TheQueen .
```

then the model should again signal an error, since now `Willem` has three parents rather than two.

Now let's see what inferences can actually be made from these assertions according to the inference patterns of OWL. From the very first statement

```
:Willem :hasParent :Beatrix .
```

along with the `rdfs:domain` information, we can infer that

```
:Willem a :Person .
```

That is, there is no need to assert that `Willem` is a `Person` before we can assert who his parent is. This behavior is at odds with the first intent; that is, we allowed `Willem` to have a parent, even though we did not know that `Willem` was a person.

What about the cardinality restriction? What can we infer from that? Three issues come into play with this. The first is the Open World assumption. Since we don't know whether `Willem` might have another parent, who simply has not yet been specified, we cannot draw any inference about `Willem`'s membership in the restriction. In fact, even if we assert just one more parent for `Willem` (along with `Beatrix`, bringing the total of asserted parents to exactly two) that

```
:Willem :hasParent :Claus .
```

we still do not know that `Willem` really does have exactly two parents. After all, there might be yet a third parent of `Willem` whom we just haven't heard about. That's the Open World assumption.

The second issue has to do with unique naming. Suppose we now also assert that

```
:Willem :hasParent :TheQueen .
```

Surely, we can now infer that `Willem` cannot satisfy the restriction, since we know of three parents, right? Even if there are more parents lurking out there (according to the Open World assumption), we can never get back down to just two. Or can we?

The Nonunique Naming assumption says that until we know otherwise, we can't assume that two different names refer to different individuals. In particular, the two names TheQueen and Beatrix could (and in fact, do) refer to the same individual. So even though we have named three parents for Willem, we still haven't disqualified him from being a member of the restriction. We haven't named three *distinct* parents for Willem.

The third issue transcends all the arguments about whether Willem does or does not satisfy the cardinality restriction. Look closely at the definition of the restriction: It is defined, as usual, as a bnode. But the bnode is not connected to any other named class in any way. That is, the restriction is not owl:equivalentClass to any other class, nor is it rdfs:subClassOf any other class (or vice versa).

What does this mean for inferences involving this restriction? On the one hand, even if we were to establish that Willem satisfies the restriction, still no further inferences could be made. Further inferences would have to be based on the connection of the restriction to some other class, but there is no such connection. On the other hand, if we could independently establish that Willem is a member of the restriction, then we could possibly draw some conclusions based on that. Since the restriction is not connected to any other class, there is no independent way to establish Willem's membership in the restriction class. Either way, we can draw no new inferences from this restriction. The AAA slogan keeps us from saying that this model is "wrong," but we can safely say that it does not support the inferences that were intended by the modeler. Unlike the case of the other antipatterns, we are not in a position to "fix" this model; the requirements of the model are simply at odds with the assumptions of modeling in the Semantic Web.

Managing Identifiers for Classes (Antipattern)

In the NCI ontology, we saw a need for identifiers for classes: The Swiss_Prot number for a gene or enzyme was listed at the class level:

```
:FABP3_Gene a owl:Class ;
    rdfs:subClassOf :Gene_Kind ;
    :Swiss_Prot "P05413" .
```

This is a direct response to the competency question "What is the Swiss Prot number for the class FABP3?" This is a common requirement of models in very formal settings: that various entities (classes, individuals, even properties) have some sort of index number that we would like to record alongside the entity in the model.

Strictly speaking, the use of a property to describe a class in this way risks confusion about whether we are describing a class or an individual. FABP3_Gene is a class because of the type triple that declares it a class, but because it has a property, it seems to be an individual. We suggested previously that this sort of ambiguity of classes and individuals should be avoided, but it seems natural to use a direct triple in this way to satisfy such a competency question.

As we shall see in Chapter 13, this distinction is not simply one of style (should we represent a class also as an individual?), but it can have ramifications in terms of the decidability of the logic. Fortunately, OWL provides a simple answer to this issue. A property can be declared as an `AnnotationProperty`, indicating that its use in such a context has no meaning in terms of the logic, and thus does not make any statement about whether a subject is a class, individual, or property.

```
:Swiss_Prot a owl:AnnotationProperty .
```

Earlier ontology languages did not support this solution, so modelers had to improvise another solution. For each class for which annotation was desired, there was a distinguished individual member of the class that would stand in for the class for the purpose of annotations. For example, one could define the following:

```
:FABP3_Gene a owl:Class ;
   rdfs:subClassOf :Gene_Kind .
:PABP3_StandIn a :FaBP3 ;
   :Swiss_Prot "P05413" .
```

This solution provides an answer to the competency question "Which gene is labeled with Swiss Prot number `P05413`?" (by following the `rdf:type` link from the stand-in back to the class), but it introduces another problem. It makes it difficult to answer, "What are all the members of the class `FABP3_Gene`?" because there is now one individual that is a member of that class that should not be considered in answering this question. With the advent of `owl:AnnotationProperty`, it is no longer necessary to use this method for annotating classes, but some models with this pattern will still be used for some time to come.

Creeping Conceptualization (Antipattern)

In most engineered systems, designing for reuse is enhanced by keeping things simple. In software coding, for example, the best APIs try to minimize the numbers of calls they provide. In physical systems, the number of connections is minimized, and most common building materials aim for a minimally constraining design so as to maximize the ways they can be combined. On the Semantic Web, the same idea should apply, but all too often the idea of "design for reuse" gets confused with "say everything you can." Thus, for example, when we include `ShakespeareanWork` and `ElizabethanWork` in our model, we are tempted to further assert that `ElizabethanWork` is a subclass of `Work`, which is a subclass of `IntangibleEntity`.

Of course, having included `IntangibleEntity`, you will want to include `TangibleEntity` and some examples of those and some properties of those examples and, well, ad infinitum. After all, you might think that modeling for reuse is best done by anticipating *everything* that someone might want to use your model for, and thus the more you include the better. This is a mistake because the more you put in, the more you restrict someone else's ability to extend your model instead of just use it as is. Reuse is best done, as in other systems, by designing to maximize future combination with other things, not to restrict it.

This kind of creeping conceptualization may seem like an odd thing to have to worry about. After all, isn't it a lot of extra work to create more classes? Economists tell us that people minimize the amount of unrewarded work they do. However, in practice, it often turns out that knowing when to stop modeling is harder than deciding where to start. As humans, we tend to have huge connected networks of concepts, and as you define one class, you often think immediately of another you'd "naturally" want to link it to. This is an extremely natural tendency, and even the best modelers find it very difficult to know when to finish, but this way lies madness.

A relatively easy way to tell if you are going too far in your creation of concepts is to check classes to see if they have properties associated with them, and especially if there are restricted properties. If so, then you are likely saying something useful about them, and they may be included. If you are including data (instances) in your model, then any class that has an instance is likely to be a good class. On the other hand, when you see lots of empty classes, especially arranged in a subclass hierarchy, then you are probably creating classes just in case someone might want to do something with them in the future, and that is usually a mistake. The famous acronym KISS (Keep It Simple, Stupid) is well worth keeping in mind when designing Web ontologies.

SUMMARY

The basic assumptions behind the Semantic Web—the AAA, Open World, and Nonunique Naming assumptions—place very specific restrictions on the modeling language. The structure of RDF is in the form of statements with familiar grammatical constructs like subject, predicate, and object. The structure of OWL includes familiar concepts like class, subClassOf, and property. But the meaning of a model is given by the inference rules of OWL, which incorporate the assumptions of the Semantic Web. How can you tell if you have built a useful model, one that conforms to these assumptions? The answer is by making sure that the inferences it supports are useful and meaningful.

According to the AAA slogan, we cannot say that any of the practices in this chapter are "errors" because Anyone can say Anything about Any topic. All of these models are valid expressions in RDF/OWL, but they are erroneous in the sense that they do not accomplish what the modeler intended by creating them. In each case, the mismatch can be revealed through careful examination of the inferences that the model entails. In some cases (like the objectification error), the requirements themselves are inconsistent with the Semantic Web assumptions. In other cases (like the exclusivity error), the requirements are quite consistent with the Semantic Web assumptions and can be modeled easily with a simple pattern.

Fundamental Concepts

The following concepts were introduced or elaborated in this chapter:

The Semantic Web Assumptions—AAA (Anyone can say Anything about Any topic), Open-World, and Nonunique Naming.

Inferencing—In OWL, inferencing is tuned to respect the Semantic Web assumptions. This results in subtleties that can be misleading to a novice modeler.

Competency Questions—Questions that scope the requirements for a model.

Modeling for Variability—The requirement (characteristic of Semantic Web modeling) that a model describe variation as well as commonality.

Modeling for Reuse—The craft of designing a model for uses that cannot be fully anticipated.

Wishful Naming—The tendency for a modeler to believe that a resource signifies more than the formal semantics of the model warrants, purely on the basis of the resource's name.

Model Testing—A process by which the boundaries of a model are stressed to determine the nature of the boundaries of the inferences it can entail.

OWL Levels and Logic

13

This book is about modeling in the context of the Semantic Web—in particular, using the W3C languages RDF, RDFS, and OWL to build and distribute those models. The meaning of these models is given by the inferences that each of these languages defines for the models. RDFS provides rudimentary inferencing about types based on class membership and properties. OWL provides a wide array of more advanced modeling features to describe how data can be related.

In Chapter 7, we introduced a subset of OWL that we called RDFS-Plus. There are a number of reasons why someone might define a subset of a language like OWL. In the case of RDFS-Plus, we were interested in a subset of the language that has considerable utility for semantic modeling but does not place a large burden on either a modeler or someone trying to understand a model. RDFS-Plus includes features that are similar to what can be found in familiar data representation systems like relational database and object-oriented systems. Researchers, implementers, and product developers have defined a number of subsets based on modeling expressivity, computational complexity, and, often, on what parts of the OWL language can best be handled by whatever inferencing system is already in place.

In the initial OWL specification, the W3C identified three particular variants (or "species") of OWL, which they called OWL Lite, OWL DL, and OWL Full. The distinction between OWL DL and OWL Full is particularly subtle, and it is the topic of much of this chapter. We will examine the motivations behind these variants and the ramifications these motivations have in terms of technology and modeling style.

Any language will grow as it is used, especially a Semantic Web language. Realizing this, the W3C processes encourage the evolution of languages to provide new functionality while maintaining backward compatibility. As we shall see, there are a number of useful modeling idioms that are clumsy or impossible in the current definition of OWL. This chapter outlines the particular features that are being considered in the ongoing process in the W3C for the OWL recommendation.[1]

---

[1]Progress and status of the OWL recommendation is documented at *http://www.w3.org/2004/OWL.*

OWL DIALECTS AND MODELING PHILOSOPHY

Normally, when we refer to different subsets of a language, we can list the language structures in one subset that are not found in the other. For instance, RDFS has `rdfs:domain`, `rdfs:range`, `rdfs:subPropertyOf`, and so on, whereas RDFS-Plus has all of those, plus some new language features like `owl:inverseOf` and `owl:TransitiveProperty`. We can define how these two languages are similar or different, based on which language terms are available in each one.

In the case of OWL Full and OWL DL, the situation is more subtle. Both OWL Full and OWL DL use exactly the same set of modeling constructs. That is, if we were to list all the properties and classes that make up OWL Full and then compile the same list for OWL DL, the lists would be exactly the same. In fact, it would be the list of OWL features that you have been reading about in this book. Everything you have learned so far applies equally well to OWL Full and OWL DL.

So what is the difference? What was so important that the W3C saw fit to make two distinct standards if they have the same language constructs and the same meanings? The distinction between these two variants—or "species," as they are often called—of OWL has to do with how the language constructs are used. The differences in allowed usage are motivated by a difference in the basic philosophy of why one builds models for the Semantic Web. We will outline these two basic philosophies—one in which the emphasis is placed on having provable models and one in which the emphasis is placed on making executable models. We examine each in turn, along with the intuitions that motivate them.

Provable Models

An important motivation for formal modeling (as opposed to informal modeling) is to be precise about what our models mean. In the context of the Semantic Web, this tells us precisely and without doubt when concepts from two different sources refer to the same thing. Does my notion of a James Dean movie correspond to yours? A formal description can help us determine whether or not this is the case. My definition of a "James Dean movie" is one that stars James Dean, but your definition of a "James Dean movie" might be movies *about* James Dean or movies with the words *James Dean* in the title. How can we tell if we have the name "James Dean movie" as the only indication of these definitions? A formal model makes these distinctions clearer. Then it becomes a simple matter of automation to decide whether two classes are the same, if one subsumes the other, or if they are unrelated.

It is this aspect of modeling that motivates a logical definition of OWL. Each construct in OWL is a statement in a formal logic. The particular logical system of OWL DL is called *Description Logic*. As the name suggests, Description Logic is a logical system with which formal descriptions of classes, individuals, and the relationships between them can be made. The inferences in OWL that have formed the basis of the bulk of this book are formally defined by a model theory based on Description Logic.

Using logic as the foundation of a modeling language makes perfect sense; we can draw upon decades, or even centuries, of development work in logical formalism. The properties of various logical structures are well understood. Logic provides a framework for defining all of the inferences that our modeling language will need. But there is one fly in the ointment: In a computational setting, we would like our logic to be processed automatically by a computer. Specifically, we want a computer to be able to determine all of the inferences that any given model entails. So, if we want to be able to automatically determine whether my notion of a James Dean movie is exactly the same as yours, we must show the set of all facts true in one are true in the others, and all facts untrue are untrue.

It is at this point that the details of the logic become important. What does it mean for our modeling formalism if we base it on a logic for which this kind of automation cannot, in principle, exist? That is, what happens if we can't exactly determine whether my notion of a James Dean movie is the same as yours? If we view this sort of provable connection as essential to the nature of modeling, then we have failed. We simply cannot tolerate a logic in which this kind of question cannot be answered by automated means in some finite amount of time.

In the study of formal logic, this question is called decidability. Formally, a system is decidable if there exists an effective method such that for every formula in the system the method is capable of deciding whether the formula is valid (is a theorem) in the system or not. If not, then the system is *undecidable*. It is not our intention in this book to go into any detail about the mathematical notion of decidability, but a few comments on its relevance for modeling are in order.

The first thing to understand about decidability is also the most surprising: how easy it is for a formal system to be undecidable. Given the formal nature of logic, it might seem that, with enough patience and engineering, a program could be developed to correctly and completely process any formal logic. One of the most influential theorems that established the importance of the notion of decidability shows that even very simple logical systems (basically, any system that can do ordinary integer arithmetic) are undecidable. In fact, it is actually quite challenging to come up with a logical system that can represent anything useful that is also decidable.

This bit of tightrope walking is the impetus behind the OWL DL sublanguage. OWL DL is based on a particular Description Logic. This means that it is possible to design an algorithm that can take as input any model expressed in OWL DL and determine which classes are equivalent to other classes, which classes are subclasses of other classes, and which individuals are members of which classes.

The most commonly used algorithm for this problem is called the *Tableau Algorithm*. It works basically by keeping track of all the possible relations between classes, ruling out those that are inconsistent with the logical statements made in the model. The Tableau Algorithm is guaranteed to find all entailments of a model in OWL DL in a finite (but possibly quite long!) time. Furthermore, it is possible to determine automatically whether a model is in fact in OWL DL so that a program can even signal when the guarantees cannot be met.

Modeling in OWL DL supports the intuition that a model must be clear, unambiguous, and machine-processable. The Tableau Algorithm provides the machinery by which a computer system can make determinations about equivalence of classes.

Executable Models

A different motivation for modeling in the Semantic Web is to form an integrated picture of some sort of domain by federating information from multiple sources. If one source provides information about the places where hotel chains have hotels and another describes what hotels appear at a particular place, a formal model can tell us that we can merge these two sources together by treating them as inverses of one another. The model provides a recipe for adding new information to incomplete information so it can be federated with other sources.

Seen from this point of view, a model is similar to a program. It provides a concise description of how data can be transformed for use in other situations. What is the impact of decidability in such a situation? Standard programming languages like FORTRAN and Java are undecidable in this sense. The undecidability of these languages is often demonstration with reference to the *Halting Problem.* It is impossible in principle to write a computer program that can take another arbitrary computer program as input, along with input for *that* program, and determine whether *that* program will halt on that input. Even though these languages are undecidable, they have proven nevertheless to be useful engineering languages. How can we write programs in these languages if we can't automatically determine their correctness or, in some sense, even their meaning? The answer to this question in these cases is what programming is all about. Even though it is not possible *in general* to determine whether any program will terminate, it is usually possible to determine that *some particular* program will terminate and, indeed, with what answer. The skill of engineering good computer programs is to write programs that not only will terminate on all input but will actually perform well on particularly interesting input.

Seen from this point of view, decidability is not a primary concern. Models are engineered in much the same way as programs. If a model behaves poorly in some situation, then an engineer debugs the model until it performs correctly. Since we are not concerned with decidability, we don't need the guarantee that any algorithm will find all possible inferences. This opens up the choice of processor for OWL to a much wider range of algorithms, including algorithms like Forgy's RETE algorithm that have enjoyed considerable popularity as processors for rule-based languages.

It's also the case that, in many Web applications, the size of datasets we would like to analyze are quite huge, dynamic, or not well represented. The question could be asked as to whether one needs a 100 percent correct model to analyze data that is itself scraped from the Web by some heuristic program that is not perfect. On the Web, people use Google because it can find good answers a lot of the time, even if it can't find perfect answers all the time. Some Semantic Web systems are targeted at this rough-and-tumble Web application space, and thus provable correctness, as opposed to efficient computation, may not be a key goal.

This executable style of modeling is the primary motivation behind the OWL Full standard. The meaning of a modeling construct in OWL Full is given in much the same way as the meaning of a construct in a programming language. Just as the meaning of a statement in a procedural programming language is given by the operation(s) that a machine will carry out when executing that statement, the meaning of an executable model is given by the operation(s) that a program (i.e., an inference engine) carries out when processing the model. Information federation is accomplished because the model describes how information can be transformed into a uniform structure.

OWL FULL VERSUS OWL DL

So far, we have described the motivation behind OWL Full and OWL DL without actually describing what the differences are in terms of the actual language. The first thing to understand about OWL DL and OWL Full is that they use exactly the same constructs. Every modeling construct you have learned in this book can be used for both. The inferences that you can draw from them are also the same, with the understanding that in the case of OWL Full, it might not be possible for an automated system to draw all correct conclusions, while in OWL DL it may not be possible to use every feature in every way.

The difference between the languages lies in the usage. Describing these differences is also problematic, since the determination of the precise boundary between OWL Full and OWL DL is a popular topic for Description Logic researchers. Many of the restrictions that were originally defined for OWL DL have since been proven to be too harsh. Inclusion of these usages has been shown not to damage the decidability of the model. For this reason, it is more important to understand the decidability-based motivation of the distinction than any particular usage distinction. Here we will outline the major kinds of restrictions on the modeling language that are enforced by OWL DL. The details of these may continue to change as research in description logic proceeds.

Class/Individual Separation

In OWL DL, classes and individuals are completely separate; that is, a model cannot specify that some resource is *both* a class and a member of a class. Recalling an example from Chapter 6, we defined a number of ranks as classes:

```
ship:Captain rdfs:subClassOf ship:Officer .
ship:Commander rdfs:subClassOf ship:Officer .
ship:LieutenantCommander rdfs:subClassOf ship:Officer .
ship:Lieutenant rdfs:subClassOf ship:Officer .
ship:Ensign rdfs:subClassOf ship:Officer .
```

We can specify the rank of an individual using membership in one of these classes:

```
:Warwick rdf:type ship:Captain .
```

By virtue of their use in `rdfs:subClassOf` triples, all of the entities mentioned here are classes. In another context, we might want to express what we know about these ranks—for instance, these ranks have a particular order, by which `Captain` outranks `Commander`, which in turn outranks `LieutenantCommander`, and so on. We could express this relationship in RDF using a series of triples:

```
ship:Captain ship:outranks ship:Commander .
ship:Commander ship:outranks ship:LieutenantCommander .
ship:LieutenantCommander ship:outranks ship:Lieutenant .
ship:Lieutenant ship:outranks ship:Ensign .
```

We represent the use of `ship:outranks` with domain and range specifications as well:

```
ship:outranks rdfs:domain ship:Rank .
ship:outranks rdfs:range ship:Rank .
```

Although this seems like a natural thing to do, it violates the separation of class and individual in OWL DL. Each rank is a class (with members who hold that rank), but the domain and range information of `ship:outranks` makes each rank also a *member* of the class rank, so they are individuals. In OWL Full, there is no condition forbidding this usage.

InverseFunctional Datatypes

In Chapter 7, we learned that `owl:InverseFunctionalProperty` is an important construct for data federation. Whenever two individuals share a value for an `InverseFunctionalProperty`, we can infer that they are the same individual. Things like social security number, employee number, driver's license number, serial number, and so on are commonly used this way. In Chapter 8 we saw that FOAF uses `foaf:mbox` this way.

Unfortunately, OWL DL has a condition that outlaws exactly these uses. It stipulates that an `InverseFunctionalProperty` must not also be a `DatatypeProperty`—that is, it cannot refer to a string, date, number, and so on. In other words, exactly the things that make up social security numbers, e-mail addresses, and dates of birth are forbidden from `InverseFunctionalProperties`. This is a stringent restriction and one that is quite often responsible for placing a model into OWL Full instead of OWL DL.

OWL LITE

Along with OWL Full and OWL DL, the original OWL specification identified a subset of OWL DL with the intention that it would be easier to implement and would accelerate the adoption of OWL. As OWL implementations mature, the significance of OWL Lite is fading. Many implementations have skipped over OWL Lite entirely and gone directly into support of OWL Full or OWL DL or, more commonly, proceeded to supporting a proprietary subset of OWL. The simplifications in OWL Lite include the following.

Limited Cardinality Restrictions: Cardinality restrictions are limited in OWL Lite to the integers 0 and 1, but, as we have seen in Chapter 10, cardinality restrictions to 0 or 1 have natural and common interpretations. Most cardinality restrictions in real models use 0 or 1 anyway.

No oneOf constructs: OWL Lite does not include `owl:oneOf` constructs. This is in line with a simplified model of cardinality.

No hasValue restrictions: OWL Lite does not include any of the `owl:hasValue` restrictions.

OTHER SUBSETS OF OWL

OWL Full, OWL DL, and OWL Lite are the only sublanguages defined in the OWL specification, but they're certainly not the only ones in use. As different companies implement OWL tools, they can decide which parts of OWL to implement. Similarly, for different modeling needs, different subsets may prove useful. We've already seen an example in this book—RDFS-Plus is defined earlier as being useful in modeling and is being implemented in some systems; however, it is not an "official" OWL language. Many other such OWL fragments have been designed and explored based on issues such as scalability and efficiency, as well as on decidability.

There is an important thing to note, however, in the use of these dialects. If the subsets use the restrictions of OWL DL, then they are in OWL DL (or OWL Lite if they use its restrictions). On the other hand, if the restrictions of

DL are not followed, then the models technically are in OWL Full. So an ontology defined in RDFS-Plus could be in OWL DL or in OWL Full depending on the details. If the RDFS-Plus model includes a property that is both an InverseFunctionalProperty as well as a DatatypeProperty, for example, then it is technically in OWL Full even though it does not use many of the OWL language terms.

In general, users working with some particular subset of OWL are usually doing so based on using a particular tool, or trying to meet a particular need. In these cases, it often doesn't really matter whether the ontology is in OWL Full, OWL DL, or OWL Lite.

BEYOND OWL 1.0

Web languages, like applications, often go through a versioning process. As new users come along with new needs, the languages evolve. Eventually, new standardization efforts can create new versions of the language. OWL is currently in a relatively early stage of its development, and thus there is an expectation that it will be extended in the future. To this end, some have taken to referring to the current OWL specification as OWL 1.0, in anticipation of future releases. In this chapter, we discuss some of the extensions that Semantic Web developers are exploring that go beyond OWL 1.0.

Metamodeling

Metamodeling is the name commonly given to the practice of using a model to describe another model as an instance. One feature of metamodeling is that it must be possible to assign properties to classes in the model. But as we have just seen, putting properties on classes typically violates the separation of class and individual that allows a model to be described in OWL DL.

A number of motivations for metamodeling exist. One such motivation is that a model often needs to play more than one role in an application: A particular concept should be viewed as a class in one role but as an instance in another role. If we are modeling animals, we might say that BaldEagle is an endangered species, thereby referencing BaldEagle as an individual. In another application, we could view BaldEagle as a class, whose members are the particular eagles in the zoo. Similarly, wine connoisseurs speak of individual wines in terms of *vintage*. For them, the vintage is an individual, but for a wine merchant who is calculating how many bottles he has sold, the bottles themselves are individual members of the class that are indicated by the vintage.

We have already seen a number of examples of this kind of metamodeling in this book. In Chapter 8, we saw how a foaf:Group is an individual that corresponds to a class of all the members of the group. In Chapter 11, we saw how the Class-Individual Mirror pattern allowed us to view a line of business either as an individual or as a class of all the subfunctions that comprise it. In Chapter 13, we saw how military ranks can be seen as both classes and individuals.

Another purpose of metamodeling is to imitate capabilities of other modeling systems (like object-oriented modeling) in which the value for some property can be specified for all members of a class at once. Metamodeling in itself is not an issue in OWL Full, since there is no restriction against using the same resource as an individual and as a class. The formal issues really arise only when trying to achieve the results of metamodeling in OWL DL. Although there is no formal issue with overloading a single resource to refer to a class and an individual, currently it is often best to keep these things separate, even in OWL Full. There really is a difference between a species and the set of animals of that species; there is a difference between Shakespeare's family and the set of people in it. These distinctions could be important to someone who wants to reuse a model. Keeping them distinct in the first place will often enhance the model's utility.

Fortunately, there are a number of possible approaches to doing metamodeling in OWL (either OWL DL or OWL Full). For most situations, we recommend the Relationship Transfer pattern from Chapter 9 or the Class-Individual Mirror pattern from Chapter 11.

Recent Description Logic research has determined that in certain cases, the Class-Individual separation constraint can be relaxed without any danger to the decidability of the logic. Thus, it is possible to have a new version of OWL DL in which metamodeling of the sort we have described here can be done as easily in OWL DL as in OWL Full. Whether or not such a proposal reaches fruition in the OWL standard, we still recommend using one of the patterns in this book whenever possible instead of resorting to overloading resource usage.

Multipart Properties

In RDFS, we have seen how properties can relate to one another using `rdfs:subPropertyOf`. This establishes a hierarchy of properties: Any relations that hold lower in the hierarchy also hold higher in the hierarchy. There are other ways in which properties can relate to one another. A common example is the notion of *uncle: A* is the *uncle* of *B* only if *A* is the *brother* of someone who is the *parent* of *B*. This is called a *multipart property*—that is, the property *uncle* is made up of two parts (in order): *parent* and *brother*.

When multipart properties are used with other RDFS and OWL constructs, they provide some powerful modeling facilities. For instance, we can model the constraint "A child should have the same species as its parent" by stating that the multipart predicate made up of `hasParent` followed by `hasSpecies` (denoted as `:hasParent + :hasSpecies`) is `rdfs:subPropertyOf hasSpecies`. Let's see how this works. Suppose we have the following triples:

```
:Elsie :hasParent :Lulu .
:Lulu :hasSpecies :Cow .
```

Now we can infer

```
:Elsie :hasParent + :hasSpecies :Cow .
```

But since the multipart predicate `:hasParent + :hasSpecies` is a `rdfs:subPropertyOf :hasSpecies`, we can infer that

```
:Elsie :hasSpecies :Cow .
```

One reason that multipart predicates were not included in OWL was that they were thought to cause undecidability, and thus could only have been available in OWL Full, not OWL DL. To add these to the language, new vocabulary terms were needed, and that would have meant that the parallel between OWL Full and OWL DL would have been changed. Recently, however, it has been shown that under certain conditions it is possible to represent multipart properties in OWL in such a way that they do not endanger the decidability of OWL DL.

Qualified Cardinality

Cardinality restrictions in OWL allow us to say how many distinct values a property can have for any given subject. Other restrictions tell us about the classes of which those values can or must be members. But these restrictions work independently of one another; we cannot say how many values from a particular class a particular subject can have. A simple example of qualified cardinality is a model of a hand: A hand has five fingers, one of which is a thumb.

Qualified cardinalities may seem like a needless modeling detail, and in fact, a large number of models get by quite fine without them. But models that want to take advantage of detailed cardinality information often find themselves in need of such detailed modeling. This happens especially when modeling the structure of complex objects.

For example, when modeling an automobile, it might be useful to say that a properly equipped automobile includes five tires, four of which must be regular road-worthy tires and a fifth that is a designated spare tire which might not have all the properties of a regular tire. Structural models of this sort often make extensive use of qualified cardinalities. Qualified cardinalities also will require syntactic extensions to OWL; in this case, however, they do work within the decidability constraints of OWL DL and thus they are likely to be added in a future version of OWL.

Multiple Inverse Functional Properties

Inverse functional properties can be used to determine the identity of individuals based on the values of the properties that describe them. If two people share the same social security number, then we can infer that they are actually the same person. This kind of unique identifier is indispensable when merging information from multiple sources.

Unfortunately, anyone who has done a lot of such integration knows that this kind of merging only scrapes the surface of what needs to be done. Far more common is the situation in which some combination of properties implies the identity of two or more individuals. For instance, two people residing at the same residence with the same first and last names should be considered to be the same person. Two people born in the same hospital on the same day and at the same time of day should be considered to be the same person. Examples of this kind of multiple identifiers are much easier to come by than single identifiers, as required for an `InverseFunctionalProperty`.

To further complicate matters, in real information federation situations, it is often the case that even these combinations of properties cannot guarantee the identity of the individuals. Two people at the same address with the same name are very likely to be the same person (but not for certain—a father could live with his son of the same name). OWL has no facility to deal with uncertainty, so there is no way to express this sort of information. Extending OWL to deal with uncertainty is a topic of current research and standardization efforts in the Semantic Web.

A few proposals have been made for how to deal with multiple inverse functional properties in OWL. However, expressing these bring up syntactic problems (how to express a relation including an arbitrary number of properties), as well as logical ones (what are the logical properties of the resulting system?). One proposal for dealing with these is to extend some or all of OWL by the use of rules, which have been proposed to be a more natural way of expressing complex relationships like this.

Rules

While OWL is the most powerful modeling system currently defined for the Semantic Web, it does have limitations. Some of these are best addressed, for the purposes of data management, using rules, and thus the development of a rules language for the Web is currently being explored.

Rule-based systems have a venerable tradition starting in the days of Expert Systems and are in common use in business logic applications to this day. A number of useful algorithms for processing data with rules have been known for many years, and many of them have been made very efficient.

Many of the issues with OWL presented in this chapter can be addressed with rules. Multipart properties (like the definition of *uncle*) are easily expressed in rules. Multiple inverse functional properties can be expressed in rules as well. There are even a number of approaches to reasoning with uncertainty in rules. Many of these have considerable research and practical examples behind them, making uncertainty in rules a relatively well-understood issue.

Given all these virtues of rules and rule-based systems, why don't they play a bigger role in modeling on the Semantic Web than they do? In fact, one could even ask why there is a need for a modeling language like OWL when there is a mature, well-understood rules technology that already exists. One could even ask this question in greater generality. Why aren't more software systems in general written in rules?

We cannot treat this issue in full detail in this book, but we can outline the answer as it relates to OWL and the Semantic Web. One of the lessons learned from the history of rule-based systems is that software engineering in such systems is more difficult than it is in modular, procedural languages. Although it is unclear whether or not this is an essential feature of rule-based systems, it is undeniable that rule-based programmers have not achieved the levels of productivity of their more conventional counterparts. This has particular ramifications in the Semantic Web. One defense for using OWL Full instead of OWL DL was that the software engineering discipline makes the notion of decidability basically irrelevant for model design. In the case of rule-based systems, software engineering cannot provide this same support. Unconstrained rule-based systems are just as undecidable as general-purpose languages like FORTRAN and Java.

Is there a way to get the best of both worlds? Could a Web-oriented rules language integrate well with OWL? It is clear that for some applications, such as the NCI Cancer Ontology discussed in Chapter 11, the class-oriented models of OWL are an excellent fit. For other applications, such as representing business processes, it may be the case that rule-based reasoning is better. At the time of this writing, there is a W3C standards group exploring the development of an interoperable rules language for the Web and trying to clearly define the relationship between this language and OWL.

SUMMARY

OWL should be considered a living language, growing in the context of the ways it is being used on the web and in commerce. As shortcomings in the language are identified, the system grows to accommodate them. Sometimes that growth takes the form of additional constructs in the language (e.g., multipart properties), sometimes as connections to other systems (rules), and sometimes progress in a language comes from specifying limitations to the language (as is the case for OWL DL and OWL Full). All of these processes are moving in parallel for the Semantic Web.

Fundamental Concepts

OWL Full—Unrestricted dialect of OWL, with all the constructs used in any combination.

OWL DL—Dialect of OWL restricted to ensure decidability; all constructs allowed but with certain restrictions on their use.

OWL Lite—Subset of OWL DL designed to encourage early adoption. Significance wanes as implementations reach OWL DL and OWL Full levels.

Metamodeling—Models that describe models, usually requires that classes be treated as individuals.

Multipart properties—Daisy-chain composition of properties.

Multiple Inverse Functional Properties—Uniquely identify an individual based on matching values for several properties.

Qualified Cardinality—Cardinality restriction whereby the class of the value being counted is specified as well as the number of distinct values.

Conclusions **14**

For those readers who are accustomed to various sorts of knowledge modeling, the Semantic Web looks familiar. The notions of classes, subclasses, properties, and instances have been the mainstay of knowledge modeling and object systems modeling for decades. It is not uncommon to hear a veteran of one of these technologies look at the Semantic Web and mutter, "Same old, same old," indicating that there is nothing new going on here and that everything in the Semantic Web has already been done under some other name elsewhere.

As the old saying goes, "There is nothing new under the sun," and to the extent that the saying is correct, so are these folks when they speak of the Semantic Web. The modeling structures we have examined in this book do have a strong connection to a heritage of knowledge modeling languages. But there *is* something new that has come along since the early days of expert systems and object-oriented programming; something that has had a far more revolutionizing effect on culture, business, commerce, education and society than any expert system designer ever dreamed of. It is something so revolutionary that it is often compared in cultural significance to the invention of the printing press. That something new is the World Wide Web.

The Semantic Web is the application of advanced technologies that have been used in the context of artificial intelligence, expert systems and business rules execution in the context of a world-wide web of information. The Semantic Web is not simply an application running on the Web somewhere; it is a part of the very infrastructure of the Web. It isn't *on* the Web; it *is* the Web.

Why is this important? What is it that is so special about the Web? Why has it been so successful, more so than just about any computer system that has come before it?

In the early days of the commercial Web, there was a television ad for a search engine. In the ad, a woman driving a stylish sports car is pulled over by traffic policeman for speeding. As he prepares to cite her, she outlines for him all the statistics about error rates in the various machines used by traffic policemen for detecting speeding. He is clearly thrown off his game, and unsure of how to continue to cite her. She adds personal insult by quoting the statistics **307** of prolonged exposure to traffic radar machines on sperm count. The slogan "Knowledge is Power" scrolls over the screen, along with the name of the search engine.

What lesson can we learn from ads like this? This kind of advertising made a break from television advertising that had come before. Knowledge was seen not as nerdy or academic but useful in everyday life—and even sexy. Or at least it is if you have the *right* knowledge at the right time. The web differed from information systems that preceded it by bringing information from many sources—indeed, sources from around the world—to one's fingertips. In comparison to Hypercard stacks that had been around for decades, the Web was an open system. Anyone in the world could contribute, and everyone could benefit from that contribution. Having all that information available was more important than how well a small amount of information was organized.

The Semantic Web differs from expert systems in pretty much the same way. Compared to the knowledge representations systems that were developed in the context of expert systems, OWL is quite primitive. But this is appropriate for a web language. The power of the Semantic Web comes from the web aspect. Even a primitive knowledge modeling language can yield impressive results when it uses information from sources from around the world. In expert systems terms, the goals of the Semantic Web are also modest. The idea of an expert system was that it could behave in a problem-solving setting with a performance that would qualify as expert-level if a human were to accomplish it. What we learned from the World Wide Web (and the story of the woman beating the speeding ticket) is that typically people don't want machines to behave like experts; they want to have access to information so *they* can exhibit expert performance at just the right time. As we saw in the ad, the World Wide Web was successful early on in making this happen, as long as someone is willing to read the relevant webpages, digest the information, and sift out what they need.

The Semantic Web takes this idea one step further. The Web is effective at bringing any single resource to the attention of a web user, but if the information the user needs is not represented in a single place, the job of integration rests with the user. The Semantic Web doesn't use expert system technology to replicate the behavior of an expert; it uses expert system technology to gather information so an individual can have integrated access to the web of information.

Being part of the web infrastructure is no simple matter. On the Web, any reference is a global reference. The issue of managing global names for anything we want to talk about is a fundamental web issue, not just a Semantic Web issue. The Semantic Web uses the notion of a URI as the globally resolvable reference to a resource as a way of taking advantage of the web infrastructure. Most programming and modeling languages have a mechanism whereby names can be organized into spaces (so that you and I can use the same name in different ways but still keep them straight when our systems have to interface).

With the World Wide Web, the notion of a name in a namespace must be global in the entire web. The URI is the web-standard mechanism to do this; hence, the Semantic Web uses the URI for global namespace identification. Using this approach allows the Semantic Web to borrow the modularity of the World Wide Web. Two models that were developed in isolation can be merged simply by referring to resources in both of them in the same statement. Since the names are always maintained as global identifiers, there is no ad hoc need to integrate identifiers each time; the system for global identity is part of the infrastructure.

An important contributor to the success of the World Wide Web is its openness. Anyone can contribute to the body of information, including people who, for one reason or another, might publish information that someone else would consider misleading, objectionable, or just incorrect. At first blush, a chaotic free-for-all of this sort seems insane. How could it ever be useful? The success of the Web in general (and information archiving sites like Wikipedia in particular) has shown that there is sufficient incentive to publish quality data to make the overall Web a useful and even essential structure.

This openness has serious ramifications in the Semantic Web, which go beyond considerations that were important for technologies like expert systems. One of the reasons why the Web was more successful than Hypercard was because the web infrastructure was resilient to missing or broken links (the "404 Error"). The Semantic Web must be resilient in a similar way. Thus, inferencing in the Semantic Web must be done very conservatively, according to the Open World assumption. At any time, new information could become available that could undermine conclusions that have already been made, and our inference policy must be robust in such situations.

In the World Wide Web, the openness of the system presents a potential problem. How does the heroine of the search engine commercial know that the information she has found about radar-based speed detection devices is correct? She might have learned it from a trusted source (say, a government study on these devices), or she might have cross-referenced the information with other sources until she had enough corroborating evidence to be certain. Or perhaps she doesn't really care if it *is* correct but only that she can convince the traffic cop that it is. Trust of information on the web is done with a healthy dose of skepticism but in the same way as trust in other media like newspapers, books, and magazine articles.

In the case of the Semantic Web, trust issues are more subtle. Information from the Semantic Web is an amalgam of information from multiple sources. How do we judge our trust in such a result even if we know about all the sources? To some extent, the same principles apply. We can trust entities that we know or have experience with, and we can trust entities that have gone through some process of authorization and authentication. When we combine information, we must also understand the impact that each information source has on the outcome and what risk we are taking if we cannot trust that source. These important issues for understanding the reliability of the Semantic Web are still a subject of research.

In this book, we examined the modeling aspects of the Semantic Web: How do you represent information in such a way that it is responsive to a web environment? The basic principles underlying the Semantic Web—the AAA slogan, the Nonunique Naming assumption, and the Open World assumption—are constraints placed on a representation system if it wants to function as the foundation of a World Wide Web of information. These constraints have led to the main design decisions for the Semantic Web languages of RDF, RDFS, and OWL.

There is more to a web than just the information and how it is modeled. At some point, this information must be stored in a computer, accessed by end users, and transmitted across an information network. Furthermore, no triple store, and no inference engine, will ever be able to scale to the size of the World Wide Semantic Web. This is clearly impossible, since the Web itself grows continually. In the light of this observation, how can the World Wide Semantic Web ever come to pass?

The applications we discussed in this book demonstrate how a modest amount of information, represented flexibly so that it can be merged in novel ways, provides a new dynamic for information distribution and sharing. SKOS allows thesaurus managers around the globe to share, connect, and compare terminology. FEARMO allows government agencies to operate autonomously while conforming to a central standard for enterprise architecture. The NCI ontology coordinates efforts of independent life sciences researchers around the globe.

How is it possible to get the benefit of a global network of data if no machine is powerful enough to store, inference over, and query the whole network? As we have seen, it isn't necessary that a Semantic Web application be able to access and merge every page on the Web at once. The Semantic Web is useful as long as an application can access and merge *any* webpage. Since we can't hold all the Semantic Web pages in one store at once, we have to proceed with the understanding that there could always be more information that we don't have access to at any one point. This is why the Open World assumption is central to the infrastructure of the Semantic Web.

This book is about modeling in the context of the Semantic Web. What role does a model play in the big vision? The World Wide Web that we see every day is made up primarily of documents, which are read and digested by people browsing the Web. But behind many of these webpages, there are databases that contain far more information than is actually displayed on a page. To make all this information available as a global, integrated whole, we need a way to specify how information in one place relates to information somewhere else. Models on the Semantic Web play the role of the intermediaries that describe the relationships among information from various sources.

Look at the cover of this book. An engineering handbook for aquifers provides information about conduits, ducts, and channels sufficient to inform an engineer about the pieces of a dynamic fluid system that can control a series of waterways like these. The handbook won't give final designs, but it will provide insight about how the pieces can be fit together to accomplish certain engineering goals. A creative engineer can use this information to construct a dynamic flow system for his own needs.

So is the case with this book. The standard languages of RDF, RDFS, and OWL provide the framework for the pieces an engineer can use to build a model with dynamic behavior. Particular constructs like `subClassOf` and `subPropertyOf` provide mechanisms for specifying how information flows through the model. More advanced constructions like `owl:Restriction` provide ways to specify complex relations between other parts of the model. The examples from the "in the wild" chapters show how these pieces have been assembled by working ontologists into complex dynamic models that achieve particular goals. This is the craft of modeling in the Semantic Web: combining the building blocks in useful ways to create a dynamic system through which the data of the Semantic Web can flow.

Frequently Asked Questions

Throughout this book, we have presented examples of modeling patterns, issues, and challenge problems to describe various modeling tasks. In the course of the text, the issues are organized in pedagogical order, starting with the simplest RDFS constructs and moving up to more advanced OWL constructs. Now that you have finished the book, you are familiar with all of these constructs.

This appendix references all the modeling examples through the kinds of modeling questions they answer. It is organized (as much as you can call it "organization") in the form of a FAQ—a list of questions, with pointers for where to find the answers.

FAQ	Challenge	Discussion
How can I represent tabular data in RDF? Construct: `rdf:type`	1, p. 46 19, p. 148	p. 32 p. 45
How do I represent IF/THEN logic in RDFS or OWL? Construct: `rdfs:subClassOf`	2, p. 108	p. 80 p. 94
How do I combine two properties into one more general property? Construct: `rdfs:subPropertyOf`	3, p. 109	p. 95 p. 248
How can I say that two properties are used exactly the same way? Construct: `rdfs:subPropertyOf`, `owl:equivalentClass`	4, p. 109	p. 142
How do I merge individuals from multiple data sources into a single class? Construct: `rdfs:subClassOf`	5, p. 110	p. 102
How can I use another property instead of `rdfs:label` to indicate the display name of a class or individual? Construct: `rdfs:subPropertyOf`	6, p. 111	p. 102 p. 108
How can I filter information based on a value for one or more properties? Construct: `owl:hasValue`	7, p. 112	p. 196

Further Reading

In this book we focused on modeling in the Semantic Web: how to use the standards and technology to build models that will assist in the interoperation of information in a web setting. In this reading list, we include pointers to other treatments of issues relating to the Semantic Web, including history, methodology, mathematical theory, business applications, and criticisms of the entire approach. This list is intended to be a starting point for the interested reader and does not claim to be comprehensive.

In addition to the references provided here, a number of tutorials on RDF, RDFS, OWL, and related Semantic Web technologies can be found at *http://www.w3.org/2001/sw/BestPractices/Tutorials.*

Selected Books

Antoniou, Grigoris, & Frank van Harmelen. *A Semantic Web Primer.* Cambridge, MA: MIT Press, 2004.

Daconta, Michael C., Leo J. Obrst, & Kevin T. Smith. *The Semantic Web: A Guide to the Future of XML, Web Services, and Knowledge Management.* New York: John Wiley, 2003.

Davies, Johan John, Dieter Fensel, & Frank van Harmelen. *Towards the Semantic WEB—Ontology Driven Knowledge Management.* New York: John Wiley, 2002.

Fensel, Dieter. *Ontologies: A Silver Bullet for Knowledge Management and Electronic Commerce.* Berlin: Springer Verlag, 2001.

Fensel, Dieter, Wolfgang Wahlster, Henry Lieberman, & James Hendler (Eds.). *Spinning the Semantic Web.* Cambridge, MA: MIT Press, 2002.

Geroimenko, Vladimir, & Chaomei Chen (Eds.). *Visualizing the Semantic Web.* London: Springer-Verlag Ltd., 2003.

Hjelm, Johan. *Creating the Semantic Web with RDF.* New York: John Wiley, 2001.

Lacy, Lee W. *OWL: Representing Information Using the Web Ontology Language.* Oxford, UK: Trafford Publishing, 2005.

Omelayenko, B. & M. Klein (Eds.). *Knowledge Transformation for the Semantic Web,* Vol. 95. *Frontiers in Artificial Intelligence and Applications.* Amsterdam: IOS Press, 2003.

Passin, Thomas B. *Explorer's Guide to the Semantic Web.* Greenwich, CT: Manning Publications, 2004.

Polikoff, Irene, Robert Coyne, & Ralph Hodgson. *Capability Cases—A Solution Envisioning Approach.* Boston: Addison-Wesley, 2005.

Pollock, Jeff, & Ralph Hodgson. *Adaptive Information: Improving Business Through Semantic Interoperability, Grid Computing, and Enterprise Integration.* New York: John Wiley, 2004.

Powers, Shelley. *Practical RDF.* Sebastapol, CA: O'Reilly, 2003.

Selected Articles

Allemang, Dean, Irene Polikoff, & Ralph Hodgson. Enterprise Architecture Reference Modeling in OWL/RDF. *Proceedings of 4th International Semantic Web Conference, ISWC 2005*, Galway, Ireland, November, 2005.

Bada, Michael, Robert Stevens, Carole Goble, Yolanda Gil, Michael Ashburner, Judith A. Blake, J. Michael Cherry, Midori Harris, & Suzanna Lewis. A Short Study on the Success of the Gene Ontology. *Journal of Web Semantics* 1, 2 (2004): 235–240.

Berners-Lee, Tim. Foreword. In Dieter Fensel, James Hendler, Henry Lieberman, & Wolfgang Wahlster (Eds.), *Spinning the Semantic Web: Bringing the World Wide Web to Its Full Potential*. Cambridge, MA: MIT Press, 2003.

Berners-Lee, Tim, James Hendler, & Ora Lassila. The Semantic Web. *Scientific American* (May 2001)—*http://www.sciam.com/article.cfm?articleID=00048144-10D2-1C70-84A9809EC588EF21.*

Brickley, Dan, & Libby Miller. *FOAF Vocabulary Specification.* 2005—*http://xmlns.com/foaf/0.1/.*

de Bruijn, Jos, Axel Polleres, Rubén Lara, & Dieter Fenser. OWL DL vs. OWL Flight: Conceptual Modeling and Reasoning for the Semantic Web. Proceedings of the World Wide Web Conference 2005—*http://www2005.org/cdrom/docs/p623.pdf.*

Decker, S., S. Melnik, F. van Harmelen, D. Fensel, M. Klein, J. Broekstra, M. Erdmann, & I. Horrocks. The Semantic Web: The roles of XML and RDF. *IEEE Internet Computing,* 2000.

Ding, Ying, & Dieter Fensel. Ontology Library Systems: The Key to Successful Ontology Re-Use. In Isabel F., Cruz, Stefan Decker, Jérôme Euzenat, & Deborah L. McGuinness (Eds.), *Proceedings of SWWS '01: The First Semantic Web Working Symposium,* 93–112. 2001—*http://sw-portal.deri.org/papers/publications/ding+01.pdf.*

Ellman, Jeremy. Corporate Ontologies as Information Interfaces. *IEEE Intelligent Systems* (January/February 2004): 79–80.

Fensel, Dieter, James Hendler, Henry Lieberman, & Wolfgang Wahlster. Introduction. In Dieter Fensel, James Hendler, Henry Lieberman, & Wolfgang Wahlster (Eds.), *Spinning the Semantic Web: Bringing the World Wide Web to Its Full Potential,* 1–25. Cambridge, MA: MIT Press, 2003.

Frey, J. G., G. V. Hughes, H. R. Mills, M.C. Schraefel, G. M. Smith, & D. De Roure. Less Is More: Lightweight Ontologies and User Interfaces for Smart Labs. *Proceedings of the 2004 UK E-Science All-Hands Meeting—http://www.allhands.org.uk/2004/proceedings/papers/187.pdf.*

Fry, Christopher, Mike Plusch, & Henry Lieberman. Static and Dynamic Semantics of the Web. In Dieter Fensel, James Hendler, Henry Lieberman, & Wolfgang Wahlster (Eds.), *Spinning the Semantic Web: Bringing the World Wide Web to Its Full Potential,* 377–401. Cambridge, MA: MIT Press, 2003.

Golbeck, Jennifer, Gilberto Fragoso, Frank Hartel, Jim Hendler, Jim Oberthaler, & Bijan Parsia. The National Cancer Institute's Thesaurus and Ontology. *Journal of Web Semantics* 1, 1 (2003): 75–80.

Gruber, Tom. A Translation Approach to Formal Ontologies. *Knowledge Acquisition* 5, 2 (1993): 199–200—*http://ksl-web.stanford.edu/KSL_Abstracts/KSL-92-71.html.*

———. 'Towards Principles for the Design of Ontologies Used for Knowledge Sharing. In Nicola Guarino & R. Poli (Eds.), *Formal Ontology in Conceptual Analysis and Knowledge Representation: Special Issue of International Journal of Human-Computer Studies* 43, 5/6 (1995)—*http://ksl-web.stanford.edu/KSL_Abstracts/KSL-93-04.html.*

———. Ontology of Folksonomy: A Mash-Up of Apples and Oranges. Keynote. First *On-Line Conference on Metadata and Semantics Research (MTSR)* 2005—*http://tomgruber.org/ writing/ontology-of-folksonomy.htm*.

Guo, Yuanbo, Zhengxiang Pan, & Jeff Heflin. LUBM: A Benchmark for Owl Knowledge Base Systems. *Journal of Web Semantics* 2, 2–3 (2005): 158–182.

Heflin Jeff, & James Hendler. Semantic Interoperability on the Web. *Proceedings of Extreme Markup Languages* 2000—*http://www.cs.umd.edu/projects/plus/SHOE/pubs/extreme 2000.pdf*.

Heflin, Jeff, James Hendler, & Sean Luke. SHOE: A Blueprint for the Semantic Web. In Dieter Fensel, James Hendler, Henry Lieberman, & Wolfgang Wahlster (Eds.), *Spinning the Semantic Web: Bringing the World Wide Web to Its Full Potential*, 29–63. Cambridge, MA: MIT Press, 2003.

Hendler, James, Tim Berners-Lee, & Eric Miller. Integrating Applications on the Semantic Web. *Journal of the Institute of Electrical Engineers of Japan* 122, 10 (2002): 676–680.

Horrocks, Ian, Peter F. Patel-Schneider, & Frank van Harmelen. From SHIQ and RDF to OWL: The Making of a Web Ontology Language. *Journal of Web Semantics* 1, 1 (2003): 7–26.

Kalfoglou, Yannis, & Marco Schorlemmer. Ontology Mapping: The State of the Art. *Knowledge Engineering Review* 18, 1 (2003): 1–31—*http://eprints.ecs.soton.ac.uk/10519/01/ker02-ontomap.pdf*.

Lassila, Ora, & James Hendler. Embracing Web 3.0. *IEEE Internet Computing* 11, 3 (2007): 90–93.

McGuinness, Deborah L. Ontologies Come of Age. In Dieter Fensel, James Hendler, Henry Lieberman, & Wolfgang Wahlster (Eds.), *Spinning the Semantic Web: Bringing the World Wide Web to Its Full Potential*, 171–194. Cambridge, MA: MIT Press, 2003.

Peter Mika. Ontologies Are Us: A Unified Model of Social Networks and Semantics. *Proceedings of the 4th International Semantic Web Conference (ISWC)*, 2005.

———. Flink: Semantic Web Technology for the Extraction and Analysis of Social Networks. *Journal of Web Semantic* 3, 2 (2005)—*http://www.websemanticsjournal.org/ps/pub/ 2005-20*.

Motik, Boris. On the Properties of Metamodeling in OWL. *J Logic Computation* 17, 617–637.

Noy, Natalya F., & Deborah L. McGuinness. *Ontology Development 101: A Guide to Creating Your First Ontology*. 2001—*http://protege.stanford.edu/publications/ontology_development/ontology101-noy-mcguinness.html*.

Parsia, Bijan. A Simple, Prima Facie Argument in Favor of the Semantic Web. 2002—*http:// monkeyfist.com/articles/815*.

Parsia, Bijan, Evren Sirin, & Aditya Kalyanpur. Debugging OWL Ontologies. *Proceedings of the World Wide Web Conference 2005*.

Shirky, Clay. Ontology Is Overrated: Categories, Links and Tags. 2005—*http://www.shirky. com/writings/ontology_overrated.html*.

Sirin, Evren, Bijan Parsia, Bernardo Cuenca Grau, Aditya Kalyanpur, & Yarden Katz. Pellet: A Practical OWL-DL Reasoner. *Journal of Web Semantics* 5, 2 (2007): 51–53.

Stumme, Gerd, Andreas Hotho, & Bettina Berendt. Semantic Web Mining: State of the Art and Future Directions. *Journal of Web Semantics* 4, 2 (2006): 124–143.

ter Horst, Herman J. Completeness, Decidability and Complexity of Entailment for RDF Schema and a Semantic Extension Involving the Owl Vocabulary. *Journal of Web Semantics* 2, 2–3(2005): 79–115.

Uren, Victoria, Philipp Cimiano, José Iria, Siegfried Handschuh, Maria Vargas-Vera, Enrico Motta, & Fabio Ciravegna. Semantic Annotation for Knowledge Management: Requirements and a Survey of the State of the Art. *Journal of Web Semantics* 4, 1 (2006): 14–28.

Uschold, Michael. Where Are the Semantics in the Semantic Web? *AI Magazine* 24, 3 (2003): 25–36.

van Hage, Willem Robert. OAEI 2006 food task: An analysis of a thesaurus mapping task. Free University Amsterdam and TNO Science & Industry, Amsterdam. Available at *http://www.few.vu.nl/~wrvhage/pdf/oaei2006food-results.pdf*.

Volz, Raphael, Siegfried Handschuh, Steffen Staab, Ljiljana Stojanovic, & Nenad Stojanovic. Unveiling the Hidden Bride: Deep Annotation for Mapping and Migrating Legacy Data to the Semantic Web. *Journal of Web Semantics* 1, 2 (2004).

Welty, Christopher A., Ruchi Mahindru, & Jennifer Chu-Carroll. Evaluating Ontological Analysis. *Proceedings of the ISWC-2003 Workshop on Semantic Integration—http://sunsite.informatik.rwth-aachen.de/Publications/CEUR-WS/Vol-82/SI_paper_16.pdf*.

World Wide Web Consortium Publications on RDF, RDFS, and OWL

RDF/XML Syntax Specification (Revised), Dave Beckett, ed.: *http://www.w3.org/TR/rdf-syntax-grammar/*

RDF Vocabulary Description Language 1.0: RDF Schema, Dan Brickley & R.V. Guha, eds.: *http://www.w3.org/TR/rdf-schema/*

RDF Primer, Frank Manola & Eric Miller, eds.: *http://www.w3.org/TR/rdf-primer/*

Resource Description Framework (RDF): Concepts and Abstract Syntax, Graham Klyne & Jeremy Carroll, eds.: *http://www.w3.org/TR/rdf-concepts/*

RDF Semantics, Patrick Hayes, ed.: *http://www.w3.org/TR/rdf-mt/*

RDF Test Cases, Jan Grant, Dave Beckett, eds.: *http://www.w3.org/TR/rdf-testcases/*

OWL Web Ontology Language Overview, Deborah L. McGuinness & Frank van Harmelen, eds.: *http://www.w3.org/TR/owl-features/*

OWL Web Ontology Language Guide, Michael Smith, Chris Welty, & Deborah McGuinness, eds.: *http://www.w3.org/TR/owl-guide/*

OWL Web Ontology Language Reference, Michael Dean & Guus Schreiber, eds.: *http://www.w3.org/TR/owl-ref/*

OWL Web Ontology Language Semantics and Abstract Syntax, Peter Patel-Schneider, Pat Hayes, & Ian Horrocks, eds.: *http://www.w3.org/TR/owl-semantics/*

OWL Web Ontology Language Test Cases, Jeremy J. Carroll & Jos De Roo, eds.: *http://www.w3.org/TR/owl-test/*

OWL Web Ontology Language Use Cases and Requirements, Jeff Heflin, ed.: *http://www.w3.org/TR/webont-req/*

Index